RONALD J. SIDER

Born in Stevensville, Ontario in 1939, Ron Sider took a degree in history at Yale University, where he also studied for his PhD. A member of the Mennonite Church and a lifelong campaigner for social justice, his spheres of activity have included race relations, voter registration, abortion, third world aid and 'simple living'. He is currently Professor of Theology and Culture at Eastern Baptist Theological Seminary in Philadelphia, Pennsylvania. He is also Executive Director of Evangelicals for Social Action and JustLife, organisations committed to developing and communicating a thoroughly Christ-centred approach to a wide range of social issues.

As an author, Ron Sider has won wide critical acclaim. His first book, *Rich Christians in an Age of Hunger* was described by Michael Green as 'one of the most important books of conscience to be written in recent years.' Of *Nuclear Holocaust and Christian Hope*, which Sider co-authored with Richard Taylor, the late David Watson commented, 'This book contains the most vital challenge facing the Church today. It is one of the most searching and disquieting books I have ever read.'

Ron Sider now lives in Philadelphia with his wife, Arbutus. The couple have two sons and a daughter.

SPIRE

By the same author

Nuclear Holocaust and Christian Hope (with Richard K. Taylor)
Rich Christians in an Age of Hunger
Living More Simply (Ed.)

SPIRE

Ronald J. Sider

EXPLORING THE LIMITS OF NON-VIOLENCE

A call for action

Copyright © 1988 by Ronald J. Sider

First printed 1988

Spire is an imprint of Hodder & Stoughton *Publishers*

British Library Cataloguing in Publication Data

Sider, Ronald J.
Exploring the limits of non-violence
1. Non-violence – Christian viewpoints
I. Title
261.8'73

ISBN 0-340-48812-6

Printed in Great Britain for Hodder and Stoughton Limited, Mill Road, Dunton Green, Sevenoaks, Kent by Richard Clay Limited, Bungay, Suffolk. Photoset by Rowland Phototypesetting Limited, Bury St Edmunds, Suffolk.

Hodder and Stoughton Editorial Office: 47 Bedford Square, London WC1B 3DP.

CONTENTS

INTRODUCTION

There are only two invincible forces in the twentieth
century – the atom bomb and nonviolence.
                    Bishop Leonidas Proano of Ecuador[1]

What good would it do for three kayaks, three canoes
and a rubber dinghy to paddle into the path of a
Pakistani steamship? Or for a tiny fishing boat with
unarmed, praying Americans aboard to sail towards an
American battleship threatening Nicaragua? Or for an
eighty year old lady in a wheelchair to stop in front of
advancing Filipino tanks?

The tanks stopped and a non-violent revolution succeeded. The American battleship left and the threat
of invasion faded. And the US shipment of arms to
Pakistan stopped.

A need for exploration

Those were just three of the more dramatic successes of
non-violent confrontation in the last two decades.
Everyone, of course, knows how Mahatma Gandhi's
non-violent revolution defeated the British Empire and
how Martin Luther King, Jr's peaceful civil rights
crusade changed American history. There are many
more cases of non-violent victories over dictatorship
and oppression in the last one hundred years. In fact,
Harvard's Dr Gene Sharp, the foremost student of non-

violence today, says that the twentieth century has seen a remarkable expansion of the substitution of non-violent struggle for violence.[2]

Surely that fact suggests a crucial area of urgent exploration in the late twentieth century. No one living in the most bloody century in human history needs to be reminded of the horror of war. A violent sword has devoured a hundred million people in a mere hundred years. The mushroom cloud reminds us of greater agony yet to come unless we find alternative ways to resolve international conflict. A method that destroys a hundred million people in one century and threatens to wipe out far more is hardly a model of success. From the ordinary layperson to the most highly placed general, it is obvious that the search for peaceful alternatives is a practical necessity.

It is also a moral demand. Christians in the just war tradition (a majority since the fourth century) have always argued that killing must be a last resort. All realistic alternatives must first be tried before one resorts to war. In a century where Gandhi, King and a host of others have demonstrated that non-violence works, how can Christians in the just war tradition claim that the violence they justify is truly a last resort until they have invested billions of pounds and trained tens of thousands of people in a powerful, sustained testing of the possibilities of non-violent alternatives?

Pacifists have long claimed that there is an alternative to violence. How can their words have integrity unless they are ready to risk death in a massive non-violent confrontation with the bullies and tyrants that swagger through human history?

In short, the concrete victories of modern non-violent campaigns, the spiralling dangers of lethal weapons and the moral demands of Christian faith all focus a clear imperative. It is time for the Christian church – indeed all people of faith – to explore, in a more sustained and sophisticated way than ever before in human history, what can be done non-violently.

The purpose of this book is to promote that exploration. The first chapter briefly surveys the history of non-violent action. The next two chapters tell the story of two very recent, dramatic non-violent campaigns. Chapters four and five plead for action – now.

Preliminary definitions

But first, a brief word on terminology and scope. Non-violence is not passive non-resistance. Nor is coercion always violent. Non-lethal coercion (as in a boycott, or peaceful march) that respects the integrity and personhood of the 'opponent' is not immoral or violent.[3] By non-violence, I mean an activist confrontation with evil that respects the personhood even of the 'enemy' and therefore seeks both to end the oppression and reconcile the oppressor.

Non-violence refers to a vast variety of methods or strategies. It includes things from verbal and symbolic persuasion through social, economic and political non-cooperation (including boycotts and strikes) to even more confrontational intervention. Dr Gene Sharp describes 198 different non-violent tactics in his classic analysis of the varieties of non-violent action.[4] This book does not focus exclusively on any one strategy. Concrete situations demand their unique mix of tactics.

Possibilities worth considering

The arenas where non-violent alternatives might possibly (at least to a great degree) replace lethal violence are basically threefold: police work at the micro level; national self-defence and international, governmental peacekeeping at the macro level; and a wide variety of middle-level situations demanding conflict resolution, from guerrilla warfare to religious conflict in a society to revolution against a dictator. I believe we ought to explore the possibilities of non-violence for all three of these areas.[5] This book, however, focuses largely on the third area.

In their peace pastoral letter, the US Catholic bishops said that 'nonviolent means of resistance to evil deserve much more study and consideration than they have thus far received. There have been significant instances in which people have successfully resisted oppression without recourse to arms.'[6] I turn now to that story of heroic struggle and astounding success.

PART I:

A GROWING VISION

1   WHAT EXISTS IS POSSIBLE

Boulding's First Law says: 'What exists is possible.'[1] From before the time of Christ to the present, hundreds of successful instances of non-violent action have occurred. Often spontaneous, and seldom organised, courageous non-violent protest, non-cooperation and intervention have stopped brutal dictators, quelled raging mobs and overthrown foreign conquerors.[2]

The full story of unarmed daring has yet to be written.[3] Here I do not try to fill that gap, for that would require a vast library rather than a brief chapter. Rather, I outline a few historical illustrations of non-violent direct action in order to show how an alternative vision for resolving social conflict has emerged.

Two Examples from the First Century

In AD 26, Pontius Pilate, the new Roman Governor of Judea, outraged the Jews by bringing military standards emblazoned with the Emperor's image into Jerusalem. Since Jewish belief condemned all representation of the human form, the religious leaders begged Pilate to remove the ensigns from the holy city. What happened is best told by the first-century Jewish historian, Josephus:

> Hastening after Pilate to Caesarea, the Jews implored him to remove the standards from Jerusalem and to uphold the laws of their ancestors. When Pilate refused, they fell

prostrate around his house and for five whole days and nights remained motionless in that position. On the ensuing day Pilate took his tribunal in the great stadium, and summoning the multitude, with apparent intention of answering them, gave the arranged signal to his armed soldiers to surround the Jews. Finding themselves in a ring of troops, three deep, the Jews were struck dumb at this unexpected sight. Pilate, after threatening to cut them down, if they refused to admit Caesar's images, signaled to the soldiers to draw their swords. Thereupon the Jews, as by concerted action, flung themselves in a body on the ground, extended their necks, and exclaimed that they were ready rather to die than to transgress the law. Overcome with astonishment at such intense religious zeal, Pilate gave orders for the immediate removal of the standards from Jerusalem.[4]

Non-violent intervention had worked!

A few years later, the Jews won an even more striking non-violent victory. Caligula was the first Roman Emperor to require that his subjects worship him as a god during his lifetime. In AD 39, Caligula sent Petronius to Jerusalem with three legions of soldiers to install his statue in the temple in Jerusalem. Outraged, the Jews organised a primitive version of a nationwide strike. Refusing to plant crops, tens of thousands of Jews took part in a 'sit-in' in front of the residence of the Roman legate, Petronius. For forty days they protested non-violently. Jewish leaders summoned for private persuasion remained firmly united with their people. They would all rather die, they insisted, than permit such a desecration of their temple.

This courage and commitment so impressed Petronius that he decided to risk his life and ask the Emperor to change his mind. Caligula was furious. He sent a messenger commanding Petronius to commit suicide. Very soon after dispatching this messenger, however, Caligula himself was murdered. Fortunately strong winds delayed the emperor's messenger, who arrived with his fatal letter twenty-seven days *after* Petronius had learnt that Caligula was dead.[5]

Non-violent direct action had succeeded again.

Attila and the Pope

In the middle of the fifth century, the conquering Attila marched to the very gates of the 'Eternal City'. Having swept through central and eastern Europe in a bloody campaign, Attila hungered for the ultimate prize — Rome. His reputation preceded him. Terrified Romans believed that '. . . the grass never grew on the spot where his horse had trod'.[6] Facing this powerful warrior stood a demoralised Roman army and a daring Roman bishop.

Some stories portray Pope Leo I riding a mule, leading a small group towards Attila's advancing army. Armed only with a crucifix and a papal crown, the brave Leo allegedly directs his men in song as they advance. Finally, they face the enemy — their backs to the Roman wall, their exposed fronts to the 'barbarians'. Now the incredible happens. Attila, alarmed and confused, turns tail and runs — never to be seen again![7] Non-violent peacekeeping at its pristine best? Perhaps, although many of the details are probably legendary.

But modern historians do believe that Leo the Great, accompanied by a Roman Senator and other official ambassadors, did confront the invading Hun. Whether the negotiators were unarmed, singing and riding on mules is open to doubt. What *is* certain is the success of the mission. According to Gibbon, in his classic work on the Roman Empire, 'The pressing eloquence of Leo, his majestic aspect and sacerdotal robes, excited the veneration of Attila for the spiritual father of the Christians.'[8] The two parties managed to hammer out an acceptable treaty. The invading army withdrew.[9] Leo the Great's willingness to intervene directly and face a brutal warrior with overwhelming military might probably saved Rome from destruction.

Neglected History

Over the intervening centuries, there were undoubtedly examples of non-violent action. Unfortunately, that history has attracted fewer historians than the bloody battles of the Charlemagnes and Napoleons. But one should not assume from the relative silence of the history books that these centuries were free from any form of non-violent resistance.

The American Revolution offers a striking illustration of this historical oversight. Almost every American knows about General Washington and his military victories in the War of Independence. Only a very few realise how successful non-violent resistance to British tyranny had been even before a shot had been fired. But a scholarly study just published demonstrates that by 1775 nine of the American colonies had already won *de facto* independence by non-violent means.[10]

The non-violent struggle in Hungary in the latter part of the nineteenth century is another exciting, yet relatively unknown, chapter in the emerging history of non-violent action. Between 1850 and 1867, Hungarians resisted Austrian imperialism non-violently and eventually succeeded without violence after armed revolt had failed miserably. In 1849 Austria crushed a popular, violent Hungarian rebellion against Austrian domination. The next year, however, a prominent lawyer, Ferencz Deàk, led the whole country into non-violent resistance. Church leaders disobeyed Austrian orders. People refused to pay Austrian taxes, boycotted Austrian goods, and ostracised Austrian troops. So successful was the non-violent resistance that *The Times* of London declared in an editorial on 24 August 1861: 'Passive resistance can be so organized as to become more troublesome than armed rebellion.'[11] In 1866 and 1867, Austria agreed to reopen the Hungarian parliament and restore the constitution.[12]

Far away in the Andes mountains, another non-violent victory occurred in the nineteenth century. In his book *Warriors of Peace*, Lanza del Vasto describes the incident this way:

> When relations between Argentina and Chile deteriorated, the two armies marched toward each other through the high passes in the Andes. But on each side, a bishop went ahead of the troops. The bishops met and exchanged the kiss of peace in the sight of the soldiers. And instead of fighting, they sealed a pact of alliance and perpetual friendship between the two nations. A statue of Christ, His hand raised in blessing, stands on the mountain to commemorate this victimless victory.[13]

By courageously placing themselves between two opposing armies, these peacekeeping bishops doubtless averted bloodshed.

A Growing Vision

As Dr Gene Sharp of Harvard's Program on Nonviolent Sanctions has pointed out, the twentieth century has witnessed an astonishing increase in the use of non-violence.[14] Some of the key figures are household names around the world: America's Martin Luther King, Jr,

India's Mahatma Gandhi, Poland's Lech Walesa, the Philippines' Cory Aquino. Many more are less familiar. But all have contributed significantly to a growing awareness of non-violent alternatives.

A Brazilian soldier named Colonel Rondon is one of the less well-known heroes. By the early 1900s, the Chavante Indian nation was violently resisting its Brazilian oppressors. The hatred and brutality were mutual. But Colonel (later General) Rondon, an officer in Brazil's army, determined to deal with the Chavante nation in a radically new, non-violent, way. Rejecting the 'Shoot the Indians on sight!' policy of the past, Rondon instructed his men, 'Die if you must, but never kill an Indian.'[15]

Success did not come overnight. Members of Rondon's peacekeeping force were wounded – some severely. Yet the 'Indian Protective Service' organised by Rondon lived up to its name. Finally, in 1946, the Brazilian government signed a treaty with the Chavante people. Rondon's protective service had taken no Indian lives since its founding some forty years earlier.[16] The treaty permitted the construction of a communication system through the Chavante's jungle home, over which General Rondon telegraphed a friend, 'This is a victory of patience, suffering and love.'[17]

While Rondon experimented with peacekeeping in the field, philosophers expounded it in the public forum. In 1910, the pragmatist William James published 'The Moral Equivalent of War'. In his article, he proposes the conscription of young people for a war against 'nature' and for social welfare.[18] James had little time for idealistic visions, suggesting that:

> Pacifists ought to enter more deeply into the aesthetical and ethical point of view of their opponents. So long as antimilitarists propose no substitute for war's disciplinary

function, no *moral equivalent* of war . . . so long they fail to realize the full inwardness of the situation. And as a rule they do fail. The duties, penalties, and sanctions pictured in the utopias they paint are all too weak and tame to touch the military-minded.[19]

To be fair, James was not advocating a new 'peace army'. He simply saw his plan as having tremendous social value. Yet many today view James' essay as the antecedent of the modern peacekeeping force concept.[20]

Mahatma Gandhi, Badshah Khan, and the Defeat of the British Empire

The philosophers of the West, however, are overshadowed by the 'Great-Soul' of the East – Mahatma Gandhi. Gandhi first began work on the idea of a nonviolent army while in South Africa in 1913. But his skeletal proposal took on flesh in 1922, when Gandhi organised a corps of peace volunteers in Bombay, India.[21] The next ten years witnessed a disciplined and growing satyagraha ('truth-force').[22] During the year-long civil disobedience of 1930, they engaged in direct, albeit non-violent, confrontation with British colonialism. Thousands of peaceful protesters suffered savage police attacks.

An American journalist, Negley Farson, recorded the following story of a volunteer Sikh repeatedly bloodied by a British officer:

[The police sergeant was] . . . so sweaty from his exertions that his Sam Browne [a leather belt] had stained his white tunic. I watched him with my heart in my mouth. He drew back his arm for a final swing – and then he dropped his hands down by his side. 'It's no use,' he said, turning to me with half an apologetic grin, 'You can't hit a bugger when he stands up to you like that!' He gave the Sikh a mock salute and walked off.[23]

Eventually, of course, Gandhi's non-violent soldiers defeated the British Empire. Rather than retell this classic non-violent victory, however, I will focus on one largely unfamiliar strand of the non-violent struggle for Indian independence.

In the annals of non-violent intervention, no episode is more astonishing than that of Badshah Khan and his non-violent army of eighty thousand Muslim Pathans.[24] The Pathans lived in the strategic Khyber Pass, the north-west gateway to India from Afghanistan and Russia. The British who tried to subdue them considered the Pathans the most savage, brutal warriors they had ever met. The Pathans' strict code of revenge obligated them to avenge the slightest insult. For a Pathan, the surest road to Paradise was to die 'with his rifle smoking'.[25] India's future Prime Minister, Jawaharlal Nehru, commented that the Pathan male, 'loved his gun better than his child or brother'.[26]

When Badshah Khan persuaded the Pathans to adopt non-violence, even Gandhi was amazed. 'That such men,' Gandhi exclaimed, 'who would have killed a human being with no more thought than they would kill a sheep or a hen, should at the bidding of one man have laid down their arms and accepted non-violence as the superior weapon sounds almost like a fairy tale.'[27]

But they did. Badshah Khan was a Pathan Muslim who became enthralled with Gandhi's vision of non-violent struggle for freedom. Khan began to dream of 'an army of nonviolent soldiers, directed and disciplined, with officers, cadres, uniforms, a flag'.[28] Calling his volunteers the 'Servants of God', Khan organised 'the first professional nonviolent army'.[29] They marched and drilled, wore a special uniform (a red shirt), and developed a careful organisational structure complete with officers – and a bagpipe corps! They also worked in the villages, opened schools, and maintained order at public gatherings.

Badshah Khan's non-violent army was ready when the Congress Party issued its historic declaration of non-violence in the struggle for Indian independence on 31 December 1929:

> We recognize, however, that the most effective way of gaining our freedom is not through violence. We will prepare ourselves by withdrawing, so far as we can, all voluntary association from the British government, and will prepare for civil disobedience, including the nonpayment of taxes. We are convinced that if we can but withdraw our voluntary help, stop payment of the taxes, without doing violence even under provocation, the end of this inhuman rule is assured.[30]

In April 1930 the great Salt Campaign began. The British government monopolised the sale of salt, and also taxed it. With Gandhi in the lead, millions of Indians broke the salt laws, illegally buying and selling millions of pounds of salt.

The British response was brutal. Soldiers beat unarmed protesters with steel-tipped staffs. They raided the offices of the Congress Party. One hundred thousand Indians landed in jail.

Nowhere was the repression as bad as in Badshah Khan's home in the strategic north-west frontier. When he called his Pathan people to non-violent resistance, Khan was quickly arrested. Non-violent civil disobedience promptly broke out everywhere among the Pathans. Bayonets and bullets were the British response. On one bloody afternoon, they killed over two hundred unarmed protesters and wounded many more.

One incredible scene involved the Garhwal Rifles, crack Indian troops commanded by British officers. When they saw unarmed men, women and children being slaughtered, they refused to obey orders to shoot. 'You may blow us from your guns, if you like,' they told their British commanders, 'but we will not shoot our unarmed brethren.'[31]

British brutality evoked massive support for the Pathans. In a very short time, Khan's non-violent army swelled to eighty thousand volunteers. Fearing this Pathan non-violence even more than their former savagery, the British did everything to destroy the 'Red Shirts' and provoke them to violence. They ordered them to strip naked in public and beat them into unconsciousness when they refused. After public humiliation, many were thrown into pools of human excrement. Everywhere, the British hunted Badshah Khan's non-violent army like animals. But the proud Pathans remained firmly non-violent.[32]

Throughout the rest of India, too, the non-violent struggle and the brutal repression raged on throughout 1930. Finally, at the end of the year, the British government summoned Gandhi to arrange a truce. For the first time, the British recognised and negotiated with Gandhi's non-violent movement for independence.

Of course, the struggle for freedom was not yet over. For the next decade and a half, Badshah Khan and his non-violent Red Shirts played a key role in the battle for independence. Always they worked for peace and reconciliation. In 1946, when thousands died in Hindu–Muslim violence, ten thousand of Khan's Servants of God protected Hindu and Sikh minorities in the northwest frontier and eventually restored order in the large city of Peshawar.[33] Finally, in 1947, Gandhi's campaign of non-violent intervention wrested Indian independence from the British Empire. Badshah Khan's peaceful army of Pathan Red Shirts deserved a good deal of the credit.

This story of non-violent direct action by Muslim Pathans with a long history of brutal violence is one of the most amazing chapters in the development of an alternative path to resolve social conflict. Khan's biographer is surely correct: 'If Badshah Khan could raise a non-violent army of a people so steeped in violence as the Pathans, there is no country on earth where it cannot be done.'[34] Perhaps Gandhi's insistence that non-violence is meant for the strong helps explain the Pathan's success. When Badshah Khan asked Gandhi why the Pathans grasped the idea of non-violence more quickly than the Hindus, Gandhi responded: 'Non-violence is not for cowards. It is for the brave, the courageous. And the Pathans are more brave and courageous than the Hindus.'[35]

Gandhi and Badshah Khan redefined courage. Towards the end of his life, this incredible liberator of India remarked:

> My non-violence does not admit of running away from danger and leaving dear ones unprotected. Between violence and cowardly flight, I can only prefer violence to cowardice. I can no more preach non-violence to a coward than I can tempt a blind man to enjoy healthy scenes. Non-violence is the summit of bravery. And in my own experience, I have had no difficulty in demonstrating to men trained in the school of violence the superiority of non-violence.[36]

Developments Between the Wars

In other parts of the world, too, non-violence was discussed and tested in the Twenties and Thirties.

In 1920, the Germans used non-violence successfully to defeat a *coup d'état*. On 13 March 1920, right-wing troops seized Berlin, the capital of Germany, and declared a new government. Spontaneously, tens of thousands of Berliners began a strike. The next day, a ringing call for a general strike echoed throughout Germany:

> The strongest resistance is required. No enterprise must work as long as the military dictatorship reigns. Therefore, stop working! Strike! Strangle the reactionary clique! Fight by all means to uphold the Republic. Put all mutual discords aside. There is only one way to prevent Wilhelm II from returning: the whole economy must be paralysed! No hand must move! No proletarian must help the military dictatorship. The total general strike must be carried through![37]

Even though some workers were shot, almost everyone went on strike. The bureaucracy refused to run the government. Within four days, the leader (Wolfgang Kapp) fled to Sweden and the rebellion collapsed. Even though the police and army had failed to resist the coup, even though the coup succeeded and the rebels seized the machinery of government, they were unable to govern. Why? Because the people would not obey. Massive non-violent resistance had defeated armed soldiers.[38]

In the Thirties, James' idea of a 'peace army' took one small step towards reality. When Japan invaded Manchuria in 1931, the League of Nations demonstrated its weakness by doing almost nothing. Even when the Chinese launched a total boycott of Japanese goods and Japan responded with brutal repression, the League failed to respond. At this juncture an amazing letter appeared in the London *Daily Express*. Signed by three well-known churchpeople (the woman preacher, A. Maude Royden, Canon H. R. C. 'Dick' Sheppard, and Dr A. Herbert Grey), the letter urged: 'Men and women who believe it to be their duty should volunteer to place themselves unarmed between the combatants [in China] ... We have written to the League of Nations offering ourselves for service in such a Peace Army.'[39] The League Secretary, General Eric Drummond, responded quickly, noting that the League Constitution prohibited consideration of 'private' proposals. At the same time, however, he promised to circulate the idea among the press in Geneva.[40] Editorials mushroomed worldwide. 'The suggestion that such an army might suitably interpose itself between the forces of two peoples at war is both intelligent and apt,' remarked the Manchester *Guardian*.[41] Across the ocean, *Time* magazine scoffed at foolish 'Occidentals willing to go to Shanghai and heroically interpose themselves between the fighting Orientals ...'[42]

Back in Britain, however, the proposal gained support. Brigadier General Frank Percy Crozier – a decorated veteran of the Western Front – volunteered almost immediately.[43] Approximately eight hundred others followed, forming an organisation called 'The Peace Army'.[44] The Army, unfortunately, existed mostly on paper and never actually served in Shanghai. Still, a precedent had been set. The proposal for a 'peace army' had drawn marked attention, and fire, from around the world.

Battling Hitler Non-violently

Brave appeals for a non-violent peace army did not however prevent the planet from slipping into the most deadly world war in human history. But even in those years, indeed precisely in many of the countries under the brutal thumb of Adolf Hitler, non-violence persisted and grew.

Hitler easily conquered Norway and established Vidkun Quisling as his puppet in 1940.[45] But when Quisling tried to establish fascist institutions, massive non-violent civil disobedience erupted. Teachers risked their lives, refusing to teach fascist propaganda. Labour unions struck and sabotaged machinery, even though their leaders were imprisoned and killed. Almost all the Lutheran clergy resigned from the state church which Quisling tried to control. When the Gestapo demanded that the Catholic Archbishop withdraw his signature from a letter supporting the defiant Lutheran clergy, he replied: 'You can take my head, but not my signature.'[46] Quisling failed in his attempt to impose fascism through the schools and church.

Norwegians succeeded in saving more than half of the country's Jews. And resistance was even more successful in this regard in Denmark, Finland and Bulgaria.[47] A secret tip-off concerning the impending arrest of Danish Jews enabled the Danes to hide and then smuggle ninety-three percent of the Danish Jews to neutral Sweden. Although allied with Germany, Finland refused to deport their Jews, even when Hitler's chief of security police threatened to cut off Finland's food supply. 'We would rather perish together with the Jews,' Finland's Foreign Minister told the astonished Heinrich Himmler.[48]

Also a German ally, Bulgaria initially passed anti-Jewish legislation. But massive resistance to anti-Jewish measures emerged at every level of society, from peasant to priest. The Metropolitan of the Belgian Orthodox Church hid the Chief Rabbi in his home. Another Orthodox bishop told the Bulgarian king he would lead a massive campaign of civil disobedience against deportation, 'including personally lying down on the railroad tracks before the deportation trains'.[49]

Not one of the fifty thousand Bulgarian Jews fell into Hitler's hands.

Overthrowing Dictators

Non-violence toppled two dictators in Central America in 1944. General Martinez seized power in El Salvador in 1931.[50] The next year, he savagely crushed a peasant revolt, killing thousands of persons. For thirteen years, the tyrannical autocrat ruled. In early 1944, he put down a revolt, torturing some and killing others. In response, university students spread the idea of a non-violent general strike. Within two weeks, doctors, lawyers, engineers, teachers, shopkeepers and railway workers all left their posts. The economy ground to a halt. After a short period, Martinez resigned and fled to Guatemala, where he explained his resignation:

> In the first few days of April, I defeated the seditionaries with arms, but recently they provoked a strike. Then I no longer wanted to fight. Against whom was I going to fire? Against children and against youths. . . ? Women also were enlisted in the movement and in this way I no longer had an objective at which to fire.[51]

General Jorge Ubico had ruled Guatemala with an iron fist since 1931. Unfortunately for him, when El Salvador's dictator fled to Guatemala in May 1944, he brought along a contagious example of non-violent resistance. The widespread opposition to Ubico's tyranny took heart. First students, then school teachers, went on strike. When the cavalry charged a silent procession of women and killed a school teacher, a total strike occurred in the capital, Guatemala City. Workers struck. Businesses and offices closed. The streets were deserted. On 1 July 1944 Ubico also gave up.[52]

Nor are the victories in El Salvador and Guatemala isolated examples. Non-violent general strikes have overthrown at least seven Latin American dictators in the twentieth century.[53]

Although finally unsuccessful, massive non-violent resistance to the Russian invasion of Czechoslovakia in 1968 denied the Soviets an early victory. The Russians had assumed that their half a million Warsaw Pact troops would overwhelm the Czechs and install a puppet government in days. But near-unanimous non-violent resistance on the part of the Czech people preserved the government of the reform-minded Alexander Dubček for eight months.[54] A decade and a half later, Solidarity in Poland again used non-violent techniques against Soviet totalitarianism. And again the people failed to achieve genuine freedom. But, with hardly any loss of life, they were able to achieve astonishing change for a short time. Even after the clampdown, substantial accomplishments remained.

Professor Gene Sharp, Director of the Program on Nonviolent Sanctions at Harvard notes:

> Each successive case of nonviolent anti-communist struggle in Eastern Europe since 1953 has been more difficult for the Soviets to crush. Resistance in East Germany in June, 1953, was crushed in two days. The improvised Czech-Slovak resistance in 1968–69 ultimately failed, but it held off Soviet control for eight months, which would have been impossible by military means. In Poland, resistance continues after five years with major achievements, including a large illegal information system that publishes papers, magazines and books.[55]

The Philippines Revolution of 1986 is of course the most recent, the most famous, and the most successful example of non-violent overthrow of dictatorship. But that story will have to wait for chapter three.

Peacekeeping by the United Nations

Since UN peacekeeping forces regularly carry weapons, their story does not actually belong in this book. But they are relevant to our theme for several reasons. Relying largely on moral power, they often never fired a shot. Their existence witnesses to the growing desire for a transnational, less violent solution to the vicious wars that modern nation-states so often fight. Thus they reflect and point to a yearning for a non-violent alternative to war. A brief overview of the UN's peacekeeping forces is therefore appropriate.

The UN, like the League of Nations before it, made no provision for peacekeeping in its charter. According to UN diplomat Brian Urquhart (Undersecretary-General for Special Political Affairs), discovering peacekeeping was 'like penicillin . . . We came across it while looking for something else.'[56] In late 1946, a special UN diplomatic commission investigated the unrest in northern Greece. Military aid from nearby communist countries (Albania, Bulgaria and Yugoslavia) was pouring across the border to likeminded guerrillas. The commission requested observation and conciliation assistance – though a speedy victory by the Greek government ended both the crisis and eventually the commission.[57]

Still, a precedent had been set. In 1948, the then Secretary-General Trygve Lie proposed a 'UN Guard' – basically a professional, international police force. Unfortunately, his novel concept was a quick casualty of the Cold War.[58] Yet Ralph Bunche (later Undersecretary-General) pursued the concept of UN peacekeeping, an idea soon put to the test by Arab–Israeli armistice efforts in 1948–1949. Following Bunche's mediation of the cease-fire, military observers were sent to the Middle East to monitor the armistice.[59] It was the first of many UN commitments.[60]

A series of flash points followed in quick succession. In 1949, UN observers arrived on the India–Pakistan border to police the demarcation line following the Kashmir cease-fire.[61] Multinational troops under the UN banner carried out full-scale military operations in Korea (1950–1953). Actual UN troops landed in the Middle East in late 1956 to help extricate the British and French armies from Egypt and the Israeli army from the Sinai. In 1958, six hundred UN military observers were sent to Beirut, facilitating the withdrawal of US troops. Two years later, twenty thousand UN troops descended on the Congo (now Zaire) – a newly independent African nation caught in the East–West crossfire. In 1962, a Pakistani contingent of limited size and mandate moved into West Irian (formerly Dutch East Indies), for a one-year period.[62]

An accurate appraisal of these first fifteen years of UN peacekeeping remains difficult. In some ways, in fact, the verdict is still out. What *is* clear is the complex character of UN missions. Most involved a curious mixture of pacific persuasion and violence, ranging from Kashmir to Korea. Peacekeepers often struggled, however, to minimise violence and maximise reconciliation. The failures are well known, the successes often obscured.

To their credit, UN peacekeepers have honestly confronted past errors in judgement. The euphemistic 'police action' of Korea, for example, is unlikely to be repeated. Speaking at Harvard University in June 1963, then Secretary-General U Thant declared, 'The idea that conventional military methods – or, to put it bluntly, war – can be used by or on behalf of the United Nations to counter aggression and secure the peace, seems now to be rather impractical.'[63] The massive commitment of troops seen in the Congo, likewise, remains equally unpopular in many quarters. The costs are simply too high and the returns often minimal.

Yet stories abound of successful – and non-violent – UN peacekeeping efforts. In the Congo, for instance, UN troops attempted repeatedly to downplay violence. Antony Gilpin (former Deputy-Chief of Civilian Operations) tells the true story of a unique rescue mission. Sudanese UN troops had been surrounded and were under shelling attack. According to Gilpin, a Nigerian *police band* '. . . marched through the lines and, under cover of martial music, led out the beleaguered Sudanese'.[64] Non-violent peacekeeping at its artistic best!

UN observers acted just as creatively (if not artistically) in Kashmir. There, the India–Pakistan border suffered repeated firefights between hot-headed soldiers. Gene Keyes quotes a memorable story of UN intervention:

> One observer who had witnessed a confrontation between an Indian and a Pakistani patrol jumped into his UN marked jeep as the two groups started shooting at each other and drove into the path of fire with the UN flag flying from his vehicle. Both patrols ceased firing, and with the arrival of more observers the fighting stopped.[65]

Once again, non-violent peacekeeping proved powerful and effective.

In the more traditional UN border actions, reviews have been mixed. In West Irian, the mandate was clear and limited. UN troops were there simply to bridge the gap between the Dutch withdrawal and the arrival of the Indonesians.[66] Their mission lasted approximately one year and was largely successful. The Middle East has proven more difficult. The 'United Nations

Emergency Force' (UNEF), established in 1956, served for over ten years. During that time, it engaged in a number of significant peacekeeping initiatives. Major General Indar Jit Rikhye (Ret.), commander of the UNEF in the late 1960s, details some of those accomplishments in his recent article 'Peacekeeping and Peacemaking':

> The [UN] peacekeepers were required to supervise the withdrawal of foreign forces from Egyptian territory, to provide security for the canal clearance operations, and to interpose themselves between the Egyptian and Israeli forces during the latter's phased withdrawal. On completion of these tasks, UNEF was deployed between the Egyptians and the Israelis along the armistice demarcation line in the Gaza Strip and along the international frontier in the Sinai. Furthermore, UNEF was made responsible to ensure the freedom of shipping through the Straits of Tiran.[67]

In 1967, however, the Egyptian President, Gamal Abdel Nasser, moved his troops dangerously close to the Israeli border and demanded a UN pull-out from U Thant. The UN complied and Egyptian forces were routed in the ensuing six-day war. Thant's decision was probably legally correct (based on the 1956 negotiations), but it was politically disastrous. Then Israeli Foreign Minister, Abba Eban, exclaimed, 'U Thant folded the umbrella just when the rain began to fall.'[68] Israel's chief ally, the United States, also complained. But the decision to withdraw had been made.

The UN pull-out would not last long, however. Following the 1973 Middle East War, the blue-helmeted troops returned to the Sinai (UNEF II) and took up new positions in the Golan Heights between Israeli and Syrian Forces (UNDOF).[69] In 1978, additional UN forces moved into southern Lebanon (UNIFIL).[70] UN presence in the Middle East continues to this day.[71]

Other border hot-spots have periodically boiled over. In 1965, war broke out between India and Pakistan, and additional UN observers moved in to beef up the original force established almost twenty years earlier.[72] A year earlier, UN troops had arrived in Cyprus – sent as a buffer between battling Greeks and Turks.[73] Those troops, and observers, continue on assignment.

Almost forty years of UN peacekeeping experience highlight several issues. First, peacekeeping has been most effective when *both* sides welcomed the third party and when the latter maintained strict neutrality. The UNEF II force in the Sinai and the UNDOF force on the Golan Heights perhaps best illustrate this. Second, and related to the above, classic border operations are far more likely to succeed than confusing internal 'policing'. Cyprus and the Congo are examples of the latter, where providing a 'buffer' carries a far different meaning than it would on the clearly demarcated Golan Heights. Third, the power of the peacekeeping troops lies not in their weaponry, but in their moral and political force. Sydney Bailey, in his *How Wars End*, argues:

> The international force is not there to impose a solution or even to enforce the cessation of hostilities: its function is partly symbolic, and the safety of UN peacekeeping personnel lies in the brassards [a cloth band with the UN insignia] or blue berets of its members and not in the weapons they carry.[74]

Roy Finch agrees: 'The arms of the UNEF troops in the Near East are only a token; the 2,000-man force could easily be crushed by either side. It is effective only because it is backed up by "world opinion" and by the big powers.'[75] In spite of admitted failures, the UN role has been largely constructive. The superpowers have yet to find a better way.

Reaching for an International Non-violent Peace Guard

The recent story probably begins in 1948. Pacifists worldwide had arranged a meeting with the man everyone viewed as their spiritual leader – Mahatma Gandhi. His assassination, however, forced postponement to December 1949. Out of this World Pacifist Conference came a proposal to form Satyagraha (Gandhi's word for non-violence) Units.[76]

The proposal lay dormant until 1957, when Vinoba Bhave of India implemented one of Gandhi's dreams by creating the 'Shanti Senas' or Peace Brigades.[77] Resolving communal conflict between Muslims and Hindus, including the quelling of raging mobs, was the special mission of this non-violent Peace Brigade. When burning and killing broke out between Hindus and Muslims, the Shanti Senas marched unarmed into the middle of the mobs, protected only by their identifying sash and their record of goodwill in all communities. By 1969, there were thirteen thousand volunteers organised in local, district, state and national levels.

The Shanti Sena also threw themselves into the gramdon movement (a movement designed to create inter-religious communal harmony at the village level). In some fifty thousand gramdon villages, the Shanti Sena were responsible for guarding the village and maintaining peace.[78]

Narayan Desai, later director of the Shanti Senas, led the group during religious riots in Ahmedabad, India. In September 1969 the city erupted in Hindu–Muslim strife. Thousands died in a rampage that devastated much of the urban area. Immediately Shanti Sena volunteers poured into Ahmedabad. They moved fearlessly throughout the city, visiting one riot-affected area after another. The Shanti Sena engaged in arbitration, clean-up, relief efforts and education. After four months of work, the volunteers celebrated success with a procession shouting: 'We may be Hindus, we may be Muslims, but above all, we are human beings.'[79]

In 1960, pacifists from both East and West met in India. Known as the 'Triennial Conference of the War Resisters International', the meeting accelerated a pacifist trend towards international peacekeeping. Two leaders in particular pressed the peacekeeping concept: Jayaprakash Narayan of India and the Spanish republican Salvador de Madariaga. Their proposal envisaged an unarmed 'Peace Guard' serving under UN auspices.[80] In a joint statement, Narayan and de Madariaga asserted:

> The presence of a body of regular World Guards or Peace Guards, intervening with no weapons whatsoever between two forces combatting or about to combat, might have considerable effect. They would not be there as a fanciful improvisation, but as the positive and practical application of a previously negotiated and ratified Additional Charter binding all United Nations members. This Charter should ensure:
>
> (1) Inviolability of the World Guards;
> (2) their right to go anywhere at any time from the day they are given an assignment by the United Nations;
> (3) their right to go and intervene in any conflict of any nature when asked by only one of the parties thereto or by third parties or the Secretary General.
>
> The World Guards would be parachutists. They should be able to stop advancing armies by refusing to move from roads, railways, or airfields. They would be empowered to act in any capacity their chiefs might think adequate for the situation, though they would never use force.[81]

Narayan and de Madariaga sent the statement to Dag Hammerskjöld at the United Nations, but never received any response. The proposal – while bold – remained theoretical.

Pacifists continued their search for concrete structures for non-violent intervention in armed conflict in the 1960s. In 1962, the World Peace Brigade was formed. The founding statement declared that its aim was to '. . . organize, train and keep available a Brigade for non-violent action in situations of potential or actual conflict, internal and international . . . [and] against all war and preparations for war, and the continuing development of weapons of mass destruction'.[82]

The fledgling Brigade did assemble for action in Zambia (then Northern Rhodesia). Kenneth Kaunda had requested that a force of primarily African marchers be ready to move into Northern Rhodesia. Kaunda was concerned that white stalling of the election process might provoke a black backlash. More than five thousand unarmed persons massed on the Northern Rhodesian border in response to Kaunda's call. Though most were Africans, some had come from Europe, Asia and the United States. In the end, the dispute was resolved peacefully and the marchers were not needed.[83]

The Shanti Sena and World Peace Brigade came together in 1962 to form the Delhi-Peking Friendship March in response to the Sino–Indian border clash. The marchers hoped to take their message of non-violence and reconciliation across the miles from Delhi to Peking. Unfortunately, the international group was denied entry by countries bordering India. Yet the march did demonstrate the growing longing for some international peace team capable of non-violent intervention in international conflict.

A Canoe Blockade of American Ports

On 14 July 1971, three kayaks, three canoes, and a rubber raft blocked the path of a huge Pakistani freighter steaming in to load arms at the port of Baltimore.[84] The next day the Foreign Affairs Committee of the US House of Representatives voted to withhold all military and economic aid from Pakistan. A dramatic form of non-violent intervention had played its part.

The Bengalis of East Pakistan (now Bangladesh) had chafed under the domination of West Pakistan. Then, in December 1970, the Awami League, which championed greater autonomy for East Pakistan, won a clear electoral victory. In response, the Pakistani dictator unleashed his army on East Pakistan on 25 March 1971. By the time the war ended, a million Bengalis had been killed, twenty-five thousand women had been raped, and nine million refugees had fled to India.[85]

As the Pakistani army continued to rampage through Bengal, the US government denied that it was aiding Pakistan. But it was. The US was shipping large amounts of war material to Pakistan from East-coast American ports.

In *Blockade*, an exciting book that reads like a first-rate novel, Richard Taylor describes the daring adventure of the 'non-violent fleet' which helped stop this flow of arms. Taylor and other Philadelphia Quakers decided to dramatise the US shipment of arms by paddling their canoes in front of the steamship *Padma* as it came into the Baltimore harbour. Obviously their lives were at risk. As it turned out, they were plucked out of the water by the US coastguard, which then escorted the *Padma* to dock. But the news coverage of their action contributed to the vote by the House Foreign Affairs Committee the next day. And the next week the block-

aders flew to Miami and persuaded the US Longshoremen not to load any more arms destined for Pakistan.

The action then moved to Philadelphia. More canoes
blockaded another Pakistani ship, the *Al Ahmadi*, as
the Longshoremen watched. The blockaders' daring
persuaded the dock workers to refuse to load the ship,
thus shutting the port of Philadelphia to all Pakistani
ships, regardless of their cargo.

Finally, in early November, the Nixon Administration ended all shipment of arms to Pakistan. Obviously
many factors led to that decision. But the activity of the
'non-violent fleet' clearly played a part.

Peace Brigades International

The groping for an international non-violent peace
guard begun in the Thirties, and continued in the
Fifties and Sixties, reached a new level of implementation and success in the 1980s with Peace Brigades
International and Witness for Peace. (The latter story
will have to wait for the next chapter.)

'Peace Brigades International' (PBI) was born at an
international consultation in Canada in September
1981. PBI is clearly based on the foundation of Gandhi,
Shanti Sena and the disbanded World Peace Brigade,
and the success of Martin Luther King's non-violent
civil rights crusade. Its founding statement reads in
part:

> We are forming an organization with the capability to
> mobilize and provide trained units of volunteers. These
> units may be assigned to areas of high tension to avert
> violent outbreaks. If hostile clashes occur, a brigade may
> establish and monitor a cease-fire, offer mediatory ser-
> vices, or carry on works of reconstruction and reconcili-
> ation . . . We are building on a rich and extensive heritage
> of nonviolent action, which can no longer be ignored.[86]

PBI is more than a philosophical statement. Its members have seen 'action' on the Nicaraguan border and within the troubled borders of Guatemala.[87]

PBI's most successful action has been its non-violent 'escort duty' for endangered mothers in Guatemala. Members of PBI accompany threatened leaders of GAM (Grupo de apoyo mutuo) twenty-four hours a day.

GAM is a group of parents (largely mothers), formed in June 1984 to protest the disappearance of their children.[88] In Guatemala, right-wing death squads frequently kidnap, torture and kill anyone involved in improving the lot of the poor. Very few of GAM's members have had any previous political involvement. But the pain of their disappeared children prompted them to place newspaper advertisements, hold regular vigils and petition the government with one simple question: 'Where are our loved ones?'

For a year, GAM was tolerated. But in March 1985, General Victores, the Chief of State, charged (falsely) that 'forces of subversion' were manipulating GAM. A barrage of anonymous death threats followed. Within a few weeks two key leaders of GAM had been murdered. One of these, Hector Gomez, was found with his head bashed in and his tongue cut out.

PBI offered to supply international, round-the-clock escorts to accompany the other leaders of GAM. Since these international escorts from PBI arrived in May 1985, no board member of GAM has been kidnapped or harmed. The task is nerve-racking. One never knows when a bullet or bomb might kill escort or friend. The work is so emotionally draining that escorts must rotate out every few weeks. But it works.

PBI has expanded its activities. It has provided a non-violent watch at the site of a labour union strike. A team went to El Salvador at the invitation of a

Lutheran bishop. PBI is also providing staff to help develop the New World Centre for Nonviolent Resolution of Conflict based in Bogota, Columbia under the auspices of the United Nations University for Peace. Conversations have begun exploring escort services for Salvadoran human rights organisations. And there are explorations with people in Sri Lanka and South Africa.[89] PBI's success in Guatemala brings the vision of an effective, non-violent international peace guard one small important step closer to fruition.

This chapter has skipped quickly over a long history of daring experimentation with alternatives to war. We explored only a few of the stories of non-violent resistance.

We could have looked at John Adams' insistence, after his extremely dangerous non-violent struggle to contain the fighting at Wounded Knee (1973), that 'at times a person has to fight for non-violence'.[90] We could have examined the Alagamar Land Struggle in Brazil (late 1970s) and Archbishop Dom Helder Camara's chasing of the landlord's cattle off the peasants' fields.[91] We might have noted the massacre that never occurred in Rio de Janeiro in 1968 because 'a dozen priests offered themselves as the first victims'.[92] We could have explored the Philadelphia Quakers' non-violent police force at the Black Panther's Convention in 1970.[93]

Because it is so well known, I hardly mentioned Martin Luther King, Jr's extremely important non-violent civil rights crusade which substantially changed American society.[94] In any comprehensive survey of the emergence of non-violent alternatives, King would deserve many chapters. In this short sketch we can only acknowledge with gratitude that, other than Gandhi, his vision and leadership have done more than anyone else's to make non-violent action a thinkable alternative to violence for millions of people.

That non-violent direct action exists is beyond dispute. That it often succeeds is an irrefutable part of the historical record. That it, therefore, attracts growing interest in the late twentieth century is hardly surprising.

That increasing attention is due in part to some very recent successes. Non-violent action has, in the last few years, helped to neutralise a guerrilla army dear to the heart of Ronald Reagan and overthrow a dictator as tough as Ferdinand Marcos of the Philippines. To those stories of peaceful daring we turn in the next two chapters.

2 NON-VIOLENT INTERVENTION IN GUERRILLA WARFARE

You take risks for peace just as you take risks for war.
Sharon Hostetler[1]

I was scared on the morning of 11 January 1985. Along with about twenty other Witness for Peace volunteers, I was riding a dusty bus down a twisting road in a remote guerrilla-infested part of Northern Nicaragua. As we wound our way down the hillside into the valley towards the small town of San Juan de Limay, we knew a thousand US-funded contras lay hidden in the surrounding hills.

The contras had announced their intention to capture the encircled town. Frequent ambushes and attacks on surrounding villages, farm houses and cooperatives had occurred. Nancy Donovan, an American Maryknoll sister from the town, had been kidnapped and then released three days earlier. In the previous month, the contras had captured and tortured many civilians. Thirty-three had died. The contras' attacks had closed all roads to the town for a month.

Our bus was the first outside vehicle to try to break that blockade. As we slowly navigated the twisting roads down the side of the hills and then drove past burnt tractors destroyed by the contras, I prayed hard that there would be no sudden burst of gunfire, no surprise ambush. There wasn't. We arrived safely in the town. (It would be bad politics to use US-supplied weapons to kill American Christians.)

I was relieved, and the townsfolk were overjoyed. Later we were told that the people of San Juan de Limay slept more securely that night than they had in weeks. They knew an attack was very unlikely while American Christians were present.[2]

My little personal pilgrimage of fear and faith is one tiny part of a much larger story. Coming in teams of about twenty each, 2300 Americans have travelled to Nicaragua with Witness for Peace.[3] One team rode a rusty fishing boat to rendezvous with a huge US warship. Eden Pastora's contras kidnapped another team while they were sailing up the Rio San Juan that flows between Nicaragua and Costa Rica. Others faced more mundane hardships – like coping with upset digestive sytems that demanded hasty, frequent treks to unfamiliar toilets.

What has prompted so many comfortable American Christians to risk disease, injury and even death in a non-violent challenge to the guerrillas invading Nicaragua?

A History of Outside Intervention

The story begins early in this century.[4] As the noted Cornell University historian Walter LaFeber has pointed out in a recent scholarly study,

> Modern Nicaragua ... was shaped by U.S. military occupation (1911–33), and then the U.S. created and supported Somoza family dynasty (1934–79). That family seized most of the wealth, including land area equal to the size of Massachusetts. Meanwhile 200,000 peasants had no land. The major causes of death were gastrointestinal and parasitic diseases, and infant maladies.[5]

Illiteracy was about sixty percent. The majority of Nicaraguans prior to the 1979 revolution faced appalling living conditions. Although Americans were obviously not responsible for a great deal of the poverty and agony, there was a connection between US policy and the conditions in Nicaragua. 'Dependency' is the word LaFeber uses to describe the relationship of Nicaragua (and Central America generally) to the US. It is a dependency that ties Central American economies to a few export crops sold to the US and leads to wealth for a ruling élite and poverty and malnutrition for the rest. Furthermore, as demonstrated in the cases of Nicaragua and Guatemala, when 'economic leverage proved incapable of reversing trends that North American officials despised and feared', the US 'intervened frequently with troops or covert operations to ensure that ties of dependence remained'.[6]

On 19 July 1979, at the cost of perhaps as many as fifty thousand lives, a broad coalition of Nicaraguan people joined in a popular insurrection to overthrow the corrupt Somoza dictatorship. To the bitter end, some powerful US interests continued to support the brutal dictator. As late as 22 June 1979, Secretary of State Cyrus Vance called on the OAS to send a 'peacekeeping force' to Somoza's aid. Some days earlier, 130 US congressmen had demanded the restoration of direct military aid to the dictator. The liberal alternatives to Somoza and the guerrillas within Nicaragua could not compete with the powerful 'Somoza lobby' in Washington. Thus the final victory was directed and led by the leftist guerrilla movement, the Sandinista Front for National Liberation (FSLN). On 19 July, Nicaragua embarked on its socialist political venture, vowing to redistribute the land among the people, educate and provide health care for the masses, and establish a mixed economy to be run, it was claimed, in the interests of Nicaraguans rather than foreign investors.

Regardless of how one views the ruling Sandinista government of Nicaragua (and I give it a very mixed review),[7] it is undeniable that the Nicaraguan revolution brought immediate benefits to the poorest segments of the population. There was new hope for a brighter future for the many poor and disadvantaged. Anthony Quainton, the US ambassador to Nicaragua in the earlier years of the Reagan administration, admitted on a number of occasions that the Sandinista government had in fact brought about significant improvement in land distribution, health, nutrition, and education for the Nicaraguan population as a whole.[8]

From the beginning, the Reagan administration was bitterly opposed to the Sandinista government. And there were reasons for concern. The anti-American rhetoric had already prompted the Carter administration to withhold some aid. Promised elections were not held for five years, and there were Marxist-Leninists in the Sandinista coalition along with nationalists and Catholics. Actions designed to undercut the independence of other centres of power such as independent trade unions occurred. All these were valid reasons for anxiety. But they hardly justified the simplistic charge that the Sandinista party was a monolithic Marxist-Leninist group determined to destroy the church and impose a Soviet-style totalitarian society. Undoubtedly some Sandinista members wanted that. Others did not.

Instead of following a balanced policy of protesting violations of human rights and democratic freedoms, the US government launched its secret war in late 1981. The US trained and financed a counter-revolutionary movement (called the contras) led by former officers of Somoza's private army. The stated aim of this 'covert' operation was to stop the flow of arms from Nicaragua to El Salvador and to 'destabilise' the Sandinista government. Later, however, when the contra army numbered over ten thousand fighters and the US offered no convincing evidence of substantial arms flow to El Salvador, the administration admitted that it had embarked on an effort to 'overthrow' the Sandinista government and to make it 'say Uncle'.[9]

The result has been enormous suffering and massacre in Nicaragua. In its brief to the World Court, Nicaragua claimed that contra violence had killed 2600 persons; maimed, raped or kidnapped 5500; and displaced 150,000 civilians.[10]

Many independent reporters and eyewitnesses have recounted widespread attacks on civilians. Contrary to the just war tradition's prohibition against targetting civilians, the contras almost daily kidnap, torture, mutilate and kill non-combatants. During my trip to San Juan de Limay in January1985, I listened to the local medical doctor describe how the contras had broken fingers, mutilated and dismembered the bodies of the thirty-three people they had killed the previous month near that one small town. The son of the woman who was to be our cook was so badly tortured and mutilated that his father could identify him only because of his belt.[11] Independent human rights organisations like America's Watch and Amnesty International have consistently reported similar contra atrocities against civilians.[12]

Many American citizens were outraged at the expenditure of their tax dollars to support this carnage.

Witness for Peace Begins

In July 1983, an interdenominational group of 150 US citizens took a dramatic new step of non-violent intervention in guerrilla warfare. They travelled to the Nicaraguan–Honduran border to be present with the people suffering attacks and to pray and keep vigil for peace. While present in the beleaguered border town of Jalapa, the delegation witnessed the terrible effects of the war on the population. They also brought hope and temporary safety. One grateful Jalapa resident told the group, 'At least tonight they won't shell us, because you are here.'[13]

An idea began to germinate among the vigilers. If their mere presence could provide security from attacks by the contras, why not establish a 'permanent presence' of US citizens to stand non-violently with the Nicaraguan people?

Before the group left Nicaragua, plans emerged for a permanent presence in Nicaragua, originally envisaged as numbering hundreds of volunteers stationed along the border. Two religious groups within Nicaragua issued a formal invitation and agreed to act as sponsors: The Evangelical Committee for Aid and Development (CEPAD), an evangelical Protestant development agency representing thirty-seven evangelical denominations, and the Antonio Valdivieso Ecumenical Center, an agency promoting religious and social research. Unfortunately, the government of Honduras rejected a request to operate there too. But the Nicaraguan government gave preliminary approval, including the important provision that the project would be politically non-aligned and would support no party in Nicaragua.

The new organisation was called Witness for Peace

(WFP). Its history is a story of transition from Spirit-inspired dream to dusty reality. The first four volunteers left the US for Nicaragua in October 1983. The earliest focus of WFP was the town of Jalapa in Northern Nicaragua. (At that time the contras hoped to capture the town, establish a provisional government, and seek 'aid' from 'friendly countries'.) WFP's initial 'modest' goal was to establish a team of ten to twenty 'permanent' witnesses who would commit themselves to a six-month stay at the Nicaraguan border. Periodically, 'Short Term Teams', staying in Nicaragua for only one or two weeks, would join them. It was hoped that the permanent presence along the border would number at least fifty at all times – a far cry from several hundred, but in itself a considerable undertaking!

In December 1983, the first Short Term Team arrived for a two-week stay. From the start the visits of the Short Term Teams were conceived as 'educational' opportunities at the same time as they were opportunities to promote peace in the war zones. The two weeks spent in Nicaragua included interviews with both opponents and supporters of the Sandinista revolution.

As 1984 unfolded, the organisation grew both in Nicaragua and in the US. Eventually a 'manageable' operation emerged, comprising a Steering Committee, a small full-time staff, plus many volunteers in the US and Nicaragua. At the heart of the operation was a 'long-term' team of between fifteen to twenty permanent volunteers in Nicaragua, and three delegations of Short Term volunteers visiting Nicaragua every month. That basic pattern was to continue for the next three years. By early 1987, 2300 WFP volunteers had visited Nicaragua.

Goals and Strategy

WFP's fundamental goal was to end the US-funded guerrilla warfare in Nicaragua. The method was non-violent direct action. WFP's official statement of purpose pledges 'to plumb the depths of the religious nonviolent tradition and continually to envision and experiment with creative, powerful nonviolent actions'. Boldly they declared themselves ready 'to take risks in the struggle for peace comparable to the risks people take in war'.[14]

The initial strategy in Jalapa was 'deterrence through interpositioning'. The contras planned to seize the town. WFP therefore hoped that by placing themselves in the town they could deter the contras, who, for political reasons, would find it costly to wound or kill American citizens.

This strategy, however, worked only for a short time because contra strategy soon changed. Aborting their effort to seize a major town, the contras began attacking isolated farms, cooperatives, and government-funded projects like schools and clinics in order to destroy the social and economic infrastructure of the country. They targetted key civilian workers and community leaders (especially teachers, doctors and agricultural specialists) for abduction, torture and assassination. It was totally unthinkable for a few dozen WFP volunteers to try to stand between even a tiny fraction of the Nicaraguan people and ten thousand guerrillas engaged in hit-and-run terrorist attacks on constantly shifting targets across Northern Nicaragua. Interpositioning, however, was not entirely abandoned. It happened dramatically in the case of the encounter with the US warship. Arnold Snyder, who led WFP's Nicaraguan team for a year, thinks it would have worked in San Juan de Limay in late 1984 and early 1985 if there had been enough volunteers.[15] Overall, however, deterrence through interpositioning does not fit the tactics of guerrilla warfare.

WFP therefore redirected its efforts towards visiting places recently attacked in order to document and publicise the targetting of civilians. The contra attack on exclusively civilian and economic targets in the town of Octal on 1 June 1984 helped shape this redirection. In their assault, the contras ignored the army base in Octal. Instead, they destroyed the country's largest lumber mill, offices of the electric company, grain storage silos, and many other vital economic plants and facilities. WFP volunteers arrived the next day to help with clean-up and reconstruction, and to publicise the atrocities. One WFP volunteer discovered a CIA-written manual designed to teach Nicaraguans how to destabilise and sabotage their government and economy.[16] Publicising the evidence of this CIA manual helped galvanise American public opinion against funding the contras.

Since 1984, in fact, the central strategy of WFP has been to mobilise public opinion to change US policy by documenting and publicising the ravaging of the civilian population. WFP publishes frequent 'Newsbriefs' based on eyewitness testimony gathered by WFP volunteers, and a bimonthly *Witness for Peace Newsletter* (with a circulation of twenty-five thousand). A regularly updated telephone 'Hotline' in the US provides a steady flow of direct information from WFP staff in Managua. Every month, three teams of short-term volunteers return to the US to speak to churches and write or stimulate articles for church and secular media. WFP has also given testimony to the US Congress. Coverage has reached a hundred million

Americans.[17] That is substantial, and has undoubtedly made a difference.

Admittedly, the coverage has been spotty and sporadic in the major news media. Unfortunately mainline US media are excessively concerned with news that sells newspapers and raises TV ratings in the US itself. Therefore the kidnapping of an American nun or the encounter of a shrimp boat full of US citizens with a US Navy frigate makes headlines. Daily mutilation and assassinations of Nicaraguan civilians do not. But even within these limitations, WFP has generated significant media coverage. As a result, its non-violent action in Nicaragua has played a crucial role in arousing US public opinion against the war.

Not surprisingly WFP's two most dramatic episodes — the encounter with a US warship, and the kidnapping along the San Juan river — attracted the most attention.

Challenging a US Warship

On 6 November 1984, President Ronald Reagan won a second term as President in a landslide victory at the polls. That same evening his government announced that US warships were tracking a Soviet freighter bound for Nicaragua's Corinto harbour. On board, it was claimed, were crates similar to those used to transport Soviet MiG fighters. Fear of war skyrocketed as the US government implied that it would never tolerate the alleged Soviet MiGs, which would 'upset the delicate balance of power in the region'.

On 7 November the Soviet freighter bearing the mysterious crates approached the Nicaraguan harbour of Corinto. It was already within Nicaraguan territorial waters, just seven miles from the coast, when two US

Navy frigates gave chase. When a Nicaraguan coast-guard cutter went to meet the Soviet ship, it was then pursued by one of the frigates, which came within five miles of the coast. An unmarked C-130 aircraft overflew the port, drawing anti-aircraft fire from onshore batteries. Fears of invasion mounted even though the Nicaraguan government repeatedly denied the presence of MiG fighter aircraft on the Soviet freighter. The government of Nicaragua called the country to mobilise for defence. The government announced that student production brigades, in all numbering twenty thousand young people, would abandon their project of picking coffee and cotton, and mobilise instead for the defence of Managua. Managua would be sold 'barrio by barrio'* if the US decided to invade. In the international arena, Nicaragua called for an emergency meeting of the United Nations Security Council. In Nicaraguan cities, people hurriedly began digging community air raid shelters and neighbourhood militia were issued arms.

It was in this charged atmosphere that twelve long-term volunteers in WFP gathered together in Managua on 8 November to share a noon meal, reflect on Scripture, pray, and plan. Their feelings are best expressed by Arnold Snyder, who was then Nicaraguan Coordinator of WFP:

> We shared a feeling that an evil force beyond all human control was propelling events toward a terrible and bloody conclusion. The time of sharing and prayer drew us together and strengthened us; the presence of the Holy Spirit was unmistakable in the coming of hope and the banishing of fear. We were moved from helplessness to a time of planning for action, trying to conceive of ways in which we could most effectively stand up to be counted as opposing the further violence our government seemed bent on imposing on the people of Nicaragua.

* A barrio is a poor community or district.

The most outlandish idea to surface was also the most inspired: that we rent a flotilla of boats and place ourselves between the US frigates and town and harbor of Corinto.[18]

'Wetness for Peace', as it was quickly dubbed, demanded speed. Two WFP Short Term delegations in different parts of Nicaragua had to be assembled. They needed government permission to enter the war zone. They rushed to notify the press, assemble food, transportation and rent a boat – all in one and a half days.

At noon on Saturday, eighty US citizens, accompanied by twenty international journalists, converged on Corinto. But their 'peace flotilla' was modest in the extreme. One rusty old shrimp boat, the *Subtiava*, would sail forth to challenge the US Navy frigate with a message of peace.

Arnold Snyder's words capture the mood of the non-violent marines:

Those of us gathered for worship in the Baptist church of Corinto continued to feel the dark threat of war around us, but there was also an unmistakable presence of God's peace in the midst of the storm, expressed by the songs that began spontaneously as we waited for the service to begin. As we have so often had to note in our work in Witness for Peace, God strengthens us in special and unexpected ways when we leave our private fears and join together in common purpose.[19]

Following a moving service and prayer of commissioning, they marched through the town to the boat, carrying banners and singing songs of hope and victory. Forty people clambered aboard and the trusty *Subtiava* pulled away from the dock in a cloud of diesel smoke. Slowly it moved towards international waters and an uncertain encounter. Those left on shore prayed together in the ruins of the fuel storage tanks destroyed by the CIA attack on Corinto in October 1983.

After two hours, a small dot appeared on the horizon. As the third hour passed, the forbidding outline of a US warship loomed ever larger. As the sun began to sink over the horizon, the little shrimp boat sailed within a kilometre of the huge ship, awesome with its constantly moving radar antennae and its artillery and missile batteries now visible. Just as the *Subtiava* came within hailing distance, the warship began to move. The little shrimper increased its speed to close the distance, but the warship suddenly turned towards the open sea and sped away.

As the Navy ship began to move away, the Rev. Stuart Taylor of the Long Term Team grabbed a loud-speaker and shouted to the US sailors on the departing warship, 'Why are you here? Why are you threatening the people of Nicaragua? Go away! Leave us and these people in peace!' But by this time the great ship was well out of earshot and turning towards open sea. David had come to speak to Goliath without so much as a sling in hand, but the giant would have none of it.

The non-violent marines in the tiny shrimp boat were disappointed. They had hoped to speak to the American sailors on board the ship, but not a single person on the frigate was visible the entire time. The final appeal had to be directed towards a huge mute machine.

But the rendezvous was a success even though the message of peace was not communicated directly to the crew of the warship. It was filmed, recorded, and reported to millions around the world from the United States and Canada to Europe, Latin America, Africa and Asia. The image of the great warship retreating from the unarmed, rusty tub conveyed its own message. At the farewell service on Thanksgiving Day, after many days of maintaining a permanent vigil on the beach of Corinto, Baptist pastor Ernesto Cordova reminded the WFP volunteers: 'The little ship did not have fire power, but it had the power of love, the power of justice, the power of God. And the weakness of God is stronger than the power of men.' One courageous act of non-violent interpositioning had played its small part in nudging leaders and national public opinion away from violent conflict. By Thanksgiving, the threats of attack and fears of invasion subsided.

Kidnapped by the Contras

Twenty-one months later, WFP volunteers again captured news headlines around the world. Travelling down the Rio San Juan in the first non-military vessel to travel on the river beyond El Castillo for over two years, fifty-six people with WFP were kidnapped by the contras.[20]

In the preceding months, tensions had risen along the Rio San Juan which flows between Costa Rica and Nicaragua. The contras were launching regular raids into Nicaragua and then retreating to the Costa Rican side. On 31 May 1985, someone killed two Costa Rican Civil Guards near the river inside Costa Rica. The Sandinistas blamed the contras and the contras blamed the Sandinistas. Many feared some new incident could provide a pretext for US intervention.

WFP decided to sail a 'peace flotilla' down the dangerous section of the river. A delegation of twenty-nine WFP volunteers and sixteen members of the press was ready to embark on 6 August 1985.

The day before, however, Eden Pastora, leader of the contras operating from Costa Rica, issued a press release announcing that he had ordered his men to fire on 'wolves in sheep's clothing'. At their press conference,

WFP responded with firmness: 'For centuries, Christian theologians have justified the risking of human life to wage war. In Nicaragua today, we are called to take risks for peace.'[21] Later, Sharon Hostetler, joint coordinator of WFP in Nicaragua, said during an interview with CBS: 'We hope to God, like all the Nicaraguans, that none of us will be killed. We are willing to risk danger . . . But we pray and reflect on the fact that the call to peace is not easy. You take risks for peace just as you take risks for war.'[22]

Flying a large WFP banner, the delegation sailed from El Castillo on 6 August. The journey downstream was peaceful. But the next morning, on the return voyage, trouble unexpectedly erupted. Shots rang across the bows and everyone hit the deck. Guerrillas ordered the boat to the Costa Rican shore and identified themselves as members of ARDE (Pastora's contra organisation).

The next thirty hours were terrifying. At the command of their armed kidnappers, everyone, including an elderly woman and an eighty year old man in the delegation, stumbled uphill through difficult jungle terrain. Sandals fell off in deep mud. Too exhausted to trudge further, they were finally allowed to rest in a thatched hut one and a half miles from the river.

Towards evening, the guerrillas decided to let the group return to the boat. People slipped and fell on the muddy downhill path, rendered more treacherous by the all-day rain. They got lost and separated from each other, finally reaching the boat only after dark. But William, the guerrilla leader, was furious, partly because of embarrassment at losing his way. Enraged, he ordered them to march up the hill to the hut again in the darkness.

The old woman collapsed on the ground, sobbing. Her

feet were bleeding. Totally exhausted, she had no energy to obey the orders and march another one and a half miles. That was the most terrifying moment of the entire episode. Many feared they would shoot the old woman. She feared others would die because of her.

Eventually William grudgingly agreed to allow everyone on board for the night, provided they kept the lights out and made no noise. Finally, in the early afternoon of the next day, they were all released. With song and prayer, they gratefully reboarded their boat and finished the return voyage.

No peace treaties were signed because of the short voyage of this peace flotilla. But radio, television and newspapers around the world broadcast a new chapter in the amazing story of non-violent resistance.

Evaluating Witness for Peace

Has WFP been successful? The war has not ended. The Sandinista government continues to commit human rights violations. The contras continue to murder civilians. And the American taxpayers continue to fund the carnage.

That was the state of affairs at the end of 1987. Then the unexpected happened in 1988. The US Congress ended funding for lethal weapons for the contras, and the Sandinistas and contras sat down to negotiate an end to the war. As this book goes to press, it is impossible to say how those negotiations – which look very hopeful at present – will finally end.

There is no doubt, however, that Witness for Peace has played a significant role in the complicated history of US–Nicaraguan relations during the Reagan era.

Occasionally, the presence of WFP has deterred attack. Documentation and publication of civilian casualties has influenced US policy. And WFP has forged another courageous model of non-violent direct action.

Deterrence of contra attack has been very modest, but not irrelevant. The presence (and publicity about the presence) of WFP in Jalapa was probably *one* factor in the contra's abandoning that objective in 1983. The contras did not attack San Juan de Limay while my delegation was there. The US warship clearly did not want to deal with a shrimp boat full of praying American Christians accompanied by international journalists.

Because of intercepted radio messages describing WFP vehicles and activities, WFP knows that the contras are informed about WFP activities and report on their movements. Only one town has been attacked while WFP volunteers were present.

Had they wished to do so, the contras could easily have ambushed WFP delegates many times as they drove the isolated roads in the war zones. Since the contras clearly do not wish to kill US citizens, this translates into a measure of protection for the Nicaraguan people while WFP volunteers are present. A highly placed Nicaraguan government official, when asked if WFP's non-violent presence deterred attack, answered unequivocally, 'Yes, it helps. Because the one thing that is feared by the Reagan government is that U.S. citizens might die ... So yes, it matters that non-violent Christians are present as a barrier.'[23]

Gilberto Aguirre, Executive Director of CEPAD, the evangelical agency in Nicaragua that has worked closely with WFP, has said the same thing: 'You have to extend and increase Witness for Peace work. We have seen that the impact of your work is very great, not only in the U.S.A. but with the contras. You could save a lot of lives.'[24]

On balance, however, one must conclude that the deterrent effect of WFP has at best been only a modest nuisance for the contras.

More important than WFP's attempt at deterrence has been its growing impact on US public opinion and indirectly on US public policy through the documentation and publication of civilian casualties. The aim is to change a policy, not simply to be willing to risk death by interpositioning oneself between warring factions. If no one is willing to take such a risk, of course, there will be nothing to tell. But if they do, the story must then be told.

And it has been. WFP estimates that fifty-one million people have heard over a thousand radio and TV interviews of returning delegations. Fifty-three million people have read over a thousand feature stories, interviews and leader columns. Nine million people have read over 650 articles in church publications. Four hundred thousand individuals have heard over eight thousand in-person presentations to local church and community groups. Over sixty million Americans saw or read national media coverage of the kidnapped delegation on the Rio San Juan. Probably a hundred million Americans in all have been reached.[25]

Reaching that many Americans even very infrequently has undoubtedly helped shape US public opinion. WFP deserves some of the credit for the fact that a majority of Americans oppose US support for the contras and persuaded the US Congress to deny funding to them from 1984 to 1986 and again in 1988. That one of the most popular presidents in American history has been unable to rally majority support for his top foreign policy objective is due in part to WFP.

Finally, WFP is having an intangible but important long-term impact. Even its modest success has opened the eyes of untold thousands to a non-violent alternative for resisting violence. The influence of thousands of returning volunteers excited about the potential of non-violent direct action is working its way through American churches like yeast in dough. Nor is the impact limited to the US. News of this effort has spread to many countries. Perhaps the comment of a (non-pacifist) Baptist leader in Nicaragua typifies the educational impact of WFP in many places: 'I didn't understand non-violence at first. I came to understand non-violent action for peace by the testimony of the witnesses [WFP volunteers] in a place where the people were being violated by force of arms.'[26]

WFP is one subplot in a living, growing story of courageous pioneers seeking alternatives to lethal violence.[27] WFP's part of that developing story demonstrates that non-violent resistance to guerrilla warfare is possible.[28] The Philippine People's Revolution, to which we turn in the next chapter, shows that non-violent revolution is also realistic.

3 WHEELCHAIRS vs TANKS

> I have decided to pursue my freedom struggle
> through the path of nonviolence . . . I refuse to believe
> that it is necessary for a nation to build its foundation
> on the bones of its youth.
>
> Benigno Aquino[1]

The most stunning non-violent victory since Mahatma
Gandhi and Martin Luther King occurred in the Philippines in early 1986. Praying nuns, nursing mothers and
old women in wheelchairs turned back bayonets and
tanks. In four breathtaking days in late February,
Filipino 'people power' toppled President Ferdinand
Marcos, one of the world's most durable dictators.

Marcos and his Opponents

The story of course began much earlier. Marcos won the
presidential election in 1965. In 1972, he declared
martial law, which was not lifted until 1981. Even
then, extra-legal powers enabled him to continue his
repressive role.

Marcos used dictatorial powers to amass great wealth
for himself, close friends, and cooperative foreign companies.[2] To promote his development policy based on
export crops, he ruthlessly suppressed workers who
demanded decent wages and land reform. (Towards the
end of his rule, the average wage for a sugar-cane cutter

working thirteen to fourteen hours a day was $7.00 a week.) Both Amnesty International and the International Commission of Jurists documented thousands of political prisoners in Marcos' jails. Electric shock torture, water torture, extended solitary confinement and beatings were common. Such measures propped up a system where a tiny portion of the population received a huge percent of the nation's total personal income.[3]

While Marcos and company stashed billions in Swiss banks, the majority of the people suffered grinding poverty. Three quarters of the people lived below the poverty line. Seventy-seven percent of all children under six suffered from malnutrition.

Not surprisingly, a Marxist guerrilla movement gained increasing acceptance. A tiny group when Marcos declared martial law in 1972, the Marxist-led New People's Army had grown into a strong national movement by the mid 1980s. Many prominent people felt civil war was inevitable. It might take ten years of bloody battle, they guessed, but no other course seemed viable.

But the assassination of Senator Benigno Aquino on 21 August 1983 ignited a fire that brought revolution by different methods.[4] Aquino held the double honour of being Marcos' most prominent political opponent and longest-held (1972–1980) political prisoner. Reading Jesus and Gandhi in prison, this conventional, self-serving politician experienced a renewal of personal faith and a transforming commitment to the poor and non-violence.[5]

Released in 1980 to obtain heart surgery in the US, Aquino prepared himself for the right moment to return home to challenge Marcos' repressive dictatorship. The non-violent tactics he intended to use were abundantly clear in a statement made to the subcommittee on Asian

and Pacific Affairs of the US House of Representatives
on 23 June 1983:

> To gather empirical data and firsthand information, I
> travelled to the Middle East, Southeast Asia, and to Cen-
> tral America. I interviewed the leaders of the most 'suc-
> cessful revolutions' and talked to both the victors and the
> vanquished, the relatives of the victims and the survivors.
> I have concluded that revolution and violence exact the
> highest price in terms of human values and human lives in
> the struggle for freedom. In the end there are really no
> victors, only victims . . .
> I have decided to pursue my freedom struggle through
> the path of nonviolence, fully cognizant that this may be
> the longer and more arduous road . . .
> I have chosen to return to the silence of my solitary
> confinement and from there to work for a peaceful solution
> to our problems rather than go back triumphant to the
> blare of trumpets and cymbals seeking to drown the wail-
> ing and sad lamentations of mothers whose sons and
> daughters have been sacrificed to the gods of violent revol-
> ution. Can the killers of today be the leaders of tomorrow?
> Must we destroy in order to build? I refuse to believe that it
> is necessary for a nation to build its foundation on the
> bones of its youth.[6]

But Aquino was not to return to his prison cell when
he stepped off the plane at Manila International Airport
on 21 August 1983. Instead, he dropped dead in a hail of
bullets in an assassination almost certainly approved
by President Marcos.

The Beginnings of Non-violent Opposition

The country erupted in outrage. Spontaneously, the
first major non-violent demonstration in the Philippines occurred. Day and night, millions moved past his
coffin in grief and silent defiance. Two million people

marched peacefully in an eleven-hour funeral procession that persisted through sunshine and rain, thunder and lightning.[7] And they responded enthusiastically when Aquino's mother and widow begged them to continue the struggle non-violently.

But this emotional outpouring did not immediately alter political reality. Marcos was still the dictator. The growing Marxist guerrilla movement (NPA) increasingly appeared to many as the only alternative as Marcos continued to crack down on opponents.

To be sure, there were a few courageous voices promoting a non-violent alternative. As early as the sixties, some poor communities organised non-violent struggles and won small but significant victories. Since the early 1970s, Francisco Claver, bishop on the desperately poor, guerrilla-infested island of Mindanao, had been promoting non-violent liberation of the poor. Marcos' army called him a Marxist. The Marxist guerrillas claimed he supported the army. Bishop Claver quietly continued forming Base Christian Communities committed to a non-violent search for justice in his diocese. He also promoted the study of non-violent social change among a small circle of Catholic bishops.[8]

Then in February 1984, a short visit by two veteran non-violent trainers crystallised more widespread interest in non-violent alternatives. Hildegard and Jean Goss-Mayr had worked for decades promoting non-violence in Europe and Latin America. Both Archbishop Dom Helder Camara of Brazil and the Nobel Prize winner Adolfo Perez Esquivel of Argentina have traced their commitment to non-violence to personal encounters with the Goss-Mayrs.[9] As they travelled through the Philippines in February 1984, they concluded that the hour was late for any non-violent effort. But they also sensed a widespread yearning for some realistic alternative to the agony of civil war.

On the last day of their visit, Butz Aquino (brother of the assassinated Benigno Aquino) met privately with them. Butz Aquino was an active leader in the ongoing protests against the dictatorship. Privately with the Goss-Mayrs, he confided his personal wrestling with the option of armed revolution:

> A few days ago the arms merchants visited us and said to us, 'Do you think that with a few demonstrations you will be able to overthrow this regime? Don't you think you need better weapons than that? We offer them to you. Make up your mind.' . . . You see it is providential that you have come just at this point of time, because ever since this visit I am unable to sleep. Do I have the right to throw our country into major civil war? What is my responsibility as a Christian politician in this situation? Is there really such a thing as nonviolent combat against an unjust system like that of Marcos?[10]

In response the Goss-Mayrs challenged him to decide for himself. But they warned that vigorous preparation for non-violent resistance is essential: 'Nonviolence is not something you do spontaneously and without preparation.'[11] They volunteered to return to do seminars if invited.

The invitation came within weeks. In the summer of 1984, the Goss-Mayrs returned for six weeks of seminars on non-violence. They ran seminars for leaders among the political opposition (including Butz Aquino), labour unions, peasants, students, and the church. Bishop Claver organised a three-day seminar for twenty Catholic bishops. Everywhere, the Goss-Mayrs advocated a twofold non-violence: non-violent opposition to the structural violence in Marcos' economic and political system, and abandonment of the inner violence in one's own heart.

The seed of the violence was in the structures, of course, and in the dictator. But wasn't it also in ourselves? It's very easy to say that Marcos is the evil. But unless we each tear the dictator out of our own heart, nothing will change. Another group will come into power and will act similarly to those whom they replaced. So we discovered Marcos within ourselves.[12]

AKKAPKA, a new Philippine organisation committed to non-violence, emerged from these seminars. AKKAPKA (formed in July 1984) is the acronym for Movement for Peace and Justice. It also means 'I embrace you' in Tagalog, the national language of the Philippines. Led by Father Jose Blanco, SJ, AKKAPKA held forty seminars on non-violent social change in thirty different provinces all over the country in its first year.[13]

The numbers seriously interested in using non-violent methods grew rapidly in late 1984 and 1985. Three weeks of seminars in Protestant circles by the American ethicist Richard Deats swelled their ranks. Even so, they were hardly ready for the surprise of 3 November 1985.

Marcos' Announcement and AKKAPKA's Initiatives

On that day, Marcos suddenly announced presidential elections for 7 February 1986. While the ideological left decided to boycott the elections, AKKAPKA quickly devoted all its energy towards trying to guarantee a fair election. They focused on three activities: encouraging the people to vote, preparing poll-watchers, and organising prayer tents.[14]

People intimidated by years of violent governmental

repression needed to be encouraged to cast fear aside, reject government bribes, and vote according to their conscience. Regularly, in previous elections, armed thugs had intimidated voters and stolen ballots. So AKKAPKA joined other religious and civic organisations to help train half a million men and women, young and old, priests and laity, to defend the ballot boxes non-violently even if attacked by armed soldiers or thugs.

AKKAPKA also set up 'prayer tents' in ten highly populated areas. One was located in the heart of Manila's banking community. Day and night, from mid-January 1986 to the end of the crisis, people came to these prayer tents to fast and pray. Hildegard Goss-Mayr, who saw these prayer tents in operation in early 1986, has underlined their importance:

> We cannot emphasize enough the deep spirituality that gave the people the strength to stand against the tanks later on. People prayed every day, for all those who suffered in the process of changing regimes, even for the military, even for Marcos . . . It makes a great difference in a revolutionary process where people are highly emotional whether you promote hatred and revenge or help the people stand firmly for justice without becoming like the oppressor. You want to love your enemy, to liberate rather than destroy him.[15]

Almost immediately after Marcos announced the 'snap' election, more and more people began to call on Cory Aquino, widow of the assassinated Benigno, to challenge Marcos at the polls. Unwilling at first, she reluctantly agreed, announcing her candidacy on 5 December 1985, just two months before the election. In the short, intense campaign, she discovered massive popular support. Clearly she was on her way to a decisive electoral victory.

Marcos, however, used massive, unparalleled fraud to steal the election. According to the Philippine Conference of Catholic Bishops, there was widespread vote-buying, intimidation of voters, dishonest tabulation of the returns, harassment, terrorism and murder.[16] In Metropolitan Manila alone, six hundred thousand people could not vote because Marcos' agents had scrambled the voters' lists.

Tens of thousands of non-violent poll-watchers with NAMFREL courageously placed their bodies in the midst of all this corruption and violence. (In the 1984 parliamentary elections, an independent organisation called NAMFREL had emerged to conduct an independent quick vote count and prevent some of the worst dishonesty.) Strong international support strengthened their hand in the 1986 presidential elections. They deployed their thirty thousand volunteers at the most critical polling stations. Six hundred nuns, nicknamed the 'NAMFREL Marines' went to the most problematic locations. During the day of voting and the subsequent vote count, these non-violent volunteers risked death many times. Twenty-four hours a day, they formed human chains and literally tied themselves to ballot boxes so the boxes could not be stolen.[17]

NAMFREL's quick count showed Cory Aquino with a substantial lead. But the official tabulation placed Marcos ahead. Then, as the parliament (Batasan) prepared to declare Marcos the winner, thirty young computer workers involved in the official vote count left their posts on 9 February to protest the deliberate posting of dishonest returns. That daring act ended any credibility still enjoyed by the official returns.

The Bishops Speak Out

At this desperate moment, the Philippine Catholic Bishops Conference decided to issue one of the more daring political pronouncements of modern times by an official church body. On 13 February, the bishops denounced the elections as fraudulent. They declared that Marcos' government could not command the people's allegiance because it lacked all moral foundation, and they called on the faithful to resist this evil with peaceful non-violence.

'We are not going to effect the change we seek by doing nothing, by sheer apathy,' the bishops insisted. In their pronouncement, read from pulpits all across the country, the bishops dared to propose non-violent resistance:

> Neither do we advocate a bloody, violent means of righting this wrong. If we did, we would be sanctioning the enormous sin of fratricidal strife. Killing to achieve justice is not within the purview of our Christian vision in our present context.
>
> The way indicated to us now is the way of nonviolent struggle for justice.
>
> This means active resistance of evil by peaceful means — in the manner of Christ . . .
>
> We therefore ask every loyal member of the Church, every community of the faithful, to form their judgment about the February 7 polls. And if in faith they see things as we the bishops do, we must come together and discern what appropriate actions to take that will be according to the mind of Christ . . .
>
> These last few days have given us shining examples of the nonviolent struggle for justice we advocate here . . .
>
> Now is the time to speak up. Now is the time to repair the wrong . . . But we insist: Our acting must always be according to the Gospel of Christ, that is, in a peaceful, nonviolent way.[18]

Hildegard Goss-Mayr believes this declaration by the bishops was the first occasion, at least in modern times, when a Catholic Bishops Conference publicly called on the faithful to engage in non-violent civil disobedience to overthrow an unjust system.[19] Cardinal Sin, the Catholic Archbishop of Manila, called it 'the strongest statement any group of bishops has produced anywhere since the days of Henry VIII [in the early sixteenth century]'.[20]

As the bishops' statement reverberated around the Philippines, Cory Aquino was meeting with 350 key advisers to plan a campaign of non-violent resistance. The Goss-Mayrs joined Cory Aquino, Cardinal Sin and others to devise scenarios and develop an extended, non-violent campaign of marches and boycotts designed to overthrow Marcos. A crowd of one million cheering supporters wildly applauded as Mrs Aquino launched her campaign of civil disobedience on 16 February. The tide had turned.[21]

Marcos, however, was determined to stay in power. He announced his intention to meet force with force. The struggle would be long and tough.

'People Power'

But surprise struck again on Saturday evening, 22 February. Unexpectedly Juan Ponce Enrile (Marcos' Minister of Defence) and General Fidel Ramos rebelled. Denouncing the fraudulent elections in a news conference, they declared Mrs Aquino the rightful President, and at 9.00 p.m., with only two hundred armed defenders, they barricaded themselves inside their camps in the middle of Metropolitan Manila. Their two hundred soldiers were at the mercy of Marcos' army of 250,000. The President could destroy them at will.

At that moment, Butz Aquino and Cardinal Sin unleashed 'people power'. Late on Saturday night, Butz Aquino called cause-orientated groups to fill the streets outside Enrile's and Ramos' campus. 'We will surround the camps and protect them with our bodies,' he announced boldly.[22]

Cardinal Sin went on the radio Saturday evening and urged the people to surround the camps. 'Go to Camp Aguinaldo and show your solidarity' with Ramos and Enrile, 'our two good friends', the Cardinal pleaded.[23] Within hours, thousands of men, women and children ringed the gates of the camps, blocking any potential movement by Marcos' army. Marcos would have to kill civilians if he chose to attack.

Before he went on the radio, Cardinal Sin called three orders of nuns. To each, he said: 'Right now get out from your cells and go to the chapel and pray ... And fast until I tell you to stop. We are in battle.'[24] No troops attacked the rebels on Saturday night.

By Sunday morning the streets around the camps were overflowing with people. Families came with children and picnic baskets. In spite of the danger, the mood was festive. All over the city, taxi and truck drivers spontaneously volunteered to shuttle people to the scene of action. Ramos and Enrile went on the air to beg for more civilians to flood the streets to act as a buffer between themselves and Marcos' soldiers. They fully expected an attack. According to a professor at the Philippine Military Academy, it was this surge of 'people power' that made the difference. 'It was the first time in history', Lieutenant Colonel Purificacion said, 'that so many civilians went to protect the military.'[25]

The non-violent soldiers of this 'classless revolution'

came from every walk of life.[26] Rich bankers, top executives and business men drove their cars to the camps. The poor walked. Men and women, children and grandparents, priest and nuns, flooded the streets. Pregnant women with babies in their arms came ready to defy advancing tanks.

Sunday afternoon at 3.00 p.m. the tanks came. A large force of marines with tanks and armoured personnel carriers headed for Enrile and Ramos' little band of rebels. Rumbling through the streets, the huge machines stopped only a kilometre from Ramos' headquarters, blocked by thousands of bodies ready to die rather than let them continue.

Amado L. Lacuesta, Jr, just one of the hundreds of thousands of civilians in the streets, offers a powerful eyewitness account of the people's raw courage.[27] As he squeezed his way through the densely packed street, he finally got close to where General Tadiar of the marines was negotiating with the civilians who totally surrounded his tanks and armoured personnel carriers (APC). The sea of kneeling people were praying, some holding small statues of the Virgin Mary. General Tadiar demanded that the people let him through, but they refused. Just then Butz Aquino arrived, clambered up on the APC and explained how people power could avoid bloodshed.

As the soldiers pushed Aquino off the huge machine, its engines roared. Weeping and praying, the people expected to be crushed. At the very front were three nuns, kneeling in prayer an arm's length from the throbbing motors. The metal mountain jerked forward once, twice, then stopped. The crowd cheered wildly. As a military helicopter made a low sweep, the people offered cigarettes to the soldiers, who looked away with a mixture of disdain and uncertainty. Again the engines roared and the machine jerked forward. Men pushed against the advancing metal wall as the nuns continued to kneel in prayer. Row after row of densely packed bodies stood ready to be pulverised by tons of metal. But again the towering monster halted. This time, after more hesitation, the APC swivelled and retreated to the deafening roar of thousands of relieved cheering voices.

Cardinal Sin tells the story of bedridden, eighty-one year old Mrs Monzon, owner of Arellano University. Everywhere she went, she used a wheelchair. But Mrs Monzon insisted on joining the people in the streets in front of the camps. When the tanks came, she wheeled in front of the advancing monsters. Armed with a crucifix, she called out to the soldiers: 'Stop. I am an old woman. You can kill me, but you shouldn't kill your fellow Filipinos.' Overcome, a soldier jumped off the tank and embraced the bold non-violent resister. 'I cannot kill you,' he told her, 'you are just like my mother.' She stayed in the street all night in her wheelchair.[28]

The marines finally withdrew without firing a shot.

Monday brought more high drama. At dawn, three thousand marines succeeded in dispersing part of the crowd with tear gas. But seven helicopter gunships with sufficient firepower to obliterate both Ramos' rebel troops and the surrounding crowds landed peacefully and defected. At 9.00 a.m. Marcos appeared defiantly on television for a few minutes and then disappeared as rebel solders seized Channel 4 TV.

Romeo Lavella, Jr, who lived near Channel 4, tells what he saw just after rebels seized the station.[29] Hearing scattered gun shots, he rushed into the streets where swarms of people stood between two groups of heavily armed soldiers. The pro-Marcos loyalists had more than twice as many men as the rebels who had just seized the station.

As sporadic gunfire erupted, a pick-up truck with a priest praying loudly slowly inched forward. As he prayed the Rosary and sang the Ave Maria, the people did the same. In the truck were statues of the crucified Christ and the Virgin Mary. Awed, the soldiers stopped shooting. As another priest and civilians helped negotiate an agreement between the soldiers, the priest and people continued to pray and sing. Channel 4, meanwhile, stayed in the hands of the people.

Hundreds of thousands jammed the streets in front of the camps on Monday. From Cardinal Sin's four auxiliary bishops to unknown slum-dwellers, the people defied the guns and tanks.

One particularly striking encounter occurred in front of the Polymedic Hospital near the camps. Several trucks with gun-wielding soldiers and two APCs slipped past the crowd by displaying yellow streamers (Cory Aquino's campaign colour). A moment later, however, the crowd discovered their mistake and people rushed to seal the street. Middle-aged ladies prayed loudly as helicopters hovered overhead. As the people stood their ground, the massive machines halted. Nobody would retreat. L. P. Flores' eyewitness account of the soldiers' reactions reveals the mystery of 'people power':

> The people pressed their bodies against the armor. Their faces were pleading but they were clothed in nothing but raw courage. In that decisive and tense moment, the soldiers atop the armored carriers pointed their guns of every make at the crowd but their faces betrayed agony. And I knew then, as the crowd, too, must have discerned: the soldiers did not have the heart to pull the trigger on civilians armed only with their convictions. The pact had been sealed. There was tacit agreement: 'We keep this

˙street corner, you retreat.' And true enough, the armored
carriers rolled back and applause echoed˙.

The face of that soldier struggling in agony for the
decision to shoot or not, on the verge of tears, will forever
remain in my memory.[30]

Dozens, indeed hundreds, of similar personal struggles ended with soldiers accepting flowers and embrac-
ing civilians. The battle was over. By Monday afternoon, a majority of the armed forces had abandoned
Marcos. On Tuesday morning, Marcos stubbornly went
through an inaugural ceremony, but his power had
evaporated. Late that evening, he fled. Mrs Aquino was
President.

Evaluating a Non-violent Success

It would be naive, of course, to suppose that unarmed
civilians in the streets singlehandedly overthrew
Marcos. International pressure (including President
Reagan's belated decision to abandon Marcos) and the
revolt of the army were clearly important. According to
an editorial in the *Philippine Daily Inquirer*, however,
it was massive non-violent resistance that made the
difference.

> When the revolution now popularly called People Power
> began, it was triggered by two Filipinos – Juan Ponce
> Enrile and Fidel Ramos. But neither of them would have
> survived if the people had not put themselves between the
> attackers and the leaders of the revolt.
> People all over the world then saw the unbelievable.
> Filipinos charging at giant tanks with Volkswagens.
> Nuns and priests meeting armored cars with Rosaries and
> prayers. Little children giving grim soldiers flowers and
> urging them not to fight for Marcos. People linking arms
> and blocking tanks, daring them to crush their fellow
> Filipinos, which they did not.[31]

Reading through the many eyewitness accounts in *An Eyewitness History: People Power, The Philippine Revolution of 1986*, one is amazed by the centrality of prayer and religious devotion. Sister Teresa was one of the Carmelite nuns ordered to fast and pray by Cardinal Sin. 'We never forgot even for an instant that we were doing battle. We daily called God in prayer to assist us all: those outside and we inside.' The radio accounts of the struggle in the streets, Sr Teresa confessed, shaped their prayers.[32]

Praying nuns and non-violent resisters armed only with religious symbols had obviously functioned as an effective deterrent:

> People were willing to die but not to kill. And I thought that even if some soldiers were willing to shoot the people, they were not willing to shoot the crucifixes. Many of them come from the provinces where they were raised to fear God. They could never shoot at people who were praying. They could have shot people who were throwing stones, as they did during the rallies. But this was the first time that they were confronted with prayers. They did not know how to react. I think this was crucial to the whole nonviolence stance.
>
> The people were there to defend the camp. They were not aggressors. We cannot pray and be violent at the same time. The religious character of the revolution made the revolution very unique. If you took away the religious flavor of the revolution, you would have removed the essence of it.[33]

Professor Randolf David, Director of Third World Studies at the University of the Philippines, concluded in amazement: 'I have been a student of revolutions, but this is the first time I have seen an assault led by the Virgin Mary.'[34]

Undoubtedly the previous training in non-violence had played a genuine role, although the convergence of the masses to protect the rebel soldiers was essentially a spontaneous emotional response rather than the result of careful organising. Not surprisingly, non-violent leaders like Father Jose Blanco, the founder of AKKAPKA, believe the Philippine revolution points the way for the rest of the world:

> What does God wish us to proclaim to the world through our nonviolent revolution? Simply this: the political problems of people can be solved without recourse to arms or violence.
>
> The world's problems are best solved if we respect the humanity, the dignity of every human person concerned. The desire to be violent or to use violence can be tamed and diminished, if we show love, care, joy to those who are unjust and wish to be violent. Violence addresses the aggressor. Nonviolence searches out and addresses the humanity in the enemy or oppressor. When that common humanity is touched, then the other is helped to recognize the human person within and ceases to be inhuman, unjust, and violent.
>
> One does not have to be a Christian to reach out to the humanity in the other.[35]

Such optimism needs tempering. One successful nonviolent revolution does not banish war. Nor dare one overlook the special circumstances that helped nonviolence succeed in this unique situation. Furthermore, simply overthrowing Marcos did not create economic justice in the Philippines. A year and a half later, it is still unclear whether President Cory Aquino will be able to correct the structural injustice that has created so much poverty in her country.

But the Filipino people did depose a powerful dictator with virtually no bloodshed. Precisely in a context where many had concluded that the only viable path was years of bloody revolution, non-violence produced a stunning victory. Non-violent revolution *is* possible.

PART II:

A CALL TO ACTION

4 MULTIPLYING SUCCESS

> Most movements of social change have only begun to experiment with the real power and flexibility of nonviolence... One of the greatest discoveries of this century is in the real power of mass nonviolent movements.
>
> Richard B. Deats[1]

Now is the time to test the limits and possibilities of non-violent resistance to injustice and oppression. The Christian community has never done that in a sustained, carefully organised and solidly financed way. Nor has any other community. In the late twentieth century, however, there are compelling reasons for experimenting with non-violence on a scale never before attempted in human history.

Why We Must Seriously Explore Non-violent Alternatives

The sheer success of numerous non-violent campaigns in itself warrants increased exploration and implementation. The previous chapters have chronicled story after story where even spontaneous, ill-prepared non-violent resistance succeeded beyond anyone's wildest dreams.

Furthermore, non-violent campaigns have again and again proved more effective than lethal violence. That is true in the very specific sense that they have accomplished their goals with far less loss of life than their violent alternatives.

When one compares the numbers of people who died in the campaigns for independence in India and Algeria, the figures are astonishing. India's non-violent struggle for independence from the British took longer than Algeria's violent victory over French colonialism (twenty-eight years, from 1919–1946, compared to seven years, from 1955–1961). But only eight thousand Indians died, whereas a million Algerian lives were lost. Even more staggering is the comparison of the numbers of dead with total population figures. Of India's three hundred million, only 1 in 400,000 died. Of Algeria's ten million, 1 in 10 was sacrificed.[2]

Solidarity in Poland accomplished more in combatting Marxist totalitarianism than did Argentina in the Falklands/Malvinas War against democratic England. But only three hundred Poles died, whereas Argentina lost a thousand in two weeks. Less than a hundred died (fifty thousand more were jailed) in the American civil rights movement. In the Cuban revolution, twenty thousand died. There were at least that many deaths (and probably more) in the Nicaraguan revolution against Somosa.[3]

One understands why Senator Benigno Aquino of the Philippines turned away from violence after a comparative study of violent and non-violent revolutions. The twentieth century has demonstrated that non-violent revolutions can be more effective.

The past century of carnage and the future prospects of much worse to come also compel us to search for non-violent alternatives. The twentieth century has been the most bloody in human history. A nuclear holocaust would make all past bloodshed seem like child's play. The ever-upward spiral of violence and counter-violence seems not only unending but ever more colossal in its destructive dimensions. Surely at a time like this, an exploration of non-violent alternatives must be high on everyone's agenda.

In May 1983, I was one of the speakers at a large conference in California on 'The Church and Peacemaking in the Nuclear Age'. In my speech, I proposed the kind of non-violent peace team on the Honduras–Nicaragua border that took shape later that year with Witness for Peace.[4] What surprised me was the positive response of another speaker, General Robert Mathis, who had recently retired as Chief of the US Air Force. Subsequent conversation helped me understand why General Mathis liked my proposal. General Mathis is so terrified by what he knows about the deadly dangers posed by nuclear weapons that he is eager to explore any realistic approach that offers non-violent alternatives for resolving international conflict. That is not to claim that large numbers of top military leaders will quickly join a coalition to implement non-violence. Such a claim would be naive. But the episode does indicate that the desire for non-violent alternatives is more widespread and urgent in our time.

Still another reason for serious testing of non-violence is that it is more democratic and therefore less subject to abuse. A non-violent struggle involves large numbers rather than a handful of highly trained, well-equipped élites who consequently possess enormous power after their violent revolution has succeeded. Gandhi pointed out that 'in nonviolence the masses have a weapon which enables a child, a woman, or even a decrepit old man to resist the mightiest government successfully'.[5]

The Nobel Peace Prize winner Adolfo Perez Esquivel

underlines this strength of non-violence with his humorous discussion of the 'battle of the elephant and the ants'. 'True the elephant is stronger. But the ants ... well, there are more of us.'[6] Hence the repeated success of non-violent masses, even when pitted against powerful and ruthless military machines.

But the virtue of non-violence lies not only in the fact that it enables unarmed masses to conquer armed opponents. It is also that there is a better chance of democratic results after the revolution, precisely because the process itself is more democratic. When small, armed élites have seized power, even in the name of 'justice for the people', the result has very often been further repression. One need only think of Stalin in Russia, Mao in China, Ben Bella in Algeria, Castro in Cuba, and Pinochet in Chile. Once chosen, violence is not easily abandoned. Violent revolution by an armed élite is one of the least effective training grounds for democratic cooperation.

Advocates of non-violence have sometimes been accused of naivete about human nature and the pervasive power of evil. But David Hoekema turns this argument on its head, precisely at the point of the abuse of lethal weapons intended only to restrain evil.

> The reality of human sinfulness means that the instruments we intend to use for good are certain to be turned to evil purposes as well. There is therefore a strong presumption for using those means of justice that are least likely to be abused and least likely to cause irrevocable harm when they are abused.[7]

A popular non-violent revolution increases the prospects of a democratic future. Its very nature prevents the emergence of small armed élites who consequently possess enormous power that is regularly abused. At the same time, non-violence schools large numbers of people in the tough skills of political struggle and respect for the humanity even of opponents.[8] The tragedy of Karl Marx is not that he saw the reality of class conflict, but rather that his way of solving the problem elevated conflict to a necessary law of history.[9] Rather than exacerbating conflict between groups in a society, on the contrary, non-violence reduces the hostility. That in turn makes more possible a future society where all can coexist in relative harmony, freedom and justice.

In the light of these compelling reasons for a new, sustained exploration of the possibilities of non-violence, it is not surprising that more and more official church documents have recently issued the call. Even so, the number and diversity are impressive.

Church Leaders' Calls For Non-violent Options

The Latin American Catholic bishops appealed for non-violence in their official statements at Puebla in 1979: 'Our responsibility as Christians is to use all possible means to promote the implementation of nonviolent tactics in the effort to re-establish justice in economic and political relations.'[10] One commentator concluded that at Puebla, conservative, moderate and progressive thinkers agreed that 'the future struggle in Latin America will depend on ... the techniques used by Martin Luther King and Mahatma Gandhi'.[11]

In 1983, Belgian and Dutch Catholic bishops both affirmed the importance of non-violence. In July, the Belgian bishops said: 'Maybe the Church of earlier times and of today should have given more emphasis to the witness of nonviolence.'[12] In May, the Dutch bishops had been more emphatic: 'The development of methods which enable people to resist injustice and to defend themselves without using violence is in keeping with the spirit of the Gospel and may not be labelled as utopian and unrealistic.'[13]

In their widely acclaimed peace pastoral of the same year, the US Catholic bishops spoke even more vigorously. Noting that Vatican II had praised those who renounce the use of violence in favour of other methods of defence, they insisted: 'Non-violent means of resistance to evil deserve much more study and consideration than they have thus far received. There have been significant instances in which people have successfully resisted oppression without recourse to arms. Non-violence is not the way of the weak, the cowardly, or the impatient.'[14]

At the conclusion of this lengthy appeal for developing non-violent means of conflict resolution, the bishops declared: 'No greater challenge or higher priority can be imagined than the development and perfection of a theology of peace suited to a civilization poised on the brink of self-destruction.'[15]

Three years later, the United Methodist bishops added their voice to the list of official church appeals for a more vigorous exploration of non-violence. Citing Harvard University's Gene Sharp and Witness for Peace, they said: 'We encourage special study of non-violent defense and peacemaking forces.'[16]

Unlike the Catholic and Methodist bishops, the National Association of Evangelicals has been largely supportive of current nuclear policy. Their *Guidelines: Peace, Freedom and Security Studies*, issued in 1986, unhesitatingly offers an ethical defence of nuclear weapons. But even in this document, one finds a repeated call for 'alternatives to violence in world politics'.[17] In a section on 'Change without Violence', they pledge to 'study and seek ways to apply that spectrum of possibilities for change without violence that runs from nonviolent forms of social organization for the defense of values to new concepts of communication and conflict resolution'.[18]

In December 1986 the Mennonite and Brethren in Christ Churches of North America completed an extensive two-year exploration of a proposal to establish peacemaking teams trained to intervene in situations of violent conflict using the techniques of King and Gandhi. Abandoning the category of 'nonresistance' as the dominant definition of their pacifism, they called for 'caring, direct challenge of evil'. And they endorsed the establishment, training and deployment of Christian Peacemaker Teams using non-violent direct action.[19]

Common Ground for Pacifists and Non-Pacifists

Non-violence is clearly on the Christian church's agenda in a dramatic new way. Not only historic Anabaptist pacifists but also Catholics and Protestants in the just war tradition are calling for a new exploration of non-violence. In fact, as the US Catholic bishops point out, non-violent resistance offers 'a common ground of agreement' between Christians who stand in the just war tradition and those who stand in the pacifist tradition.[20]

In fact, one must put it much more strongly. To have any integrity, both the pacifist and just war traditions demand a massive commitment to non-violence.

According to the just war tradition, lethal violence must always be a last resort. How then can Christians in the just war tradition claim that they are justified in resorting to war until they have devoted vast amounts of time and money to explore the possibilities of non-violence? In a century where Martin Luther King and Mahatma Gandhi are two of the most revered international religious leaders; in a century where success after success has been registered in non-violent campaigns against oppression, injustice and dictatorship; at such a time, no one can honestly deny that non-violence is often a realistic alternative to war or violent revolution. The only way that the just war criterion of 'last resort' can have any integrity at all in our time is if Christians in that tradition commit themselves to a sophisticated and sustained testing of the possibilities of non-violent alternatives.[21]

Pacifist premises demand a similar commitment. Pacifists hotly reject the charge that their refusal to bear arms is a callous or cowardly disregard of their obligation to defend the weak and defenceless against bullies and tyrants. If pacifists think they have an alternative to war, then they must have the guts and integrity to prove it in the brutal world of Hitlers, Somosas, Pinochets and Pol Pots. If pacifists are not ready to run the same risk as soldiers in non-violent struggle against evil, they have no moral right to pretend that they know a better way. Only pacifists ready to risk death by the thousands will have credibility in a century that has witnessed the greatest bloodshed in human history. Costly pacifist involvement in successful non-violent campaigns is perhaps the most effective way to convince doubting contemporaries that there is an alternative to war. Pacifist premises and goals demand a much more vigorous commitment to non-violent defence of freedom, justice and peace.

A new non-violent movement in the Christian church

possesses a twofold virtue. It offers the promise of greater integrity to the stated positions of both pacifist and just war Christians. It also offers a channel, not for ending their ongoing debate, but for throwing the emphasis on mutual cooperation in non-violent resistance as both focus on what the US Catholic bishops have rightly called the 'common ground of agreement'.[22]

A Call For a New Exploration of Non-violent Alternatives

Now is the time to move from spontaneous, ill-prepared non-violent skirmishes to a serious and sustained global exploration of the full power of non-violent alternatives. Harvard's Gene Sharp, probably the most important contemporary analyst of non-violence, underlines the difference:

> Nonviolent action has almost always been improvised without significant awareness of the past history of this type of struggle. It has usually been waged without qualified leadership, or without . . . wide popular understanding of the technique, without thorough comprehension of its requirements for effectiveness, without preparations and training, without analyses of past conflicts, without studies of strategy and tactics, without a consciousness among the actionists that they were waging a special type of struggle. In short, the most unfavorable circumstances possible have accompanied the use of this technique. It is amazing that the significant number of victories for non-violent struggle exist at all, for these conditions of the lack of knowledge, skill and preparations have been to the highest degree unfavorable.
>
> In contrast, for many centuries military struggle has benefited from conscious efforts to improve its effectiveness in all the ways in which nonviolent action has lacked.[23]

Many today honestly believe we must maintain massive nuclear and non-nuclear weaponry. Others disagree. Without settling that disagreement, however, both can unite in a new exploration of the possibilities and limits of non-violence. Could we not all agree that it would be worthwhile to see what would happen if for two decades we spent at least one-tenth as much on non-violent methods as we do on preparation for lethal violence? Concretely that would mean massive new activity in at least three areas: study centres to analyse the history of previous non-violent successes and failures; training centres to prepare large numbers of people in the strategy and tactics of actual non-violent campaigns; and the launching of new non-violent movements. In different ways, study centres, training centres and actual campaigns would all serve to popularise the possibilities of non-violence.

Study centres

Harvard University's Program on Nonviolent Sanctions in Conflict and Defense offers a model that ought to be duplicated at scores of colleges and universities around the world. Directed by Dr Gene Sharp and located in Harvard's Center for International Affairs, the Program on Nonviolent Sanctions attracts a growing circle of scholars. They are producing an expanding stream of articles and books that offer detailed analyses of specific non-violent campaigns, comparative studies of tactics, methods and outcomes, and theoretical analyses of power and politics from the perspective of non-violence.[24]

If the Christian church is serious about exploring non-violence, then we must develop financial resources and the scholars to make possible scores of new study centres on non-violence around the world. Individuals, foundations and denominations can provide the money. Colleges and universities can develop the centres to produce both scholarly studies and popular materials.[25]

Training centres

We also need new training centres. We saw in chapter 3 how important were the short-term training institutes conducted for key Philippine leadership by the Goss-Mayrs. The Fellowship of Reconciliation sponsors training seminars and Witness for Peace does short training sessions for its volunteers. Other modest training programmes exist and limited materials have been prepared.[26] But much more is required. We need a number of action-orientated training centres that can produce trained non-violent activists familiar with the tactics of Gandhi and King, and ready to lead non violent campaigns.

Some training centres could concentrate on producing generalists – trainers of trainers. Others could prepare people for specific campaigns like Witness for Peace and/or new ventures. In both cases, key components would include spiritual formation and the techniques of non-violent direct action. The development of a biblical spirituality of prayer, Bible study and worship focused on the heavy emotional demands of costly non-violent intervention would be essential. Each volunteer should be supported by a 'home-town' support group and prayer chain committed to regular prayer plus all-night intercession during emergencies.

All the concrete strategies, techniques and tactics learnt in the many campaigns of King, Gandhi and others need to be studied carefully.[27] Role-playing scenarios of intervention, ambush, crowd control and injury would be important. When training for action in a specific locale, extensive study of the geography, history, economics, politics and culture of the area would be an additional crucial component.

New non-violent movements

Launching new non-violent movements is so difficult as to seem almost impossible. But congregations, denominations and interdenominational bodies could decide to call, train and equip new teams familiar with the history, theory and tactics of non-violence and ready to move into situations of violent conflict. Such teams could reduce both killing and oppression by their direct intervention and also serve as the trainers and catalysts for provoking the widespread adoption of non-violent methods by much larger numbers of people. In the last chapter, we saw that the Mennonites of North America had decided to launch new Christian Peacemaker Teams ready to intervene peacefully in conflict situations both in North America and abroad. If violence is truly to be a last resort for churches in the just war tradition, then they will need to do the same.

Could not the Christian church set the target of training, by the year 1995, five thousand volunteers per year for an ever-expanding, worldwide Christian peace brigade? Trained volunteers could spend one to three years in new non-violent campaigns all around the world. A growing body of 'non-violent reserves' would be available for special emergencies.

Frequently, these teams would work in their own country and culture. Frequently, too, however, as Peace Brigades International and Witness for Peace have shown, international teams would be desirable and effective.

Non-violent Strategies, Tactics and Principles

It is impossible in a book such as this to describe the precise scenarios for the actual intervention of Christian Peacemaker Teams. But we do know the places where they are needed as well as the places where new groupings and proposals for non-violent intervention are emerging. An extremely creative new non-violent proposal for the struggle against apartheid has just appeared.[28] Non-violent tactics are increasingly being explored by Palestinians on the West Bank in Israel.[29] As this book goes to press, a substantially non-violent campaign in the West Bank has captured world headlines for several months. In South Africa, black Church leaders are making plans for a new Church-based non-violent campaign against apartheid. A hundred other places of violent agony from Sri Lanka to Northern Ireland to El Salvador cry out for non-violent alternatives.

While the specific tactics of Christian Peacemaker Teams (CPTs) in all these places cannot be decided abstractly ahead of time, certain general principles and criteria of intervention are fairly clear.

- CPTs would be *non-partisan in outlook* and not seek to promote or destroy any nation or group, although in specific situations a particular aspect of the policy of one nation or group would be challenged.
- Therefore CPTs would always, at every phase of their activity, *seek to establish and maintain dialogue* with all parties to a conflict. They would never attempt to impose a specific political, constitutional or economic proposal, but rather seek to create a context where the warring parties themselves could peacefully negotiate solutions appropriate for their unique setting.

- At the same time, CPTs would not be indifferent to the biblical call for justice and freedom for all people. Therefore, CPTs would always *seek to act in ways that promote religious and political freedom*, including freedom of worship, speech, democratic elections and equality before the law. They would also *seek to foster economic justice* where all are genuinely free to enjoy adequate food, housing, clothing, education, health care and meaningful work to earn their own keep.

Several criteria for intervention would be basic.

- CPTs would intervene only after a careful attempt to dialogue with, understand and affirm the legitimate concerns of all parties to a conflict.
- CPTs would intervene only after at least one major party in the conflict had issued an invitation and agreed to give them the freedom to operate in their area.
- CPTs would always seek to operate in the territory of both sides to a conflict, and would decide to operate exclusively in the territory of one side only after their offer to operate on both sides had been rejected.
- CPTs would intervene only when they believed that they could operate non-violently in a way that would probably promote peace, justice and freedom.
- CPTs would place a high priority on sharing the vision and techniques of non-violence with the people wherever they serve.

What kinds of interventions might be possible for CPTs? The history of non-violent action suggests a wide variety of possibilities.

Interpositioning involves placing oneself between two warring parties. Perhaps the most dramatic interpositioning has occurred in India where Gandhi and then the Shanti Sena movement intervened physically between rioting Hindu and Muslim mobs. Interpositioning can occur in a number of ways:

- *patrolling* demarcation lines, demilitarised zones or borders to deter invasion, violations or disturbances.
- *denying access* to certain areas or buildings (e.g. a town under attack by guerrillas, as in the beginnings of Witness for Peace in Northern Nicaragua).
- *separating hostile groups* (e.g. Hindus and Moslems engaged in inter-religious killing).
- *disarming persons or groups* (a Quaker team did this during the struggle of Native Americans at Wounded Knee).[30]
- *protecting persons or groups* by living and travelling with them (as in the case of Peace Brigades International in Honduras).

Not all non-violent direct action involves physically placing oneself between two warring parties. It is totally impossible for fifty or even five hundred volunteers in Witness for Peace in Nicaragua to physically stand between Nicaragua's almost three million civilians and twelve thousand guerrillas. Much of their work has been to *record and report* the many instances of torture, kidnapping and death. Of course, interpositioning is also involved, since careful documentation is possible only if one is present in the battle zone. However, the primary focus is not on preventing attacks by interposing one's body, but rather on changing public opinion through more accurate information about the atrocities.

CPTs might also engage in *temporary police work* in a destabilised situation. This might happen if CPTs replaced an *ad hoc* military force or even a United Nations military unit. (This seemed possible in Cyprus in 1973.)[31]

Perhaps some new non-violent tactic might be found

to intervene to *dramatise* the evil of apartheid. What would happen if Billy Graham, the Archbishop of Canterbury and Pope John Paul II led an international team of CPTs to join a new inter-racial campaign of non-violence within South Africa?

Interpositioning, documentation and reporting, temporary police work and dramatisation of injustice would all be possible types of intervention for CPTs.

But would they ever succeed? What is the basis of power of non-violent action?[32]

The Power of Non-violence

Too often, power is understood only in terms of lethal coercion. (Mao said power is what comes from the barrel of a gun.) Certainly power includes the ability to control people's actions by the threat or use of lethal violence. But the people also possess non-violent collective power because they can choose to withdraw their support from rulers. The political scientist Karl Deutsch points out that 'the voluntary or habitual compliance of the mass of the population is the invisible but very real basis of the power of every government'.[33] The potential choice by large numbers to withdraw that compliance represents enormous collective power. Consequently, without any arms at all, the people can exercise non-violent power either by doing what they are not expected or required to do or by refusing to do what they are expected to do.[34] Large numbers of people using non-violent techniques possess enormous non-violent collective power.

But non-violence does not require large numbers to have power. Witness for Peace and Peace Brigades International have demonstrated that even small groups can exercise substantial power.

Non-violent activists possess strong moral power. Praying, reconciling CPTs risking their lives for others would share something of the moral power Jesus exercised in the temple. He was able single-handedly to drive the crowds of angry, oppressive moneychangers out of the temple, not because he was stronger or his disciples were more numerous: it was because deep in their hearts they knew he was right.

International public opinion would also be powerful. The daring of the CPTs would sometimes be headline news around the world. Any group or nation that battered or killed prominent, internationally famous Christian leaders or even ordinary members of CPTs would suffer substantial international disapproval.

A mandate also provides authority and therefore power. A mandate to intervene internationally, if issued by an organisation such as the Organization of African States or the United Nations, could legitimise CPTs. So too – at least to a certain, if lesser, degree – would an invitation by prominent Christian leaders and established churches, as well as recognised leaders of other religious groups.

Self-sacrificial love weakens even vicious opponents. Though not always of course. People ready to suffer for others sometimes get crucified. But often, too, they evoke a more human, loving response, even from brutal foes.

The discipline, training and coordination of an organised body with visible symbols of identity and cohesion are also powerful. Part of the power of a large group of police or soldiers lies in their uniforms, careful coordination and ability to act quickly, decisively and collectively. Highly trained and disciplined CPTs would possess some of this same power.

Finally, there is the divine power of the Lord of

history. What the Almighty will do if thousands of praying, loving Christians non-violently face death in the search for peace and justice will remain shrouded in mystery – at least until we have the courage to try it. But what believer will doubt that there may be surprises ahead?

We do have to be honest and realistic. We never dare pretend that no one would get hurt. Tyrants and bullies callously torture and murder. Opponents would intimidate, threaten, wound, torture and massacre even praying CPTs. But we have always assumed that death by the thousands, indeed even millions, is necessary in war. Would it not be right for non-violent CPTs to be ready to risk death in the same way soldiers do? Certainly we must not seek death. Martyr complexes are wrong. But a readiness to lay down one's life for others lies at the heart of the gospel.

Death will be tragically intertwined with any serious test of the effectiveness of non-violence. But that will not prove that the effort has failed. It will only underline the depth of human sin. And also the fact that Christians are willing to imitate the One they worship.

5 THE MORAL EQUIVALENT OF WAR

> The War against war is going to be no holiday excursion or camping party.
>
> William James[1]

In a now famous essay, 'The Moral Equivalent of War', William James argued that the struggle for non-violent alternatives would be a long and costly battle. Why? Because 'history is a bath of blood'.[2] War has been central to human history because violent instincts are deeply embedded in the human heart.

The costly demands of non-violent action

Anyone seeking to reduce war, James argued, must realise that in important respects war represents human nature at its best. Not only does war smash the dull boredom of ordinary life, it also summons forth high virtues such as courage, self-sacrifice, intense discipline and total dedication. War disciplines the slack, rewards the daring, evokes one's last ounce of energy and breeds loyalty to the larger community. How, James concluded, can any peace movement succeed unless it offers meaningful substitutes for the glamour and appeal of war?

If James' essay poses a valid question, then vigorous non-violent action offers the answer. Non-violent resistance to tyrants, oppressors and brutal invaders is not for fools or cowards. It demands courage and daring of the highest order. It requires discipline, training and a willingness to face death. It produces collective pride in the group or society that successfully, as in the Philippines, stands together and overcomes a brutal foe.

Are there tough, brave volunteers for that kind of costly, demanding battle? Would the people be there if the Christian church – and people of other faiths as well – called for a vast multiplication of our efforts in non-violent alternatives to war? Would the scholars and trainees emerge if we doubled and then quadrupled our study and training centres on non-violence? Would the non-violent troops be available to be trained by the thousands and then tens of thousands to form disciplined Christian Peacemaker Teams ready to walk into the face of danger and death in loving confrontation of injustice and oppression? We will not know until courageous Christian leaders, organisations and denominations decide to issue the call and spend the money.

But the time has never been more right. At no time in history, perhaps, has the concrete evidence of the tangible success of non-violence been clearer. At no time has the need to break the escalating cycle of violence and counter-violence been greater. As late twentieth-century people glance back in anguish at history's most violent century and peer ahead fearfully to far worse potential catastrophes, a new sustained exploration of the possibilities of non-violence seems to be a prerequisite of sanity.

The ultimate risk

But the battle will be long and costly. To argue that non-violence is less costly in human lives than is warfare is not to pretend that no one will be wounded or killed. Some will die. Everyone must be ready to face death.

Are there enough people for such a struggle? The history of warfare and of non-violent action proves that danger does not deter volunteers. Throughout history, millions of bold souls have gladly risked death for a noble cause and a grand vision. Walter Wink is surely right that 'there is a whole host of people simply waiting for the Christian message to challenge them for once to a heroism worthy of their lives'.[3]

Death of course, is not the point. To seek martyrdom would be naive and immoral. The way of Christ is the way of life, not death. But the Christian martyrs of all ages provide testimony that the way to abundant life sometimes passes through the dark valley where the cross stands stark and rugged. Those who dare in loving obedience to shoulder that old rugged cross will exchange it some day for a crown of *shalom* in the peaceful kingdom of the reconciling Lamb.

NOTES

Introduction

1　Quoted in Adolfo Perez Esquivel, *Christ in a Poncho: Testimonials of the Nonviolent Struggles of Latin America,* ed. Charles Antoine, trans. Robert R. Barr (Maryknoll, NY: Orbis Books, 1983), p. 87.

2　Gene Sharp, *The Politics of Nonviolent Action,* 3 vols (Boston: Porter Sargent Publishers, 1973), 1., p. 98.

3　See the helpful discussion and literature cited in Duane K. Friesen, *Christian Peacemaking and International Conflict: A Realist Pacifist Perspective* (Scottdale, PA: Herald Press, 1986), pp. 143–157.

4　Sharp, *Politics of Nonviolent Action,* 2., pp. 117–435.

5　I have dealt with national self-defence in Part 4 of Ronald J. Sider and Richard K. Taylor, *Nuclear Holocaust and Christian Hope* (London: Hodder and Stoughton, 1983), pp. 229–292. Taylor is also working on a book that includes a discussion of non-violent methods for police work.

6　Pastoral Statement of the National Conference of Catholic Bishops, *The Challenge of Peace: God's Promise and Our Response* (Boston: St Paul Editions, 1983), No. 222, p. 58.

Chapter 1: What Exists is Possible

1　Kenneth Boulding, quoted in Jerome D. Frank, *Sanity and Survival: Psychological Aspects of War and Peace* (New York: Vintage Books, 1968), p. 270.

2　Gene Sharp has divided non-violent action into the three broad categories mentioned here: protest and persuasion, non-co-operation, and intervention; see Gene Sharp, *The Politics of Nonviolent Action,* 3 vols (Boston: Porter Sargent Publishers, 1973), 2., pp. 114–448.

　　In this book, I focus largely on the third, but all three are dealt with and are in fact inseparably interrelated.

3　Gene Sharp's book (see note 2) is one of the best. See also the Bibliography, especially the books by William Robert Miller (see note 11) and Anders Boserup and Andrew Mack (see note 37).

4   Josephus, *Wars*, ii. 9., in Hugh R. Trevor-Roper, *Josephus: The Jewish War and Other Selections* (Union Square, NY: Twayne Publishers, Inc., 1965), pp. 201, 202.

5   This story is told by Josephus; see *Antiquities*, xviii. 8. and *Wars*, ii. 10., in Trevor-Roper, *Josephus*.

6   Edward Gibbon, *The Decline and Fall of the Roman Empire*, vol. 2 (New York: Random House, 1954), p. 289.

7   Lanza del Vasto, *Warriors of Peace: Writings on the Technique of Nonviolence* (New York: Alfred A. Knopf, 1974), p. 197.

8   Gibbon, *Decline and Fall*, p. 293. See also, T. Walter Wallbank and Alastair Taylor, *Civilization Past and Present*, vol. 1 (Dallas, TX: Scott, Foresman, 1976), p. 215.

9   Attila was discovered dead in his bed soon after this incident. He had expired during one of his many honeymoon celebrations.

10 Walter H. Conser, Ronald M. McCarthy, David J. Toscano and Gene Sharp (eds), *Resistance, Politics and the American Struggle for Independence, 1765–1775* (Boulder, CO: Lynne Rienner Publishers, 1986).

11 Quoted in William Robert Miller, *Nonviolence: A Christian Interpretation* (New York: Association Press, 1964), p. 239.

12 For the story, see Miller, *Nonviolence*, pp. 230–243 and the short summary in Ronald J. Sider and Richard K. Taylor, *Nuclear Holocaust and Christian Hope* (Downers Grove, IL and Ramsey, NJ: InterVarsity Press/Paulist Press, 1982), pp. 235–237.

13 del Vasto, *Warriors of Peace*, p. 202.

14 Sharp, *Politics of Nonviolent Action*, 1., p. 98.

15 See Charles C. Walker, *A World Peace Guard* (Hyderabad, India: Academy of Gandhian Studies, 1981), p. 65, and Allan A. Hunter, *Courage in Both Hands* (New York: Ballantine Books, 1962), p. 90.

16 Walker, *Guard*, p. 65.

17 Quoted in Hunter, *Courage*, p. 92.

18 See the analysis of Weinberg, *Instead of Violence*, p. 303.

19 William James, 'The Moral Equivalent of War', in John K. Roth (ed.), *The Moral Equivalent of War and Other Essays* (New York: Harper & Row, 1971), p. 10.

20 Walker, *Guard*, pp. 65, 66.

21 *Ibid.*, p. 69.

22 Joan Bondurant provides this definition of satyagraha in her classic work *Conquest of Violence: The Gandhian Philosophy of Conflict*, (1958; revised edition, Berkeley, CA: University of

California Press, 1971), p. 16. In his autobiography (trans. Mahadev Desai), Gandhi offers the following interpretation: 'Sat = truth, Agraha = firmness'; see *Gandhi: An Autobiography by Mohandas K. Gandhi* (Boston, MA: Beacon Press, 1957), p. 319.

23   Quoted in Bondurant, *Conquest of Violence*, p. 96.
24   This section is based on Eknath Easwaran, *A Man to Match His Mountains: Badshah Khan, Nonviolent Soldier of Islam* (Petaluma, CA: Nilgiri Press, 1984).
25   *Ibid.*, p. 99.
26   *Ibid.*, p. 20.
27   *Ibid.*
28   *Ibid.*, p. 110.
29   *Ibid.*, p. 111.
30   *Ibid.*, p. 118.
31   *Ibid.*, p. 123.
32   *Ibid.*, p. 126–128.
33   *Ibid.*, p. 175.
34   *Ibid.*, p. 189.
35   *Ibid.*, p. 195.
36   Quoted in George Estey and Doris Hunter, *Nonviolence* (Waltham: Xerox College Publishing, 1971), p. 92.
37   Quoted in Anders Boserup and Andrew Mack, *War Without Weapons: Non-Violence in National Defense* (New York: Schocken Books, 1975), pp. 123–124.
38   Sharp, *Politics of Nonviolent Action*, 1., pp. 79–81.
39   Quoted in Gene Keyes, 'Peacekeeping by Unarmed Buffer Forces: Precedents and Proposals', in *Peace and Change: A Journal of Peace Research* 5/2,3 (1978), pp. 3–4.
40   Walker, *Guard*, p. 67.
41   Quoted in Keyes, 'Peacekeeping', p. 4.
42   Quoted *ibid.*
43   A general turned pacifist, Crozier greatly admired Gandhi and saw the 'Peace Army' as an outgrowth of Gandhian principles.
44   Keyes, 'Peacekeeping', p. 4.
45   See Sider and Taylor, *Nuclear Holocaust*, pp. 238–241 for a summary and the bibliographical sources. See also, Paul Wehr, 'Nonviolent Resistance to Nazism: Norway, 1940–45', *Peace and Change: A Journal of Peace Research* 10/3,4 (1984), pp. 77–95; and Paul Wehr, *Conflict Regulation* (Boulder, CO: Westview Press, 1979), pp. 69–100, which has a good study of the Norwegian communications network.
46   Quoted in Eivine Berggrar, 'Experiences of the Norwegian Church in the War', *The Lutheran World Review* 1/1 (1948), p. 51.

47 See Sider and Taylor, *Nuclear Holocaust*, pp. 242–246 for the sources.

48 Quoted in Nora Levin, *The Holocaust: The destruction of European Jewry, 1933–1945* (New York: Schocken Books, 1973), p. 401.

49 Quoted in Frederick B. Charry, *The Bulgarian Jews and the Final Solution 1940–1944* (Pittsburgh: University of Pittsburgh Press, 1972), p. 90.

50 See Patricia Parkman, *Insurrection Without Arms: The General Strike in El Salvador, 1944* (unpublished PhD dissertation, Temple University, 1980), for this story.

51 Quoted *ibid.*, p. 169.

52 See Sharp, *Politics of Nonviolent Action*, 1., pp. 90–93.

53 See Elizabeth Campuzano *et al.*, *Resistance in Latin America* (Philadelphia: American Friends Service Committee, 1970).

54 Sharp, *Politics of Nonviolent Action*, 1., pp. 98–101.

55 Gene Sharp, 'Philippines Taught Us Lessons of Nonviolence', *Los Angeles Times*, 4 April 1986, Section 2, p. 5.

56 Quoted in Madeleine G. Kalb, 'The U.N.'s Embattled Peacekeeper', *The New York Times Magazine*, 19 December 1982, p. 46.

57 Henry Wiseman, 'The United Nations Peacekeeping: An Historical Overview', in Henry Wiseman (ed.), *Peacekeeping: Appraisals and Proposals* (New York: Pergamon Press, 1983), pp. 23–25.

58 Andrew W. Cordier and Wilder Foote, *The Quest for Peace: The Dag Hammarskjöld Memorial Lectures* (New York: Columbia University Press, 1965), p. 113.

59 The observers served under the UNTSO banner – 'United Nations True Supervision Organization' – in Palestine. UNTSO personnel continue on assignment at the time of writing.

60 Kurt Waldheim, *The Challenge of Peace* (New York: Rawson, Wade Publishers, 1980), p. 135.

61 The United Nations Military Observer Group in India and Pakistan (UNMOGIP) continues to serve, though in a reduced capacity.

62 Kalb, 'Peacekeeper', p. 46, and Sydney D. Bailey, *How Wars End: The United Nations and the Termination of Armed Conflict*, vol. 1 (Oxford: Clarendon Press, 1982), pp. 4, 5.

63 Quoted in Charles C. Walker, *Peacekeeping: 1969* (Philadelphia: Friends Peace Committee, 1969), p. 2.

64 Antony Gilpin, 'Non-Violence in the U.N. Peacekeeping Operations', in Ted Dunn (ed.), *Foundations of Peace and Freedom* (Wales: Salesbury Press, 1975), p. 279.

65 Keyes, 'Peacekeeping', p. 3.
66 Kalb, 'Peacekeeper', p. 48.
67 Indar Jit Rikhye, 'Peacekeeping and Peacemaking', in Wiseman, *Peacekeeping*, p. 6.
68 Quoted in Kalb, 'Peacekeeper', p. 48.
69 Waldheim, *Challenge*, pp. 83–84.
70 *Ibid.*, pp. 93–95.
71 It should be noted, however, that the UNEF II mandate expired in 1979, due largely to a Soviet veto threat in the Security Council.
72 Kalb, 'Peacekeeper', p. 48.
73 P. N. Vanzis, *Cyprus: The Unfinished Agony* (London: Abelard-Schuman, 1977), p. 1.
74 Bailey, *How Wars End*, 1., p. 369.
75 Quoted in Miller, *Nonviolence*, p. 120.
76 *Ibid.*, pp. 119–120 and Walker, *Guard*, pp. 71–72.
77 Walker, *Guard*, pp. 71–72.
78 See Narayan Desai, 'Gandhi's Peace Army: The Shanti Sena Today', *Fellowship*, November 1969, pp. 23–25.
79 See Narayan Desai, 'Intervention in Riots in India', in A. Paul Hare and Herbert H. Blumberg (eds), *Liberation Without Violence: A Third Party Approach* (Totowa, NJ: Roman & Littlefield, 1977), p. 83.
80 Miller, *Nonviolence*, p. 123.
81 Cited in Keyes, 'Peacekeeping', p. 8.
82 Cited in Charles C. Walker, 'Nonviolence in Eastern Africa 1962–1964', in Hare and Blumberg, *Liberation*, p. 157.
83 *Ibid.*, pp. 160–167. For a broader discussion of non-violence in Africa, see Charles C. Walker, 'Nonviolence in Africa', in Severyn T. Bruyn and Paula M. Rayman, (eds). *Nonviolent Action and Social Change* (New York: Irvington Publishers, 1979), pp. 186–212. For another attempt at non-violent peacemaking, see A. Paul Hare (ed.), *Cyprus Resettlement Project: An Instance of International Peacemaking* (Beer Sheva: Ben-Gurion University of the Negev, 1984).
84 For this story, see Richard K. Taylor, *Blockade: A Guide to Non-Violent Intervention* (Maryknoll, NY: Orbis Books, 1977).
85 *Ibid.*, p. xiii.
86 From a PBI brochure; for more information on PBI, write to Charles C. Walker, the Coordinator of Peace Brigades International, at the address in note 89.
87 See *Peace Brigades* ('A publication of Peace Brigades International'), 2/1 (1984).
88 The following information about GAM comes from Philip

McManus, 'Refusing to Disappear', *Fellowship*, July–August 1985, pp. 12–14.

89 For further information, write to PBI, 4722 Baltimore Avenue, Philadelphia, PA 19143, or Charles Walker, Box 199, Cheyney, Pa. 193/9.

90 John P. Adams, *At the Heart of the Whirlwind* (New York: Harper & Row, 1976), p. 119.

91 See Hildegard Goss-Mayr, 'Alagamar: Nonviolent Land Struggle', *IFOR Report*, July 1980, pp. 15–16.

92 Penny Lernoux, *Cry of the People* (New York: Penguin Books, 1982), pp. 313–314.

93 See Lyle Tatum, 'Friendly Presence', in Hare and Blumberg, *Liberation*, pp. 92–101.

94 For King's writings, see the extensive collection in James Melvin Washington (ed.), *A Testament of Hope – The Essential Writings of Martin Luther King, Jr* (San Francisco: Harper & Row, 1986). Stephen Oates has written a comprehensive biography, *Let the Trumpet Sound: The Life of Martin Luther King, Jr* (San Francisco: Harper & Row, 1982). See also the important TV documentary called *Eyes on the Prize*, which was released in 1987, and the companion volume ed. Juan Williams, *Eyes on the Prize: America's Civil Rights Years, 1954–1965* (New York: Viking Penguin, Inc., 1987).

Chapter 2: Non-violent Intervention in Guerrilla Warfare

1 Quoted in Witness for Peace Documentation Project, *Kidnapped by the Contras: The Peace Flotilla on the Rio San Juan, Nicaragua, August 1985* (Washington DC: Witness for Peace Documentation Project, 1985), p. 9.

2 For a longer account of that trip, see Ronald J. Sider, 'Why Me Lord?: Reluctant Reflections on the Trip to Nicaragua', *The Other Side*, May 1985, pp. 20–25.

3 As of February 1987. See *Witness for Peace Newsletter*, February–March 1987, p. 4.

4 I want to thank Dr Arnold Snyder for granting me permission to make generous use of an unpublished paper, 'Witness for Peace in Nicaragua', that he wrote in early 1985. From 15 February–15 December 1984, Arnold was the Coordinator of Witness for Peace in Nicaragua. He is now Assistant Professor of History and Peace Studies at Conrad Grebel College, University of Waterloo, Waterloo, Ontario, Canada.

5 Walter LaFeber, *Inevitable Revolutions: The United States in*

Central America (New York: Norton, 1984), p. 11. See also Richard Millett, *Guardians of the Dynasty: A History of the US Created Guardia Nacional de Nicaragua and the Somoza Family* (Maryknoll, NY: Orbis Books, 1977).

6   LaFeber, *Inevitable Revolutions*, p. 18.
7   See my article 'Why Me Lord?'. For a very critical view of the Sandinistas, see Humberto Belli, *Breaking Faith: The Sandinista Revolution and Its Impact on Freedom and Christian Faith in Nicaragua* (Westchester, IL: Crossway Books, 1985). For a positive evaluation, see James and Kathleen McGinnis, *Solidarity with the People of Nicaragua* (Maryknoll, NY: Orbis Books, 1985), pp. 5–25. See also Mario Vargas Llosa's lengthy study, 'Nicaragua', *The New York Times Magazine*, 28 April 1985, p. 37.
8   In conversations with Arnold Snyder (see n. 4).
9   *New York Times*, February 22, 1985.
10 Figures cited in WFP Documentation Project, *Kidnapped by the Contras*, p. 42.
11 Sider, 'Why Me Lord?', p. 22.
12 See Amnesty International, *Nicaragua: The Human Rights Record* (London: Amnesty International, 1986), pp. 32ff., and Americas Watch, *Human Rights in Nicaragua: 1985–6* (Washington: Americas Watch, 4 March 1986), pp. 86ff.
13 Quoted in Snyder, 'Witness for Peace', p. 5.
14 Cited in WFP Documentation Project, *Kidnapped by the Contras*, p. 40.
15 Snyder, 'Witness for Peace', p. 15.
16 The copy I possess has the title: 'Manual del Compatiente Por La Libertad.'
17 See note 25 below.
18 Snyder, 'Witness for Peace', pp. 19–20. In this whole section, I am relying on Snyder's eyewitness account.
19 *Ibid.*, p. 21.
20 For the following story, see WFP Documentation Project, *Kidnapped by the Contras* (see note 10 above).
21 Quoted in *ibid.*, p. 9.
22 Quoted in *ibid.*, p. 6.
23 Quoted in Snyder, 'Witness for Peace', p. 36.
24 Quoted in WFP Documentation Project, *Kidnapped by the Contras*, p. 47.
25 Estimates published by WFP in a 1986 promotional letter.
26 Quoted in Snyder, 'Witness for Peace', p. 38.
27 A complete evaluation of WFP would go way beyond this brief sketch. Among other things, I believe WFP has been too hesitant to criticise Sandinista violations of human rights and

democratic freedoms. WFP has, however, challenged the Sandinista government a number of times. For example, in meetings with Sandinista officials, including President Ortega, representatives of WFP have criticised various aspects of government policy, including mistreatment of Miskito Indians, failure to provide for conscientious objectors in the draft law, incommunicado detention of prisoners, and President Ortega's trip to the Soviet Union.

When President Ortega suspended certain civil liberties in October 1985, the WFP November–December newsletter said, 'We oppose the decision to suspend civil liberties ... We are deeply saddened by developments in Nicaragua restricting human rights.'

In 1985 and 1986 WFP loaned a staff person, Mary Dutcher, to the Washington Office on Latin America. Using WFP resources, she produced two widely publicised reports entitled 'Nicaragua: Violations of the Laws of War by Both Sides'. These reports criticised human rights violations by both the contras and the Nicaraguan government.

In the summer of 1985, when WFP delegates were kidnapped by the contras, a WFP spokesman, Dennis Marker, criticised several specific Sandinista practices during a nationally televised interview on the McNeil-Lehrer Report.

28 For two other recent treatments of WFP, see Joyce Hollyday, 'The Long Road to Jalapa', and Jim Wallis, 'A Venture of Faith', in Jim Wallis (ed.), *The Rise of Christian Conscience* (New York: Harper & Row, 1987), pp. 30–46.

Chapter 3: Wheelchairs vs Tanks

1 Quoted in Douglas J. Elwood, *Philippine Revolution, 1986: Model of Nonviolent Change* (Quezon City, Philippines: New Day Publishers, 1986), p. 19.
2 For much of the following data, see Ricki Ross, 'Land and Hunger: Philippines', Bread for the World Background Paper, No. 55, July 1981.
3 According to Virginia Baron, 'The Philippine Example', *Fellowship* 53/3 (1987), p. 4, two per cent of the population received fifty-five per cent of the total personal income.
4 My sources for this chapter include the following:
   • Monina Allaray Mercado (ed.), *An Eyewitness History: People Power, The Philippine Revolution of 1986* (Manila: The James B. Reuter, SJ, Foundation, 1986). Hereafter cited as *People Power*, this magnificent book of eyewitness

accounts and splendid pictures also contains short synopses of developments and valuable historical notes (pp. 308–314) on which I have relied for many of the historical details.
- Several articles in the March 1987 issue of *Fellowship* 53/3.
- Peggy Rosenthal, 'Nonviolence in the Philippines: The Precarious Road', *Commonweal*, 20 June 1986, pp. 364–367.
- Elwood, *Philippine Revolution 1986* (see note 1).
- Bel Magalit, 'The Church and the Barricades', *Transformation* 3/2 (1986), pp. 1–2.

5   Hildegard Goss-Mayr, 'When Prayer and Revolution Became People Power', *Fellowship* 53/3 (1987), p. 9.
6   Quoted in Elwood, *Philippine Revolution, 1986*, p. 19.
7   Mercado, *People Power*, pp. 10, 304.
8   Goss-Mayr, 'When Prayer and Revolution Became . . .', p. 8; Rosenthal, 'Nonviolence in the Philippines', p. 366. For earlier examples of nonviolence, see Esther Epp-Tiessen, 'Militarization and Non-Violence in the Philippines', *The Ploughshares Monitor* 7/2 (1986), p. 3 and Richard L. Schwenk, *Onward Christians! Protestants in the Philippine Revolution* (Quezon City, Philippines: New Day Publishers, 1986), p. 37.
9   Rosenthal, 'Nonviolence in the Philippines', p. 364
10 Quoted *ibid.*, p. 365. See Hildegard Goss-Mayr's account in 'When Prayer and Revolution Became . . .', p. 9.
11 Quoted in Rosenthal, 'Nonviolence in the Philippines', p. 365.
12 Goss-Mayr, 'When Prayer and Revolution Became . . .', p. 9.
13 *Ibid.*, p. 10.
14 *Ibid.*
15 *Ibid.*
16 See the bishop's official declaration, quoted in Mercado, *People Power*, p. 77.
17 *Ibid.*, pp. 43, 67, 68, 71.
18 Quoted *ibid.*, pp. 77–78.
19 Rosenthal, 'Nonviolence in the Philippines', p. 367.
20 Quoted in Elwood, *Philippine Revolution, 1986*, p. 5.
21 Rosenthal, 'Nonviolence in the Philippines', p. 367; Mercado, *People Power*, p. 67.
22 Quoted in Mercado, *People Power*, p. 106.
23 Quoted *ibid.*, p. 105.
24 Quoted *ibid.*
25 Quoted *ibid.*, p. 120.
26 *Ibid.*, pp. 1, 109, 122; and Elwood, *Philippine Revolution, 1986*, p. 14.
27 Cited in Mercado, *People Power*, pp. 125–127.
28 Cited *ibid.*, p. 127.
29 Cited *ibid.*, pp. 203–204.

`30` Quoted *ibid.*, p. 207.

31 An editorial in the *Philippine Daily Inquirer* 27 February 1986, quoted in Mercado, *People Power*, p. 246.

32 Quoted *ibid.*, p. 254.

33 Vicente T. Paterno, quoted *ibid.*, p. 257.

34 From a statement on Philippine television after the revolution, and shared with me by Melba Maggay, an evangelical Protestant leader deeply involved with the struggle.

35 From his 'Epilogue' in Mercado, *People Power*, p. 306. See Gene Sharp's more cautious but similar comments in 'Philippines Taught Us Lessons of Nonviolence', *Los Angeles Times*, 4 April 1986, Section 2, p. 5. AKKAPKA continues promoting nonviolent social change in the Philippines. See Richard Deats, 'Fragile Democracy in the Philippines', *Fellowship*, Oct.–Nov., 1987, pp. 14–16.

Chapter 4: Multiplying Success

1 Richard B. Deats, 'The Way of Nonviolence', in Thérèse de Coninck (ed.). *Essays on Nonviolence* (Nyack, NY: Fellowship of Reconciliation, n.d.), p. 18.

2 Figures from Walter Wink, *Jesus' Third Way* (Philadelphia: New Society Publishers, 1987), pp. 41–42.

3 *Ibid.*, p. 42.

4 I do serve on WFP's Advisory Board, but I do not mean to suggest that my speech prompted the emergence of WFP later that year.

5 Quoted in de Coninck, *Essays on Nonviolence*, p. 2.

6 Adolfo Perez Esquivel, *Christ in a Poncho: Testimonials of the Nonviolent Struggles of Latin America*, ed. Charles Antoine, trans. Robert R. Barr (Maryknoll, NY: Orbis Books, 1983), p. 32.

7 David A. Hoekema, 'A Practical Christian Pacifism', *The Christian Century*, 22 October 1986, p. 918.

8 I owe this point to Wink, *Jesus' Third Way*, pp. 56–57.

9 Bernard Häring, *The Healing Power of Peace and Nonviolence* (New York: Paulist Press, 1986), pp. 83–84.

10 No. 533 of their declaration, quoted in Esquivel, *Christ in a Poncho*, p. 52.

11 Penny Lernoux, *Cry of the People* (New York: Penguin Books, 1982), p. 447.

12 Quoted in Häring, *Healing Power*, p. 34.

13 Quoted *ibid.*

14 Pastoral Statement of the National Conference of Catholic

Bishops, *The Challenge of Peace: God's Promise and Our Response* (Boston: St Paul Editions, 1983), No. 222, p. 58.

15 *Ibid.*, No. 230, pp. 60–61.

16 The United Methodist Council of Bishops, *In Defense of Creation: The Nuclear Crisis and a Just Peace* (Nashville: Graded Press, 1986), p. 80.

17 National Association of Evangelicals, *Guidelines: Peace, Freedom and Security Studies* (Wheaton, IL: National Association of Evangelicals, 1986), p. 26. See also pp. 3, ii and *passim*.

18 *Ibid.*, p. 28.

19 The concept was first proposed in a speech by Ronald J. Sider at the Mennonite World Conference in Strasbourg, France, in July 1984; the speech was reprinted with the title 'Are We Willing to Die for Peace?' in the *Gospel Herald*, 25 December 1984, pp. 898–901. For the December 1986 gathering, see 'Christian Peacemaker Team Proposal Revised, Approved', *Evangelical Visitor*, February 1987, pp. 14–17. For further information, write to Christian Peacemaker Teams, Peace Section, Mennonite Central Committee, Akron, Pennsylvania 17501.

20 Catholic Bishops, *The Challenge of Peace*, No. 224, p. 58.

21 See further, John Howard Yoder, *When War is Unjust: Being Honest in Just-War Thinking* (Minneapolis: Augsburg, 1984), pp. 76–78.

22 Catholic Bishops, *The Challenge of Peace*, No. 224, p. 59.

23 Gene Sharp, 'The Significance of Domestic Nonviolent Action as a Substitute for International War', in Severyn T. Bruyn and Paula M. Rayman (eds), *Nonviolent Action and Social Change* (New York: Irvington Publishers, 1981), p. 245.

24 For further information, write to The Program on Nonviolent Sanctions, Center for International Affairs, Harvard University, 1737 Cambridge Drive, Cambridge, MA 02138.

25 Both Bernard Häring (*Healing Power*, p. 120) and the US Catholic Bishops (*Challenge of Peace*, No. 228, p. 59) call for new study centres. For a list of current Peace Studies courses in US colleges and universities, see Ronald J. Sider and Richard K. Taylor, *Nuclear Holocaust and Christian Hope* (Downers Grove, IL and Ramsey, NJ: InterVarsity Press/Paulist Press, 1982), pp. 310–311.

26 See Charles C. Walker, *A World Peace Guard* (Hyderabad, India: Academy of Gandhian Studies, 1981), pp. 34, 44, 47–48; Theodore Olson and Lynne Shivers, *Training for Nonviolent Action* (London: Friends Peace Committee, 1970); William Moye, *A Nonviolent Action Manual* (Philadelphia: New Society Press, 1977); Ken Butigan, *et al, Basta! A Pledge of Resistance*

Handbook (San Francisco: Emergency Response Network, undated); Ed Hedemann, ed. *War Resisters League Organizer's Manual* (New York: War Resisters League, 1981); Richard K. and Phyllis B. Taylor and Sojourners, *The Practice of Peace: A Manual and Video for Nonviolent Training* (1987) and available from Sojourners, Box 29272, Washington, D.C. 20017.

27 For a brief discussion of many different non-violent strategies, see Deats, 'The Way of Nonviolence', in de Coninck, *Essays on Nonviolence*, pp. 15–17, and Mubarak E. Awad, 'Nonviolent Resistance: A Strategy for the Occupied Territories', in *Nonviolent Struggle in the Middle East* (Philadelphia: New Society Publishers, n.d.), pp. 28–36. For a much longer, more scholarly analysis, see the superb treatment in Gene Sharp, *The Politics of Nonviolent Action*, 3 vols (Boston: Porter Sargent Publishers, 1973), 2., pp. 117–435.

28 In Wink, *Jesus' Third Way* (see above note 2).

29 See Nat Henthoff, 'Can Israel Create its Own Gandhi, Muste or King?', *Village Voice*, 28 June 1983; the series of articles in the *Jordan Times*, 16–19 November 1986, reporting a conference on non-violence held in Amman; Mubarak E. Awad, 'Nonviolent Resistance: A Strategy for the Occupied Territories' (see note 27); and R. Scott Kennedy, 'The Druze of the Golan: A Case of Nonviolent Resistance', in *Nonviolent Struggle*, pp. 5–21.

30 See Walker, *World Peace Guard*, p. 19.

31 *Ibid.*, p. 25.

32 See the discussion *ibid.*, pp. 13–21.

33 Karl Deutsch, *The Analysis of International Relations* (Englewood Cliffs, NJ: Prentice Hall (1978). See the discussion in the excellent book by Duane K. Friesen, *Christian Peacemaking and International Conflict: A Realist Pacifist Perspective* (Scottdale, PA: Herald Press, 1986), pp. 147–149.

34 Friesen, *ibid.*, p. 148, summarising Gene Sharp.

Chapter 5: The Moral Equivalent of War

1 William James, 'The Moral Equivalent of War', in John K. Roth (ed.), *The Moral Equivalent of War and Other Essays* (New York: Harper & Row, 1971), p. 3. The essay originally appeared in 1910.

2 *Ibid.*, p. 4.

3 Walter Wink, *Jesus' Third Way* (Philadelphia: New Society Publishers, 1987), p. 34.

SELECT BIBLIOGRAPHY

Adams, John P. *At the Heart'of the Whirlwind* (New York: Harper & Row, 1976)

Awad, Mubarak E., and R. Scott Kennedy. *Nonviolent Struggle in the Middle East* (Philadelphia: New Society Publishers, 1985)

Bailey, Sydney D. *How Wars End: The United Nations and the Termination of Armed Conflict*, vol. 1 (Oxford: Clarendon Press, 1982)

Bedau, H. A., (ed.). *Civil Disobedience: Theory and Practice* (Nyack, NY: Fellowship of Reconciliation, 1982)

Bondurant, Joan. *Conquest of Violence: The Gandhian Philosophy of Conflict*, revised edition (Berkeley, CA: University of California Press, 1965)

Boserup, Anders, and Andrew Mack. *War Without Weapons: Non-Violence in National Defense* (New York: Schocken Books, 1975)

Bruyn, Severyn T., and Paula M. Rayman, (eds). *Nonviolent Action and Social Change* (New York: Irvington Publishers, 1979)

Camara, Dom Helder. *Revolution Through Peace*, trans. Amparo McLean (New York: Harper & Row, 1971)

de Coninck, Thérése, (ed.). *Essays on Nonviolence* (Nyack, NY: Fellowship of Reconciliation, n.d.)

Conser, Walter H., McCarthy, Ronald M., Toscano David J., and Sharp Gene, (eds). *Resistance, Politics and the American Struggle for Independence, 1765–1775* (Boulder, CO: Lynne Rienner Publishers, 1986)

Desai, Narayan. *Towards Nonviolent Revolution* (India: Sarva Seva Sangh Prakashan, 1972)

Douglass, James W. *The Non-Violent Cross: A Theology of Revolution and Peace* (New York: Macmillan, 1966)

Easwaran, Eknath. *A Man to Match His Mountains: Badshah Khan, Nonviolent Soldier of Islam* (Petaluma, CA: Nilgiri Press, 1984)

Ebert, Theodor. *Soziale Verteidigung* (Waldkirch: Waldkircher Verlagsgesellschaft mbH, 1981)

Elwood, Douglas J. *Philippine Revolution, 1986: Model of Nonviolent Change* (Quezon City, Philippines: New Day Publishers, 1986)

Esquivel, Adolfo Perez. *Christ in a Poncho: Testimonials of the Non-violent Struggles of Latin America*, ed. Charles Antoine, trans. Robert R. Barr (Maryknoll, NY: Orbis Books, 1983)

Friesen, Duane K. *Christian Peacemaking and International Conflict: A Realist Pacifist Perspective* (Scottdale, PA: Herald Press, 1986)

Galtung, Johann. 'Violence, Peace, and Peace Research', *Journal of Peace Research* 3 (1969), pp. 167–191

Gandhi, M. K. *Gandhi: An Autobiography of Mohandas K. Gandhi* (Boston, MA: Beacon Press, 1957)

Haring, Bernard. *The Healing Power of Peace and Nonviolence* (New York: Paulist Press, 1986)

Hope, Marjorie, and Young, James. *The Struggle for Humanity: Agents of Nonviolent Change in a Violent World.* (Maryknoll: Orbis, 1977)

King, Martin Luther. *Stride Toward Freedom* (New York: Harper & Brothers, 1958)

idem. Why We Can't Wait (New York: New American Library, 1963)

Laffin, Arthur J., and Anne Montgomery, (eds). *Swords into Plowshares: Nonviolent Direct Action for Disarmament* (San Francisco: Harper & Row, 1987)

Lakey, George. *Strategy for a Living Revolution* (San Fancisco: W. H. Freeman, 1968)

Lernoux, Penny. *Cry of the People* (New York: Penguin Books, 1982)

Mercado, Monina Allaray, (ed). *An Eyewitness History: People, The Philippine Revolution of 1986* (Manila: the James B. Reuter SJ Foundation, 1986)

Miller, William Robert. *Nonviolence: A Christian Interpretation* (New York: Association Press, 1964)

Millett, Richard. *Guardians of the Dynasty: a History of the US Created Guardia Nacional de Nicaragua and the Somoza Family* (Maryknoll, NY: Orbis Books, 1977)

Oates, Stephen. *Let the Trumpet Sound: The Life of Martin Luther King, JR* (New York: Harper & Row, 1982)

Olson, Theodore, and Shivers, Lynne. *Training for Nonviolent Action* (London: Friends Peace Committee, 1970)

Parkman, Patricia. *Insurrection Without Arms: The General Strike in El Salvador, 1944* (unpublished PhD dissertation, Temple University, 1980)

Pastoral Statement of the National Conference of Catholic Bishops, *The Challenge of Peace: God's Promise and Our Response* (Boston: St Paul Editions, 1983)

Schwenk, Richard L. *Onward Christians! Protestants in the Philippine Revolution* (Quezon City, Philippines: New Day Publishers, 1986)

Sharp, Gene. *Exploring Nonviolent Alternatives* (Boston: Porter Sargent Publishers, 1970)

idem. Making Europe Unconquerable: The Potential of Civilian-Based Deterrence and Defense (Cambridge, MA: Ballinger, 1985)

idem. Making the Abolition of War a Realistic Goal (New York: Institute for World Order, 1981) (pamphlet)

idem. The Politics of Nonviolent Action, 3 vols (Boston: Porter Sargent Publishers, 1973)

Part 1: *Power and Struggle*

Part 2: *The Methods of Nonviolent Action*

Part 3: *The Dynamics of Nonviolent Action*

Sider, Ronald J. *Christ and Violence* (Scottdale, PA: Herald Press, 1979)

Sider, Ronald J., and Taylor, Richard K. *Nuclear Holocaust and Christian Hope* (London: Hodder & Stoughton, 1983)

Snyder, C. Arnold. *The Relevance of Anabaptist Nonviolence for Nicaragua Today* (Akron, PA: Mennonite Central Committee Peace Section, 1984)

Taylor, Richard K. *Blockade: A Guide to Non-Violent Intervention* (Maryknoll, NY: Orbis Books, 1977)

United Methodist Council of Bishops. *In Defense of Creation: The Nuclear Crisis and a Just Peace* (Nashville: Graded Press, 1986)

del Vasto, Lanza. *Warriors of Peace: Writings on the Technique of Nonviolence* (New York: Alfred A. Knopf, 1974)

Walker, Charles C. *Peacekeeping: 1969* (Philadelphia: Friends Peace Committee, 1969)

Walker, Charles C. *A World Peace Guard* (Hyderabad, India: Academy of Gandhian Studies, 1981)

Wallis, Jim, (ed.). *The Rise of Christian Conscience* (New York: Harper & Row, 1987)

Washington, James Melvin (ed). *A Testament of Hope – The Essential Writings of Martin Luther King, JR* (New York: Harper & Row, 1986)

Wehr, Paul. *Conflict Regulation* (Boulder, CO: Westview Press, 1979)

idem. 'Nonviolent Resistance to Nazism: Norway, 1940–45', *Peace and Change: A Journal of Peace Research* 10/3, 4 (1984), pp. 77–95

Windsor, Philip, and Adam Roberts. *Czechoslovakia 1968: Reform, Repression and Resistance* (New York: Columbia University Press, for the Institute of Strategic Studies, London, 1969)

Wink, Walter. *Jesus' Third Way* (Philadelphia: New Society Publishers, 1987)

Witness for Peace Documentation Project. *Kidnapped by the Contras: The Peace Flotilla on the Rio San Juan, Nicaragua, August 1985* (Washington DC: Witness for Peace Documentation Project,

1985) available from Witness for Peace Documentation Project, PO Box 29241, Washington, DC

World Council of Churches. 'Violence, Nonviolence and the Struggle for Social Justice', *The Ecumenical Review* 25/4 (1973)

Yarrow, C. H. Mike. *Quaker Experiences in International Conciliation* (New Haven, CT: Yale University Press, 1978)

INDEX

▶Religious Education◀

across the curriculum

TOPICS

for the Primary School

▶**John Rankin** ▼

LONGMAN GROUP UK LIMITED.
Longman House, Burnt Mill, Harlow,
Essex CM20 2JE, England
and Associated Companies throughout the world.

© Longman Group UK Limited 1991

First published 1991

Set in 10/13pt Helvetica Light, Linotron 202
Produced by Longman (FE) Ltd
Printed and bound in Great Britain by
Butler & Tanner Ltd, Frome and London

ISBN 0 582 06052 4

John Rankin
formerly Head of Religious Studies at the West Sussex
Institute of Higher Education

Alan Brown
RE (Schools Officer), Church of England Board of Education;
Director, The National Society's RE Centre, London

Mary Hayward
Deputy Director of the York Religious Education Centre,
College of Ripon and York St John

Responsibility for each section is as follows.

  Section 1 (for 5–7 year olds): Alan Brown

  Section 2 (for 7–9 year olds): John Rankin

  Section 3 (for 9–11 year olds): Mary Hayward

General editor: **John Rankin**

We are grateful to the following for taking part in consultations:

Mary Appleyard	Whingate Primary School, Leeds 12
Susan Ashe	Belton CE School, nr Doncaster
Anne Bond	Churwell School, Leeds 27
Judith Hunt	East Garforth Junior and Infant School, Leeds 25
Ruth Newton	Humberside Local Education Authority
David Pike	Easingwold County Primary School, N. Yorkshire
Stella Senior	Cottingley Primary School, Leeds 11
Dorothy Spiers	Little London Primary School, Leeds 7
Sheila Stavely	Grimes Dyke Primary School, Leeds 14
Norman Webster	St Martin's CE School, Fangfoss, York
Janet Wharrier	Barrowcliff County Infant School, Scarborough
Diana Zanker	Brudenell Primary School, Leeds 6

We wish to acknowledge the generous co-operation of the staffs at the National Society's RE Centres in York and London. We particularly thank Sue Thomason, Resources Officer in the York RE Centre, for invaluable help in compiling the resources lists; Jean Metcalfe and Julia Jones for help with the typing; and Peter Doble, Director of the York Centre, for his ready advice and encouragement.

Although the authors take full responsibility for what finally appears, we wish to thank the following for contributing useful material and many exciting ideas which have been used in the book:

David Barton	RE Adviser, Diocese of London
Janet Evans-Lowndes	CEM and the West Sussex Institute of Higher Education
Erica Musty	Co-ordinator for RE and Special Educational Needs at the West London Institute of Higher Education
Liz Wolverson	RE Adviser, Diocese of London

Contents

About this book

Topic titles

Topic titles are umbrellas which teachers use as an aid in grouping different parts of the curriculum together. Some aspects of Religious Education may fit quite well under several titles, and teachers may find the material they need under a title differing from the one they are currently using. (Consult the charts on pages 170–173.)

Relevance

We wish to make the plea that a so-called 'religious' aspect should not be included in a topic simply because of some accidental word association. There is no 'religious' point, for example, in telling of Jesus riding on a donkey into Jerusalem simply because the theme happens to be 'transport'. It may be interesting to study the development of transport through history, but 'transport' itself does not have a substantive religious dimension and it is better not to look for a way of dragging it in.

Scope

It is important to note that this book makes suggestions *only* on the RE treatment of the themes and makes no attempt to indicate how those themes might figure in other curriculum areas in the primary school.

Each unit begins with a 'star chart' which simply indicates some of the directions lesson planning might take in treating *the RE dimension*. The approaches which are subsequently described appear in boxes on the chart. It is by no means suggested that the book treats any theme exhaustively.

Resources

Some resources are indicated in the course of each unit. Others are listed at the end. Again, it is not suggested that these are exhaustive, but those mentioned have been found useful and are mostly readily available.

Age ranges

We have used the same age-range divisions as in the first book, but in the present one there is no actual repetition of themes across the age ranges. We have allocated topics to the age range in which they are most commonly treated, but themes are of course not exclusive to any age group, and teachers will adapt material from one division to another as it suits them.

About the Chichester Project

This book is a result of long consultation with primary teachers under the auspices of the Chichester Project. The Project acknowledges the financial support received from the United Society for Christian Literature and the National Society in carrying this out. These bodies are in no way responsible for the text as it appears.

The Chichester Project is an independent Trust set up in 1977. The impetus came from the *Shap Working Party on World Religions in Education*.* It was felt that there was a need to carry out research into the teaching of Christianity as a world religion. This initial research led to the publication of ten books for pupils in the secondary school. These have been influential in helping to foster a new approach to the teaching of Christianity. In 1987 there appeared also *Teaching Christianity: A World Religions Approach*, a symposium written by authors and teachers associated with the Chichester Project. It reflects the approach developed by the Project over a period of ten years.

In 1989 the Project produced *Religious Education Topics for the Primary School*, introducing an explicit approach to the teaching of RE for that age group. That publication looked across the spectrum of religions, an approach continued in this current publication. The Project is now actively engaged in producing a resource book on Christianity for teachers of pupils of all ages.

Alan Brown
Director, Chichester Project

* The Shap Handbook on *World Religions in Education 1987* is a useful source for all teachers. It can be obtained from the Commission for Racial Equality (Elliot House, 10–12 Allington Street, London SW1E 5EH) at £4.50.

1 Myself

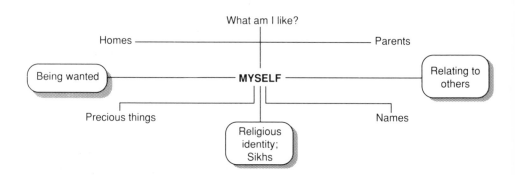

What am I like?

Homes ———————————— Parents

Being wanted

MYSELF ———— Relating to others

Precious things

Names

Religious identity; Sikhs

Aims

> The main aims of this unit are to help pupils recognise that each person is unique though sharing with others common values, activities and beliefs. A further aim is to explore an awareness of oneself linked to belonging to a religious tradition.

Self

An exploration of oneself in relation to others can form the basis of important later development. Poems and stories provide an introduction.

My Face

My face isn't pretty,
Nor is it quite plain.
I suppose it's an ordinary
Face in the main.
My Mum says, 'Even if
You had your hair curled,
You wouldn't exactly be Miss World.
But cheer up my lovely,
Don't look glum all the while.
You'd look so much nicer
If only you'd smile!'

(Anon, from *Pictures and Poems*, 'Ourselves 1', Philip Green Educational)

Everybody Says

Everybody says
I look just like my mother.
Everybody says
I'm the image of Aunt Bee.
Everybody says
My nose is just like my father's
But I want to look like ME!

(Dorothy Aldis, from *The Walker Book of Poetry*, Walker Books 1983)

Arthur

Arthur was a very ordinary dog. He lived in Mrs Humber's Pet Shop with many other animals, but Arthur was the only dog. All the other dogs had been sold because dogs were very popular — all the dogs except Arthur. He was just an ordinary brown dog, who dearly wanted a home, with a pair of old slippers to chew.

On Monday morning Mrs Humber put some rabbits in the window. By the end of the day the window was empty, except for Arthur. Nobody wanted an ordinary brown dog. Everybody wanted rabbits. So that night, when all was quiet, Arthur practised being a rabbit. He practised eating carrots and poking out his front teeth and making his ears stand up straight. He practised very hard until he was sure he could be a rabbit.

Next morning Mrs Humber put some snakes in the window. By the end of the day the window was empty, except for Arthur. Nobody wanted an ordinary brown dog, not even one who acted like a rabbit. Everybody wanted snakes. So that night when all was quiet, Arthur practised being a snake. He practised hissing and slithering and sliding and looking cool. He practised very hard until he was sure he could be a snake.

Next morning Mrs Humber put some fish in the window. By the end of the day the window was empty, except for Arthur. Nobody wanted an ordinary brown dog, not even one who acted like a rabbit and a snake. Everybody wanted fish. So that night when all was quiet, Arthur practised being a fish. He practised swimming and blowing bubbles and breathing under water. He practised hard until he was sure he could be a fish.

Next morning Mrs Humber put some cats in the window. By the end of the day the window was empty, except for Arthur. Nobody wanted an ordinary brown dog, not even one who acted like a rabbit and a snake and a fish. Everybody wanted cats. Arthur felt that he would never find a home with a pair of old slippers to chew.

Next morning Mrs Humber put the rest of her pets in the window. There were two hamsters, a cage of mice, three canaries, a blue budgerigar, a green frog, one sleepy lizard and Arthur. Arthur jumped and squeaked and nibbled cheese, purred, croaked and even attempted to fly. By the end of the day the window was empty, except for Arthur. He had collapsed exhausted in the corner of the window. Now he was certain he would never find a home, whether he was a rabbit, a snake, a fish, a cat, or a purple, spotty, three-headed wombat. Arthur decided that he might as well be just an ordinary brown dog.

Late that afternoon, just before Mrs Humber was to close the shop, a man came in with his granddaughter. 'Excuse me,' said the man, 'Melanie tells me that you have rather an extraordinary dog, who performs all sorts of tricks.' 'The only dog I have', replied Mrs Humber, 'is Arthur.' 'There he is Grandpa, in the window!' said Melanie. She rushed to pick up Arthur, who gave her the biggest, wettest, doggiest lick ever.

Arthur knew he had found a home, with a pair of old slippers to chew.

(Amanda Graham and Donna Gynell, Spindlewood 1985)

Activities

1 Looking at a picture or describing an event often helps young children to think about their own appearance and their identity. Using individual photographs taken at school, ask pupils to talk about 'themselves', their interests and things which are important to them. When every child has been given a chance to take part (some may not wish to do so and should not be forced), a class photograph can then be introduced around the theme 'although we are all different, we belong together'. The poems 'My Face' and 'Everybody Says', and the story of Arthur might be a starting point for exploring questions like:

What do you feel about the way you look?
How do you feel about the way other people see you?
Is it always easy to smile?
Can we tell from a person's face how they are feeling?
How often do we try to be wanted?
Should we try to please other people?

2 Children are fascinated by the uniqueness of fingerprints and handprints. These can easily be recorded using finger/posterpaints or an ink pad. Try footprints too! Also talk about the uniqueness of our teeth and the pattern of heartbeat, felt by taking each other's pulse.

Self and others

Most classes will have children with a wide range of ability, and where children with special needs are integrated into mainstream education it is particularly important to encourage the development of self-value and worth. So often we read about helping the 'handicapped', and ignore the fact that *all* children have talents as well as finding some skills difficult to learn. Picture lists of 'Things I Can Do' and 'Things I Find Difficult' (including the teacher!) will help. Every child, however handicapped, is able to smile, and to express emotions. The following story is one example of a wide range of fiction published about children with disabilities. When these stories are shared together, pupils learn to develop attitudes of respect, care and tolerance for other people.

Don't Forget Tom

Tom is handicapped. Do you know what that means? It means that part of you won't work properly. With Tom it's part of his brain and this means he can't understand as quickly as you or I. He needs more time to learn and to do things.

When Tom wakes in the morning, he gets up straight away and has his breakfast. He likes to eat it by himself but it isn't easy and sometimes his mother helps him so that his food doesn't get cold. After breakfast Tom sometimes has to take pills which the doctor gives to help to keep him well all day. When he was little, he made a fuss, but now he understands that they do him good.

One of Tom's troubles is that his brain can't tell him fast enough when he wants to wee, which is a real nuisance. So he has some special nappies and this is a great help.

Because Tom's brain doesn't work properly, it's important that he doesn't get overtired, for then he feels cross and unhappy. So every day he has a rest on the sofa or in his bed.

Tom's Mum makes sandwiches for dinner. She cuts them small and thin so that he can manage by himself. And she pours his milk into a heavy cup which doesn't easily tip over, and this helps Tom not to have a spill.

In the evening, Tom looks forward to the time when his Dad gets home from work. They usually have supper together and whilst they are eating, they have a lot to talk about.

I hope you enjoyed meeting Tom.

He's nearly always happy, but he would so much like to do all the things that his brother and his friends manage so easily.

But he knows he can't and sometimes he gets jealous and cross without really meaning to.

Most people have learned to understand and are kind and helpful.

And if he has a sulk or a tantrum now and then, try to remember that it isn't Tom's fault.

Perhaps you will meet someone who is handicapped. If you do — don't forget Tom and all you have heard about him.

(shortened version of *Don't Forget Tom* by H Larsen, A & C Black)

My Treasures

I keep all my treasures in my basket. I take my basket with me everywhere. I even take it when we go shopping.

I take it with me to the beach and put my picnic in it. I put shells in it to carry home. When we go to the woods I put acorns and nuts in my basket. I keep so many treasures in my basket!

My favourite treasures are a police car, a fire engine, an ambulance and a dump truck. I play with my treasures all at the same time. One day there was a surprise in our house. I had a baby brother. I love to play with my baby brother and to show him my treasures. Mummy sometimes worries that I might hurt my baby brother. But I love him and one day I will give him all my treasures.

(adapted from *My Treasures* by Chiyoko Nakatani, Bodley Head)

Activities

1   Pupils can talk about helping others. What activities do they need help with? Whom do they help at home and how?

2   Much of Tom's experiences are concerned with feelings. Pupils could make a personal book about their responses to events in their own lives. For example: When my wobbly tooth fell out I felt...; When my baby brother scribbled on my picture I was...then I...; When I saw the doll's pram on my birthday I felt like...

3   Ask children if they have an object which is precious to them. What is it? Why is it precious? With older pupils ask them to think of two rules about how they would like people to treat their precious object.

Sikh religious culture

Children bring to school many situations and life-styles which will reflect their culture and faith. Learning about and observing different styles of dress, celebration, diet and so on are prerequisites to a later understanding of what it is that religion is expressing through symbol and practice.

This approach takes Sikhism as an example of how 'Myself' can be developed within a religious tradition. The same type of approach can be used with other faiths.

Names

Names are of special significance to Sikhs. A Sikh child receives its name at a special naming ceremony in the *gurdwara* (place of worship). The name is chosen by opening the Guru Granth Sahib (holy book) at random and selecting the first letter of the first word of the first verse on the left-hand page. The parents then choose a name beginning with this letter.

Place of worship

Sikhs worship in a gurdwara. The name means 'house of God', or 'at the guru's door'. Guru is the name for a religious teacher. In Great Britain there are many kinds of buildings used as a gurdwara, but they all have several things in common:

• a copy of the Sikh holy book kept in a special room;

• a triangular yellow flag with the Sikh emblem (Khanda) flying above the building;
• a large kitchen, called a *langar*, where food is cooked for the congregation.

Sikh gurdwaras are always distinguished by their flag. Here a new flag is being put in place at the festival of Baisakhi.

KIRPAN

KANGHA

KARA

KACCHA

KESH

The 'five Ks' of Sikhism.

Dress Guru Gobind Singh ordered that Sikhs should wear five items as a reminder of their faith. The articles all begin with the letter K and they are often referred to as 'The Five Ks'.

• **Kesh**—uncut hair, symbolic of faith in God
• **Kara**—a steel bracelet worn on the right wrist, symbolic of the unbreakable union between humankind and their Guru and with each other
• **Kirpan**—a small sword, representative of justice and of freedom
• **Kangha**—a comb, a symbol of cleanliness
• **Kach**—a pair of knee-length shorts which assisted rapid movement on the battlefield

Guru Nanak, the first Sikh guru, pictured with a garland in a Sikh home.

Food

Guru Nanak taught his followers to share food as a sign of the equality of all people, regardless of caste or creed. Today all gurdwaras will have a kitchen where food is prepared and shared on special occasions and after worship.

A small amount of each kind of food is set apart from the remainder and placed in front of the Guru Granth Sahib (holy book) before being mixed with the remaining food of the same kind.

Karah parshad is a dessert made from semolina, *ghee* (clarified butter), sugar and water. It is made in the gurdwara by men and women who are required to maintain strict codes of cleanliness while they are preparing it. Before being shared among the congregation, it is taken in a bowl covered by a clean cloth and carried to the prayer room and placed on a table beside the Guru Granth Sahib. At the end of the service it is blessed before being distributed to the congregation. Great care is taken not to waste any and the share for very small children and babies is given to parents. Sometimes relatives of sick people will take some home to share with them. Karah parshad is a reminder of common 'brotherhood' and symbolic of the belief that no person should go hungry.

5 Holy book

The Sikh holy book was compiled by Guru Arjan, the fifth guru. It is the most precious possession of a Sikh community, and regarded as the 'everlasting guru'. Before reading from it, Sikhs will cover their heads and wash their hands as a sign of respect. When it is not in use it is stored covered and each night it is either left under the canopy in the gurdwara or kept in a special room, set aside for the purpose.

All important religious functions and ceremonies are performed in the presence of the Guru Granth Sahib. The text is written in Gurmukhi script and the writings have not been changed since it was first written. There are 1,430 pages and 5,894 hymns and verses.

A Sikh story

The Donkey and the Tiger Skin

Once Guru Gobind Singh was riding through the city of Anandpur when he saw a donkey crying in pain because it was carrying a very heavy load. People were pointing and laughing at the poor donkey, but the Guru was worried and wondered if people would treat a fierce animal in the same way.

That night he found an old tiger skin and the next day he hung it over the donkey's back. When he let the animal go it walked through the city but this time people ran from it in fear. The donkey really enjoyed eating all the fruit and vegetables in the market place—it had a great time. However, the people banged drums to frighten the 'tiger' away. They were amazed that the 'tiger' was frightened and even more surprised when instead of roaring it went 'Hee-Haw, Hee-Haw'. Then the tiger skin caught on the branch of a tree and they saw it was a donkey.

Guru Gobind Singh sat the people down, calmed the donkey and talked about what had happened. 'Sikhs', he said, 'must wear the Khalsa uniform and they must be brave and noble.'

(adapted from *Stories of the Sikh World* by R J Singh, Macdonald 1987)

Activities

1 One of the first things children learn is the sound of their name, and an interest in the origin and meaning of names often continues into adulthood. Learning about names across different cultures and religions not only develops skills but it can help to nurture positive attitudes to other people. Ask pupils to find out why their parents chose their name. Did the family attend a special naming ceremony? Do any of the children's names have a religious significance? Do any of the children have nicknames? If they have, do they know why? Make charts of the names and genders of the pupils in the class.

2 Visiting a place of worship will help to bring religion 'alive' for children,

especially if it can be arranged at a time members of the community are present in the building.

Continuing the theme of Sikhism, arrange to visit a gurdwara. It will be important that the children understand they are entering a 'special' place and that taking off shoes and covering heads before going inside is a mark of respect to God and to the Guru Granth Sahib. How do pupils greet guests who visit their home? What do they do when they visit someone else's home? Do they take a gift with them? What are the Sikh community bringing to the gurdwara? How might the gifts be used? Do some children know about other religious buildings? Is there a 'special' or holy place set aside? What happens there? Can anyone see which parts of the gurdwara are special? Where do people pray? Where is the holy book kept? Where do the congregation go to play music, share meals, learn about their religion? Why are there no chairs or seats?

3   Religions often use symbols to express their beliefs. Inside the gurdwara, can the children find any pictures of the gurus? What does the symbol of the Khanda (two scimitars, a double-edged sword and a circle) represent? Are any of the congregation wearing special clothes?

4   Make *Karah parshad* and share small portions. It will be important to remind the children that it should be prepared in a clean kitchen and that they wash thoroughly before cooking.

Karah parshad is shared by a member of the gurdwara at the end of worship. Eating it together is a powerful symbol of equality and unity.

Karah parshad

Ingredients

1 cup semolina
1 cup ghee (clarified butter)
1 cup sugar
2 cups water

Method

Boil the sugar and water to make a syrup. Remove from the heat. Put the ghee and the semolina in a separate saucepan and cook on a medium heat until it is golden brown, stirring all the time. Add the syrup and continue stirring until all the water is absorbed and the mixture blends together. The karah parshad is ready to serve when it is thick.

Resources

Books
M Pollard, *Yourself*, Wayland 1989
M Pollard, *Your Friends*, Wayland 1989
M Pollard, *Your Family*, Wayland 1989
M Pollard, *Your Community*, Wayland 1989
(An information series, *Your World*, with colour pictures and simple text which helps children to explore themselves in relation to others)

On Sikhism
Roshan gets dressed, ILEA 1984
(One of a series of 9 *Phototalk* books for parents/teachers to talk about with their children. This one focuses on a Sikh boy; useful notes for using the series too. Address for obtaining ILEA resources: Harcourt Brace Jovanovich, Foots Cray High Street, Sidcup, Kent DA14 5HP)
O Bennett, *Kikar's Drum*, Hamish Hamilton 1984
O Bennett, *Our New Home*, Hamish Hamilton 1990
O Bennett, *A Sikh Wedding*, Hamish Hamilton 1985
(3 books which focus on aspects of Sikh family and community life and would help to illustrate themes in this unit)
M Aggarwal, *I am a Sikh*, Franklin Watts 1984
J Wood *Our Culture: Sikh*, Franklin Watts 1988
(2 picture books (some pictures overlap) with simple text about the Sikh way of life)

AVA
I'm Special Myself, ILEA/ACER
(A pack to help young children (age 3–7) explore ideas about themselves and how they feel. Photographs and books in full colour and teacher's notes. An excellent set of 6 posters has also been produced from this pack. Both available from ACER Centre, Wyvil Road, London SW8 2TJ)

2 Family

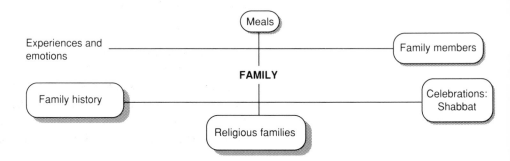

Meals

Experiences and emotions

Family members

FAMILY

Family history

Celebrations: Shabbat

Religious families

| Aims |

This unit aims to help children begin to understand the importance of family life, and such ideas as 'belonging', 'interdependence', 'responsibility', 'security and affection'. It is hoped that these will be explored later in the context of religious groups and communities which are sometimes thought of in terms of a family.

Belonging

All children will experience a sense of 'belonging' to a family, but great care should be taken to avoid the often misleading stereotype of a family as a unit cared for by a mother and father figure. Increasingly pupils come from one-parent or extended families. Therefore it might be best to introduce the topic under some of the following headings:

Things families do
- working together—including helping around the home and caring for family members
- eating together—including everyday experiences, special occasions
- playing together—including recreation, holidays, watching television etc.
- quarrelling and reconciliation—including acceptance of differences
- being parted—including hospital stays, holidays; separation: divorce, being looked after by a babysitter
- worship—at home and in the religious community; special occasions: festivals, baptism and naming ceremonies, initiation, marriage

Family members
- roles—taking care to include non-stereotype gender roles
- siblings—including step-brothers and -sisters, adopted members, those who may share the home
- grandparents and other relatives
- neighbours
- pets

Memories
- stories
- photographs
- heirlooms
- people who no longer live with us—including those separated through death

Activities

1 For most families, mealtimes are set aside for sharing everyday events and sometimes for celebrating a special occasion, eg Shabbat or a birthday.

Young children role-play family events in the play-house/home-corner and often this will include 'preparing' a meal and laying the table. It is therefore very important to provide authentic cooking utensils, eg for an Indian home:

- kadai—a cooking dish
- chapati rolling pin and board
- spices (saffron, cumin)
- empty ghee tin

2 Make salt and water dough 'items of food', representative of the kinds which children eat. Paint and varnish them.

Different breads, either dried in a slow oven or placed in a microwave oven to remove the moisture, will make a lovely display and are almost indestructible when polyurethaned. NB: do not put rolls/bread with sesame seeds in a microwave—the result is a kitchen full of black smoke!

3 Invite family members to come to school and show children how to cook special foods, eg:

- samosas (recipe in story on page 20)
- challah, Jewish plaited loaf (recipe on page 23)
- hot cross buns (recipe on page 25)
- raita, a mixture of yoghurt, spices (see below)

Banana and yoghurt raita

Ingredients	Method
3 bananas	(1) Peel and slice the banana.
1 tsp chopped coriander	(2) Place all the ingredients in a bowl and mix well.
Small carton natural yoghurt	
Pinch salt	(3) Put in the refrigerator to chill for about an hour.

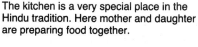

The kitchen is a very special place in the Hindu tradition. Here mother and daughter are preparing food together.

Nadeem makes samosas

Mummy and I were standing at the bus stop. 'Where are we going?' I asked. 'To the shops,' said Mummy. First we went to the sweet shop. The sweets looked lovely. Then I saw some samosas. 'Can I have a samosa, Mummy?' I asked. 'Let's make some instead,' she replied.

We went to the greengrocer's. Mummy chose some vegetables for the samosas. When we got home Mummy gave me an apron to wear. I washed my hands in the sink. My little sister looked in. 'Can I help too?' she asked. Mummy told me which spices to get out of the cupboard. She put out the flour, salt, water, ghee and vegetables. First we mixed some flour and water to make a dough. Mummy showed me how to knead it. Then she washed the potatoes. She peeled them and cut them into little pieces.

Then she cooked them with some peas and some spices. They smelt lovely. I made little balls out of the soft dough. I flattened them ready for Mummy to roll out. Mummy rolled out each ball until it was very thin. Then she cut each circle in half. She folded each half into a cone shape. I spooned some of the vegetables into the cones. Mummy stuck the edges of the cones together with a little water.

When we had made lots of samosas, Mummy fried them in hot oil. As soon as they were cooked she put them on a plate. I put the plateful of crispy samosas on the table. 'They look good,' I said. I took a bite. It was delicious! 'Leave some for us, Nadeem,' laughed Mummy.

(adapted from *Nadeem Makes Samosas* by S Stone (English/Urdu edition, Hamish Hamilton 1987)

4   Collect pictures of dishes from different cultures. Paste them on to paper plates and display them on the classroom wall.

Families and religious culture

Religious cultures will include those to which the children belong and those in the local community.

The strong emphasis on family life in the religious traditions means that examples of family celebration are easily brought into school. Some religions, among them Judaism, place great emphasis on the celebration of religious life in the home.

Shabbat is the weekly Jewish festival reminding Jews that God is the Creator and that he brought the Jews out of slavery in Egypt. On the Shabbat table, at the start of Shabbat on a Friday evening is:

- a cup of wine
- two loaves of bread (called *challah*) covered with a cloth until ready to be eaten. These are often white plaited loaves covered with poppy seed. They are sprinkled with salt before cutting.
- a white cloth on the table, and best crockery and cutlery
- two candles in candlesticks

The woman of the house lights the candles, the man says a blessing over the wine, then the Sabbath evening meal can begin.

Shabbat

It is Friday. Ruth and David come in early from school. They help polish the candlesticks, the Kiddush Cup and the little silver wine cups. They help lay the table with a white cloth and use the best plates and knives and forks. Their mother puts Challah loaves on the bread board and puts it on the table. David puts the knife and the salt next to it and Ruth covers it with the Challah cloth. Then they bath and put on clean clothes.

When the candles are to be lit, Mother covers her head and lights the candles and says a blessing. Then she pours wine into the cups. Then Father says a blessing over the wine and the loaves, reminding the family that God created the world in six days and rested on the seventh. Then, when they have all eaten a little of the Challah and sipped a little of the wine, dinner begins!

(adapted from *Shabbat* by Olga Deaner, JSMH Society for Special Care and Educational Needs 1982)

Activities

1 Prepare a table as for Shabbat (see photograph on page 23) and share a small piece of bread quietly. Ask the children what they feel as they share with one another. Discuss the taste of the bread, the table set with candles. Does it remind them of other special occasions?

Do they have special ceremonies/rituals at family meals at home?

2 Christian families may say grace before meals, go to church together, visit special places. Pupils can make an Advent crown and light the candles in the four weeks before Christmas. (See *RE Topics for the Primary School*, pp 9–10.)

Family history

Family history also contributes to the sense of 'belonging'. This is not meant in the sense of research into centuries-old history, but simply parents, grand-parents, perhaps also great-grandparents.

With the increase of one-parent families for various reasons, it is important too that children are able to talk about and read about situations which reflect their own experiences. Whilst it would not be appropriate to pry into home life, making a class book about the 'Person/People in my Family' allows each child to contribute something about the importance of the person or people who care for them.

Activities

1   Read the poem 'From Me to You'.

From Me to You
by Paul Rogers

I came headfirst into this world eighty years ago.
Inside, all lamps and firelight, outside was white with snow.
Or so my mother told me.
What does a baby know?
Two brothers and a sister:
Harry, James and Tess.
And who's that in the Christening robe — that baby
Can you guess?
My gran sewed all the lace by hand on that little dress.
We had some fun, the four of us.
Once we tossed a pie in Mrs Morgan's knickers hanging up to
    dry.
And Father spanked us one by one.
And I saw Harry cry.
James became a carpenter.
Harry went to sea.
And Tess became a lady and had us all to tea.
Alone at night, I used to dream what might become of me.
I fell in love with Grandad.
My mother found that lace.
She pinned it on my wedding dress, then stitched it into place.
Soon we had a little girl, born one summer's day.
I trimmed the crib with lace, where your Mummy lay.
And now I'm getting very old.
Some things I just can't do — like climb this hill!
But I can still stitch a thing or two.
Look what I have made with the lace that was left.
Do you like it?
It's for you.

(by Paul Rogers (adapted), Orchard Books 1987)

---

2 Invite parents to send or bring a small item of special significance to their family (not necessarily of monetary value). What does it tell about the family and the people to whom it belongs?

Shabbat begins on Friday evening with the lighting of candles and a short prayer which is normally made by the woman in a household.

Challah

Ingredients

175g strong plain white flour
175g wholemeal flour
1 tsp salt
1 sachet easy-blend dried yeast
1½ tbsps vegetable oil
1 beaten egg (reserve some for glazing)
1–2 tbsp dark brown sugar or honey
175ml tepid water
1 tbsp poppy seeds

Set oven at 200°C (400°F, Gas Mark 6)

Equipment

2 large mixing bowls
baking tray
chef's knife
a glass
chopping board
pastry brush
(food processor)

Method

(1) Place the flour, salt, yeast, oil, egg (remembering to check for blood spots) and sugar (or honey) into a large mixing bowl or a food processor.

(2) Mix the ingredients together and gradually add water until a soft dough is formed.

A challah loaf.
(The word comes from the same root as
Alleluia.)

(3) If using a food processor, knead with the steel blade for 1½–2 minutes. If kneading by hand, knead the dough until it has lost all its stickiness and feels smooth and silky.

(4) Form the dough into a ball and place in a greased mixing bowl with a slightly damp teatowel over it.

(5) Leave the dough to one side until it has doubled in size.

(6) Remove the dough from the mixing bowl and place on to a board. Knead thoroughly for about 1 minute and then shape it.

(7) Shaping: roll the dough until it resembles a sausage.

(8) Take the chef's knife and cut the dough longways into three equal parts, ensuring that it is still joined at the top.

(9) Take the left-hand strand and place it over the middle one.

(10) Take the right-hand strand over so that becomes the middle one.

(11) Repeat steps 9 and 10 until there is no more dough to plait.

(12) Dip your fingers into a little cold water and stick the ends together. Place the loaf on a baking tray.

(13) Dip the pastry brush into the reserved beaten egg and gently brush it over the loaf. Sprinkle the top with poppy seeds.

(14) Cover the loaf with the damp teatowel and leave it until it has doubled in size (about 30 minutes).

(15) Place in the preheated oven for 25–30 minutes. Remove from the oven, turn the plait over and bake for a further 5 minutes.

Hot Cross Buns

Ingredients

250g plain flour
½ tsp salt
½ tsp mixed spice
1 tsp cinnamon
25g brown sugar
25g margarine
½ sachet dried yeast
1 small egg
70ml warm milk
50g currants
10g mixed peel

Method

(1) Grease a baking tray.

(2) Sift flour, salt and spice. Add the sugar.

(3) Rub in the margarine. Add yeast, egg, milk and fruit. Mix.

(4) Turn onto a floured surface and knead for 10 minutes until soft.

(5) Place in a greased bowl and cover. Leave for 1 hour.

(6) Divide the dough into 6–8 pieces. Shape the buns and place onto the greased baking tray.

(7) Mark a cross on the top of each bun with a sharp knife.

(8) Cook the buns at 200°C (400°F) for 15–20 minutes.

(9) Eat while still warm.

Resources

Books
J Baskerville, *New Baby*, A & C Black 1985
S Perry and N Wildman, *Brothers & Sisters*, A & C Black 1987
(2 books in the *Celebrations* series; excellent colour pictures and relevant to belonging to and needing a family)
A Morris and H Larson, *Uzma's Photo Album*, A & C Black 1989
(A story about visiting family members in another country and 'preserving' memories in a photo album.)
M Pollard, *Children Need Families*, Wayland 1988
(Produced with Save the Children, for junior children but useful for ideas; it explores the concept of family and has a world-wide dimension.)
M Pollard, *Your Family*, Wayland 1989
C Zolotow, *My Grandson, Lew*, World's Work 1974
(A story of family relationships, as Lew and his mother share memories of Lew's grandfather)
Relating to a Jewish family celebrating Shabbat, see:
V Barnett, *A Jewish Family in Britain*, RMEP
(For middle years, but useful background here)
Available from the Jewish Education Bureau, 8 Westcombe Avenue, Leeds LS8 2BS:
Come let us Welcome Shabbat
(Exploration of Shabbat; black-and-white pictures; music, crafts. Large type for young readers. Intended for Jewish children — useful resources for teaching)

AVA
What is a Family?, Development Education Centre 1985
(Photographs and activities about families in Britain. Intended for use with age 8+ to adult. Photos are black and white. Resource for teachers to draw on. Available from The Development Education Centre, Selly Oak Colleges, Bristol Road, Birmingham B29 6LE.)
A05 *Families 1* }
A06 *Families 2* } Philip Green Educational Centre 1985
(2 sets of A4 high-quality pictures with poems)

3 Beginnings

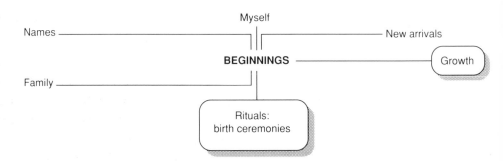

Myself
Names ———————————————————— New arrivals
BEGINNINGS ——————— Growth
Family ————————————
Rituals:
birth ceremonies

Aims

The aims of this unit are to help pupils reflect on milestones in their own lives and to encourage them in an understanding of how different religions express new beginnings through worship, ceremony and ritual.

New arrivals

New beginnings are usually thought of as an exciting, positive time with new circumstances to look forward to, but for all of us, they can also be times of anxiety, and children in the primary school will need to develop positive attitudes towards change. The theme 'Beginnings' will often form a natural part of topic work on Homes, Myself, Families, but there is plenty of scope to explore a religious dimension.

The following poem might also provide a starting point for exploring the kinds of questions which some children may be asking themselves.

Some things don't make sense at all
by Judith Viorst

My Mum says I'm her sugar plum.
My Mum says I'm her lamb.
My Mum says I'm perfect, just the way I am.
My Mum says I'm a super-special wonderful
Terrific guy.
My Mum just had another baby.
Why?

(from *Philip Green Pictures and Poems; Families*, Philip Green Educational)

The well-known story of the Ugly Duckling has a message of hope and although not directly about human experience, it offers opportunities to explore themes such as: preparing for birth; relationships with family members; fear; reconciliation; acceptance.

The Ugly Duckling

This is the story of someone who had a very sad beginning. Once upon a time there were two ducks who built a nest. The mother duck laid some beautiful eggs and they all hatched out one by one. All the water birds and the river creatures admired the new brood of ducklings until they noticed that the last one to hatch was different from all the others. He wasn't the same colour and he walked in a strange way. And that wasn't all. He made the most dreadful noise when he cheeped!

The other ducklings were very unfriendly towards him and even Mr and Mrs Duck had to admit that he was very ugly . And when he tried to make friends with the farmyard animals they were frightened of him and ran off. When he tried to stay in the chicken house the other birds chased him away.

The little ugly duckling was so sad that he hid in the rushes on the river bank and cried big tears. Suddenly he heard a loud honking noise and when he looked up he saw mother swan with her cygnets who looked just like he did. They all swam across and welcomed him and told him that he was a cygnet too and that something must have gone wrong when he was born to Mrs Duck.

The ugly duckling grew bigger and as he did so he changed. His feathers turned white and his neck became long and graceful until he was no longer ugly but a beautiful swan.

Activities

1   A selection of new-born size baby clothes might be a springboard to talking about growth since birth. Where parents have kept an item which a child wore, personal associations may help to nurture feelings of wonderment and instil attitudes of self-worth and personal identity which will be the foundations for the later development of respect and concern for other people. Discovering how personal needs change as babies become toddlers and young children will also raise issues of dependence/independence.

2   A time-line on which symbols are drawn to mark significant events in children's lives from birth until the present day will provide a pictorial 'story' of their lives so far. Special events might include: birthdays, initiation ceremonies, new teeth, staying away from home for a night, starting school.

3   The arrival of a new baby in a family may also cause feelings of jealousy. Stories which have human experience themes may help children to distance

themselves from their own anxiety and to put themselves in the shoes of another so that they are able to explore their emotions in a 'safe' environment. Some suggestions are:

Peter's Chair by E J Keats, Bodley Head 1968
From Me to You by P Rogers, Orchard Books 1987
Changing Baby Hollie, ILEA, Phototalk Books
Jenny's Baby Brother by P Smith, Collins 1981
Janine and the New Baby by I Thomas, André Deutsch 1986
A New Baby by T Berger, Macdonald 1979
The Joy of Birth by C Jessel, Methuen 1982
Being Born by S Kitzinger, Dorling Kindersley 1986

Birth ceremonies

Most young children will have a younger child in their family or know a home which has. Talking about the arrival of a new baby will involve birth ceremonies and celebrations and these can be explored according to the religious traditions of the pupils. Beliefs and ceremonies vary between religious communities and families but there are some common elements:

- thanksgiving
- celebration
- naming ceremonies
- symbolism, eg water, light/darkness
- worship
- the use of sacred scripture
- the giving of gifts
- sharing food

In some **Hindu** homes a new baby is ceremonially washed after birth and the syllable AUM (OM) is inscribed on the child's tongue with a gold pen dipped in honey. After the parents have consulted lunar astrological charts a naming ceremony will take place and a priest will suggest suitable names. Some Hindu babies may be taken to the temple to have the hair with which they were born shaved in the presence of an image of Shiva.

In a **Muslim** home the birth of a baby is usually marked by a family celebration and readings from the Qur'an (holy book). Shortly after the birth, the father usually performs *Adhan* (the call to prayer), speaking into the right ear of the child. This if followed by *Iqamah*, spoken into the left ear of the baby, which tells of the greatness of God and invites the new-born child to submit to Allah.

Sikh parents greet a new baby with rejoicing and thanksgiving. As soon as possible after the birth, special prayers are said in the home by either a *granthi* or the baby's grandmother. While the baby is still very young, it is taken to the *gurdwara* (place of worship) by the parents for a blessing and naming ceremony. Relatives and friends gather in front of the Guru Granth Sahib (holy book), which is opened at random and read. The first letter of this reading, or the first letter of the first word on the left-hand page, is given to the parents and a name with a corresponding letter is chosen for the child. The name is announced to the congregation. A boy's second name is always Singh, meaning 'Lion' and a girl's is Kaur, meaning 'Princess'.

In common with many others, **Christian** families usually announce the birth of a child to their relatives and friends, who often send gifts and cards to the baby. In

The Adhan prayer is whispered into a new born baby's ear.

some churches the mother may have a thanksgiving for the safe delivery of her child as soon as possible after birth. Baptism is usually carried out when the child is a few months old. This includes a naming ceremony where the child has water poured over, is given a Christian name, and is signed with the symbol of the cross. In some churches this is done by a priest, in others by a member of the Church. Some Christian traditions choose godparents who make promises on behalf of the child, which the child will affirm at confirmation. A boy has two godfathers and one godmother; a girl, two godmothers and one godfather. Some Baptist and Free churches hold a service of thanksgiving to God for a new baby and they dedicate the parents and the child to God, promising to give the child a Christian upbringing. For all Christians who perform infant baptism, the ceremony is symbolic of cleansing from sin and acceptance into the Church.

NB. The Salvation Army hold a service of dedication, and the Religious Society of Friends welcome a new baby during a Sunday meeting. There is no baptism.

In **Jewish** homes there is great rejoicing when a child is born. On the eighth day after birth, boys are circumcised (Brit Milah) by a *mohel* (registered circumciser) and the baby is blessed and given a religious name which is kept throughout life. Other names may also be chosen.

On the 31st day after a first-born Orthodox baby boy's birth his parents will perform a ceremony in which they offer the child to a priestly family (with the surname Cohen) and then 'buy' him back (redeem him) by offering five silver coins. The baby boy is then dedicated to the service of God.

Girls are generally taken to the synagogue (place of worship) on the Sabbath after they are born and a name is chosen, often in memory of a dead relative. In Reform and Liberal synagogues a special service of thanksgiving may take place for both boy and girl babies.

Activities

1   Children might be encouraged to bring small items to school which are a reminder or a record of their birth or naming ceremony. It is important to stress the 'value' of such items to the families and faith communities from which the children come and to give parents assurance that they will be treated with care and respect.

2   Pupils who are able might write a short account of a birth or naming ceremony which they have attended. They could put these in a special book about 'religious families'.

A baby is baptised into the Greek Orthodox Church — a time of happiness and celebrations.

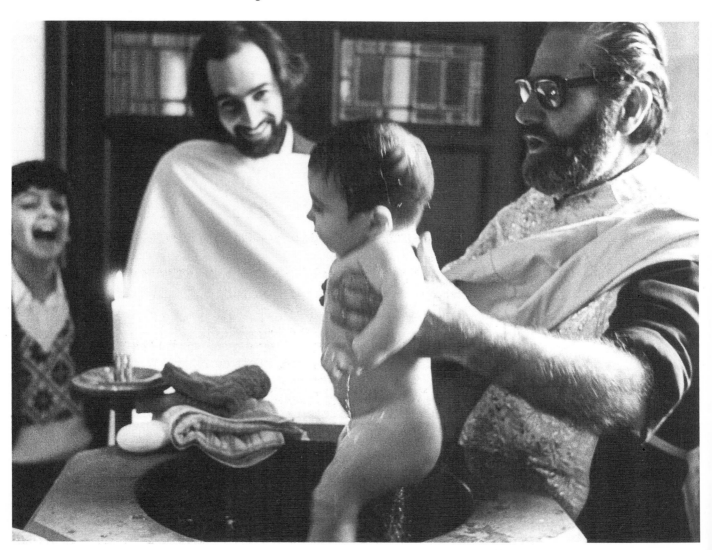

3 Where a member of a faith community is willing to visit school he or she might bring religious artefacts associated with birth ceremonies/celebrations.

4 A visit to a place of worship to see where special ceremonies take place might include:

- a church, to look at the font, Paschal candle, register of baptism;
- a gurdwara to see the Guru Granth Sahib and to share karah parshad with the congregation.

5 If there are Muslim pupils present, they might remember their first impressions of the reciting of the Qur'an or be able to tell how they learned their first Arabic words.

Resources

Books

In addition to those on new babies included above, the following explore birth ceremonies in different faiths.

O Bennett, *Colin's Baptism*, Hamish Hamilton 1986
J Jones, *Shakoor is Born*, Blackie 1986
(Looking at birth in a Muslim context — simple telling of events)
K McLeish, *Let's Celebrate: Birthdays*, Ginn 1987
(Available as one of a set of 6 books — *Spring, Harvest, Friends, Weddings, Story Book* are the others — plus teacher's notes)
J Mayled, *Birth Customs*, Wayland 1986
(Exploration of customs in 7 traditions)
Teachers may find the following more detailed adult book useful:
J Prickett (Ed), *Initiation Rites*, Lutterworth 1978
And a book with useful information, written for secondary schools, is:
C Collinson and C Miller, *Milestones*, Edward Arnold 1984

AVA

E270 *Birth Rites*, Pictorial Charts Educational Trust
(4 wall charts about Chinese, Hindu, Christian and Muslim traditions)
Primary RE Materials: Islam Wallet — Birth, Centre for Study of Islam and Muslim Christian Relations/Regional RE Centre (Midlands)
(One of a series of 8 resources wallets which provide information for the teaching of Islam in primary schools. Available from: Primary RE Materials, Regional RE Centre (Midlands), Westhill College, Weoley Park Road, Selly Oak, Birmingham B29 6LL)

4 Animals

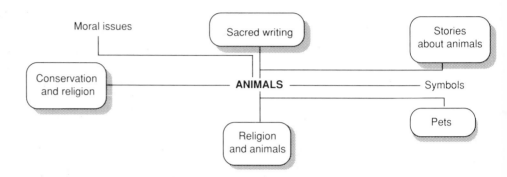

Moral issues

Sacred writing

Stories about animals

Conservation and religion

ANIMALS

Symbols

Religion and animals

Pets

Aims

The aims of this unit are: to encourage children to reflect on the interdependence of human and animal life and to support positive attitudes concerning the responsibility of humankind towards the created world; to help children towards an understanding of how different religions express their teaching about, and their concerns for, animals, through story and literature.

Pets

'Animals' is a popular theme, but so often in RE the topic begins and ends with the story of Noah. World religions have many stories about creatures, particularly concerning their dependence on humankind for care and protection.

We use animals in many ways. They are our companions, the providers of food and clothing, and their bodies are used for medical research. Most children will respond with a natural sensitivity to animal life, and in RE a topic on the theme of animals can develop a more sensitive awareness of the beauty, mystery and complexity of creation, which will in turn help them to ask questions of a more explicitly religious nature.

Many schools keep pets and most children will either own a pet at home or know someone who does. Themes might include those things upon which animals are dependent on humankind, For example:

- food
- affection/friendship
- sleeping places
- protection against illness
- exercise

Greyfriars Bobby

In the city of Edinburgh there is a long street with a drinking fountain at the end. On the top of the fountain there is a bronze sculpture of a little terrier dog.

The memorial in Edinburgh to the faithful little dog — Greyfriars Bobby.

A long time ago there was a man who sold newspapers near Greyfriars Church. He owned a little dog who sat with him while he worked and the two friends always went to a café at lunchtime. The man had his dinner there and the little dog was given a bone to chew.

Then a very sad thing happened. The newspaper seller became very ill and died. Bobby the dog still went to the café for his bone just as he had always done. The café owner heard that Bobby's master had died, and he followed the dog home one day to see where he was living.

Bobby went to the churchyard where his master was buried, sat down on the grave and chewed the bone he had been given. Lots of people tried to give Bobby a home but he always went back to the churchyard, so the people of the city made him a kennel so that he could live close to his master's grave-side.

The little dog stayed in his kennel for fourteen years until he became very old and died. The people of Edinburgh did not forget the love which Bobby had for his master, and they built a fountain in memory of him. The fountain is still there and there is a sign underneath which says:

> 'A tribute to the loyalty of Greyfriars Bobby. In 1858 this faithful dog followed the coffin of his master to Greyfriars Churchyard and stayed near the spot until he died in 1872.'

Activities

1 A class graph of the pets which children have at home will reveal many kinds. Talking about why children chose a particular animal might develop into discussion about animals as companions.

Designing a poster on the lines of 'A dog is for life, not just for Christmas' would reinforce the idea that taking on pets as companions demands commitment to their welfare.

2 Often we talk about caring for animals while omitting to explore the many ways in which they are used by humankind. Younger children might look at 'animals at work' and make a collage which includes some of the following:

guide dogs
husky dogs
sheep dogs
camels
oxen
police dogs

An older age-group might like to explore a historical dimension of working animals including those which are used for entertainment and sport.

3 It is a fact of life that when children become attached to a pet they are then open to the pain and sadness of loss when it becomes ill or dies. But it is only through an understanding of death as a natural process in the created order that

children are prepared for the bereavement of someone close to them later on and that they will begin to understand the importance of death and mourning rituals in religions. Death is all around us. Very young children may simply be made aware of it through their attention being drawn to the flowers which were beautiful at the beginning of the week, but are wilted on Friday; or the fly which has died on the classroom windowsill. Top infants might share in experiencing the loss of a classroom pet who has died, and be helped towards an understanding that 'dead' means being still, cold, not breathing, etc. It will be important for them to participate in the preparation for a simple burial ceremony, too, and to be given an opportunity to express their responses through written work, drama and art, remembering the happy times and reflecting on the value of the relationship with the pet as well as on their sadness.

Stories and poems about death may help children to realise that they are not alone in the grief and sadness that they are feeling.

Religion and animals

World religions often include in their teaching and sacred writings reference to the natural world, including the need for conservation of the created order and compassion for animal life. By the end of the infant years, pupils should have heard a range of stories, fables, legends, myths and prayers from different traditions. Asking questions about the stories, such as, 'Why do you think he/she did that?', 'How would you feel if someone did that to you?', 'Have you ever felt like that?', will help children to understand and to interpret literature according to their own level of understanding. Some faiths have laws regarding the treatment of animals, and many have strict rules about the eating of animal flesh.

Judaism teaches that animals are part of God's creation and that Adam gave names to all living creatures (Genesis 1: 20–25). It also emphasises that the responsibility for animal welfare lies with humankind. Indeed, a person is allowed to break the law of the Sabbath for the sake of helping an animal in distress. There are strict laws in Judaism in order to protect animals from cruelty, including the demand that creatures, like humans, should rest on the Sabbath.

The care for animals is shown in the story of Noah, in which God ensured the survival of a male and a female of each species after the flood.

Christianity shares with Judaism the teaching that God created nothing unnecessarily and that it is through the interdependence of human and animal life that the beauty of the universe is brought to fulfilment and perfection. In Britain, Harvest Thanksgiving is an expression of gratitude to God for the abundance of the earth including the food and clothing provided by animals.

Animals figure in the beginning of the New Testament narratives at the birth of Jesus (Luke 2: 6–9) and just before his death when he rode into Jerusalem on a donkey (Matthew 21: 1–11).

Some Christians, including Francis of Assisi, have tried to encourage others to care for animal life and in his 'Canticle of Brother Sun' the saint called the creatures his brothers and sisters. In the nineteenth century, William Wilberforce and Lord Shaftesbury fought for the prevention of cruelty towards animals, and today several Christian organisations provide animal sanctuaries.

Islam teaches that the entire universe is God's creation and that humankind must do everything possible to tend and care for the earth. There are numerous stories concerning the teaching of the Prophet Muhammad about the welfare of animals and reward in the afterlife for consideration of them.

The animals around the crib at Christmas are well known but here Christians celebrate the entry of Jesus into Jerusalem on Palm Sunday — on a donkey.

Islamic law relates to the humane treatment of all creatures and forbids the torture or killing of them for sport. It also forbids the over-loading of beasts of burden.

The **Hindu** religion is permeated by a reverence for life and an awareness that all living things are bound to each other within the rhythms of nature. This is shown in the veneration of the cow, known as 'mother' because she provides so much for the family, including food, drink and fuel.

One of the daily requirements of a householder is to feed the animals.

Animals are associated with gods and goddesses and the sacred scriptures include many stories about these.

Dairy products are used in Hindu ritual worship and also form an important part of the diet. Most orthodox Hindus are strict vegetarians and strongly support the philosophy of *ahimsa* (non-violence). Since the cow is sacred, the eating of beef is strictly forbidden, but some Hindus may eat fish, poultry and mutton and, very occasionally, pork.

Sikhism shares a philosophy of reverence for all living creatures. Sikhs are usually less strict than Hindus about the eating of meat, although it is not served in the gurdwara kitchen (*langar*). The majority of Sikhs do not eat beef and some orthodox Sikhs will not eat eggs since they are a source of life.

Activities

1   The value of story is widely recognised in primary education, and stories about animals fall into several categories:

- teachings of religious leaders
- accounts in sacred literature
- fiction based on stories, myths, legends, fables found in the literature of world religions

The well-known story of St Francis and the wolf is not only a 'good' story; it provides an opportunity for children to explore issues like conflict resolution by peaceful means and to explore questions such as: 'How do you feel when you are very fond of someone?', 'How would you feel if you knew that you might be attacked?'

Observing the world from the perspective of an animal might form the basis of work in drama. This could include consideration of how an approaching person might look to a small creature.

St Francis and the Wolf

St Francis lived a long time ago. He loved the animals and the birds and called them his brothers and sisters. They grew to love him and would come to talk to him in the deep dark forest near his home.

One day he had to go on a journey. He took his few belongings and set off on his little grey donkey.

'Do be careful,' begged his friends, 'there is a large and ferocious wolf roaming the country and everyone is afraid.' 'I'm not afraid,' said St Francis. 'Brother wolf won't hurt me.' And he waved a cheery 'goodbye'.

Snow was falling when he reached the hills, and as he went on, it got deeper and deeper. That evening he came to a little town nestling in a valley, so he decided to stay there until he and his donkey had rested. Everyone was talking of the fierce wolf. Brave hunters had gone out to catch him — but the wolf was far too cunning... He slunk in through the gates of the town and frightened people in their beds. He chased the pompous old schoolmaster round the town in his nightshirt, and no one has forgotten it to this day. He sprang amongst the woodcutters at their work, and they fled in fear. And when the moon was full, his howls echoed across the valley.

So the people were afraid to open their doors and windows and kept their shutters barred. On hearing about this, St Francis declared: 'I will go and see this wolf.' The people laughed. 'How can such a funny little man as you talk to a wolf?' 'I mean it,' insisted St Francis, 'this sort of thing must stop.' When they saw that he was serious, the people grew sad, 'Oh, no, he will kill you,' they said. But St Francis took no notice. He began to climb the path that led to the wolf's lair. Suddenly he stopped. Coming towards him was the biggest, fiercest animal he had ever seen. Gr-rr-rr!

St Francis stood quite still and waited. When the wolf saw that he was not afraid he, too, stopped. 'Come here, brother wolf,' ordered St Francis, and the wolf obediently lay at his feet. St Francis told the wolf how wrong it was to eat people and said he would ask the townsfolk to put out some food each day. 'Would you leave the people alone then?', he asked. The wolf promised that he would. He went down to the town with St Francis and met the people, who were to become his friends. A large bowl of food was prepared and the wolf gobbled it up. He was very, very hungry. All the people came to see him . . . to begin with from a safe distance. When the plate was licked clean he sat back on his haunches and grinned happily around him — then the people knew he would keep his promise.

Long and loud was the rejoicing when the people found they need no longer be afraid. 'Let there be music and dancing,' they cried. They all donned their best clothes and danced in the streets, and they laughed and sang and were merry for the first time for many months. There was a great feast with St Francis and the wolf as guests of honour. 'Three cheers for St Francis! Hurrah! Hurrah! Hurrah!'

After the feast the wolf was taken to see a small house which had been specially built for him. Soon he became sleek and fat. He was a great favourite with the children, who played with him and used to ride on his back. He was the happiest wolf in the world.

Now what a change came over the town; the people slept peacefully at night, the woodcutters had no fear as they chopped down the trees, and the schoolmaster, a much less pompous man, even forgave the wolf for making him look so silly.

As for St Francis, he went on his way, leaving a much happier town behind him.

(adapted from *St Francis and the Wolf* by M Kasuya, Dent 1979)

---

2   At a time when humankind is reminded of the need for conservation and protection of the environment, stories which reflect the teachings and example of religious leaders can make a valuable contribution to children's knowledge and understanding of the subject. Where it is possible to have a small conservation or 'wild' area within the school grounds pupils will begin to develop positive attitudes towards the natural world. The following story might help top infants to

explore why the Prophet Muhammad thought it important to protect the ants and whether insect life is of less significance than animal life. Perhaps they could write their own story about how they made someone aware of conservation and concern for living things.

The Little Ants

Muhammad and his followers once stopped to have a rest when they were on a long journey. Muhammad walked around the place where they had set up camp and he saw that somebody had lit a fire to keep himself warm. The Prophet walked over to the fire to talk to the man and suddenly he saw an ant hill very close to where the flames were burning. He was very upset to see this and afraid that some of the ants might be burned. 'Quick!', the Prophet shouted, 'put out the fire!' The man, obeying at once, took a blanket and beat out the fire. Then he realised that there had been ants near the fire and that was why the Prophet in his mercy had asked that the fire should be put out.

The man always remembered after this to look around carefully before he lit a fire, to make sure that it would not harm any living creatures. 'Allah forbids that humankind should hurt animals,' he said.

(adapted from *Love All Creatures*, The Islamic Foundation 1981)

3 Hinduism has many stories about animals, and some of the gods and goddesses take the form of animals or use them as their 'vehicles'. Visiting a Hindu temple or looking at small statues of some of these deities in the classroom will help children begin to understand religious symbolism. Some possible examples are:

- Ganesh the elephant god
- Hanuman the monkey king
- Nanda the bull

There are excellent illustrations in *Hindu Gods and Goddesses* by K Oldfield (CEM 1987).

How Ganesh got his Elephant Head

Once there was a beautiful goddess called Parvati, who was married to the god Shiva. They were very happy except for one thing. They had no children.

Ganesh, the son of Shiva, is the god in the Hindu tradition who can remove obstacles and who gives protection to householders.

39

One day Shiva went out to pick some flowers on the mountain and he left his wife bathing in the royal palace. Before Parvati took her bath she rubbed lots of dead skin off her body, and she moulded it into a little human figure and breathed life into it. She called the little boy Ganesh and said to him, 'Go and guard the palace while I have my bath.'

Ganesh stood outside the palace gates, and when Shiva arrived home Ganesh did not know who he was and refused to let him in. Shiva was so angry that he cut off the child's head.

Parvati was terribly upset when she saw that the boy was dead and she demanded that her husband should bring him back to life.

Shiva sent his servants out and told them to bring back the first person they found sleeping with his or her head facing north. But they could not find anyone in that position. At last however they found a baby elephant asleep in the right direction, so they chopped off its head and took it to Shiva. The god attached the elephant's head to the boy's body and immediately Ganesh came to life as half child and half elephant. Parvati was delighted and the family lived happily ever after.

(adapted from *Hindu Stories* by V P (Hemant) Kanitkar, Wayland 1986)

---

4   There are many pictures of Ganesh and other Hindu gods in animal form. Look at the pictures with the pupils. Discuss the characteristics they associate with elephants, monkeys, etc.

Above: Vishnu in three different forms — a boar, a tortoise and a fish.
Far left: Ganesh in the form of an elephant.
Left: Hanuman the monkey god.

Resources

Books

E J Keats, *Pet Show*, Picture Puffin 1972

L Parr, *Flowers for Samantha*, Hicks Smith & Son & Pty Ltd 1975

H Wilhelm, *I'll Always Love You*, Picture Knight 1986

J Wagner, *John Brown, Rose and the Midnight Cat*, Kestrel 1977

(4 stories focusing on the interrelationship of people and animals)

R Brown and P Emmett, *Multi Faith Fables*, Mary Glasgow Publications 1989

(A set of 6 attractively presented story books (one story each from Buddhism, Christianity, Hinduism, Islam, Judaism, Sikhism) and teacher's notes. Available as set)

A Bahgat { *The Elephant of Abraha* / *The Hoopoe of King Solomon* } Shorouk International 1983

(Retelling of 2 stories from the Qur'an)

B Candappa, *Tales of South Asia: Legendary Creatures*, Ginn 1984

(One of a set of 4 books with teacher's notes — for an older age-group but can be adapted for telling to younger children)

M S Kayani, *Love all Creatures*, Islamic Foundation 1981

(8 stories from the life of Muhammad, showing compassion and kindness for all creatures)

V P (Hemant) Kanitkar, *Hindu Stories*, Wayland 1986

J Snelling, *Buddhist Stories*, Wayland 1986

(Both books include some reference to animals)

M Mayo, *Saints Birds and Beasts*, Kaye & Ward 1980

(An anthology on Christian saints and animals)

AVA

Animals and Religion, CEM/RSPCA 1985

(Pack including leaflets on RSPCA and a useful book, *Christian Attitudes to Animals* by A Linzey

Sitakumari, *Animals in Indian Classical Dance*

(Set of slides of animals and mudras showing how different creatures are portrayed in dance)

Sitakumari, *Tirukkulakunram and the Holy Kites*

(Slides of a Hindu temple where care is taken of the kites)

Slides available from Sitakumari, Allied Mouse, Brixton Village, Brixton Hill, London SW2 13F

5 Colour

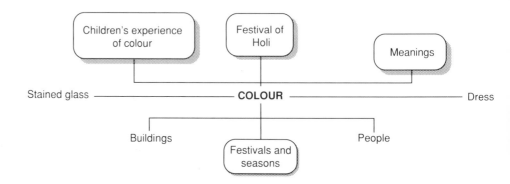

Aims

This unit aims to develop in the pupils a recognition that colour has an important place in religious practice and to help them recognise the use of colour as a symbol.

Different colours

One aspect of the topic will be to help pupils be more sensitive to colour—colour in the classroom, colour in nature, colour as a symbol, and the way in which colours are mixed to create other colours.

The Rainbow
by Dineshi Kodituwakku, age 12

My class are built up with different cultures
We are different —
In shapes
And sizes
And colours —
A bit like a rainbow.
We come from different places.
We have learned about each other's backgrounds.
Some of us are
Brown,
Some pink,
Some tanned,
And others shades of colour.
But all of us are flesh coloured.
If we weren't different,
The rainbow would not be.
So in the end,
We produce a beautiful rainbow!

(taken from *Colours, Pictures and Poems*, Philip Green Educational)

Seeds

by James Reeves

A row of pearls
Delicate green
Cased in white velvet —
The broad bean.

Smallest of birds
Winged and brown,
Seeds of the maple,
Flutters down.

Cupped like an egg
Without a yolk,
Grows the acorn,
Seeds of the oak.

Autumn the housewife
Now unlocks
Seeds of the poppy
In their spice-box

Silver hair
From an old man's crown
Wind-stolen
Is thistledown.

Yellow

by David McCord

Green is go,
and red is stop,
and yellow is peaches
with cream on top.

Earth is brown,
and blue is sky;
yellow looks well
on a butterfly.

Clouds are white,
black, pink or mocha
yellow's a dish of
tapioca.

Colour Song

Take a little bit of yellow
And a little bit of blue,
Put it in a bowl and mix it up do,
We've got a colour we've never had before,
What have we got? We've got green.
    We can mix lots of colours
    All the colours you've ever seen,
    We can mix lots of colours
    Yellow and blue make green.

Take a little bit of yellow
And a little bit of red,
Put it in a bowl and what have you got instead?
We've got a colour we've never had before.
What have we got? We've got orange.
    We can mix lots of colours
    All the colours you've ever seen,
    We can mix lots of colours
    Yellow and red make orange,
    And yellow and blue make green.

43

Take a little bit of red
And a little bit of blue,
Put it in a bowl and mix it up do,
We've got a colour we've never had before,
What have we got? We've got purple.
    We can mix lots of colours
    All the colours you've ever seen,
    We can mix lots of colours
    Red and blue make purple,
    Yellow and red make orange
    And yellow and blue make green.

Ride on a Rainbow
by David Moses

I took a ride on a rainbow,
Went to see the colour king and queen.
They asked me to tea,
And then they said to me,
'Please choose the nicest colour you can see'.
So I stopped . . .
And I looked . . .
And I thought . . .

Green is the colour of the swings in the park,
Of lime juice, and cat's eyes that shine in the
    dark.
Frogs can be green, so can leaves on trees,
Spinach is green; so are garden peas.

I took a ride etc.

Red is a colour that's easy to see,
My blood is red when I cut my knee.
Cars can be red, and fire-engines of course,
Strawberries are red, and tomato sauce.

I took a ride etc.

Blue is the colour of a cloudless sky,
A police patrol car has a blue flashing light.
On a warm summer day, the sea can look blue,
Some sweets are that colour, and medicine too.

I took a ride etc.

Brown is the colour of sand on the shore,
It's hard work to polish a brown wooden floor.
Water looks brown in a pond or lake,
Coffee is brown, so is chocolate cake.
Mmmmm . . .

Activities

1   In the classroom, following the advice in the 'Colour Song' mix the colours.

2   Using the colours, paint the rainbow. A prism with light passed through it will show the rainbow colours on the wall.

3   A collection of seeds in the classroom will show many different colours—and shapes. You could have a nature table, and notice the different colours as well as the different plants.

4   Colours are often connected with emotions—green with envy, red with embarrassment, blue with cold. Encourage the class to make a list of things they associate with particular colours.

5   Children could touch things of different colours in the room. Collect things that are red, blue, green etc. Count classmates wearing particular colours. Or you could even make a simple graph of the colours worn, colour of eyes, hair, schoolbags, shoes, lunch boxes etc.

Meanings

Colour is used every day in our world as a symbol.

In a simple walk down a street we may see traffic lights, where red means stop, amber is a warning and green means go. Traffic signs reflect the same use of colour, with red signalling the need for caution. Blue and green are used on maps to denote the difference between motorways and other roads. On water taps, red indicates hot, and blue cold.

The idea of conveying meaning with colour is usually learned quite rapidly.

To convey sadness many people wear black or dark colours. At times of joy bright colours generally predominate.

Colour blindness may be an interesting area to pursue. The school nurse will have a series of charts which determine whether someone is colour blind. This could lead into an interesting discussion and work with red and green.

Activities

1   Children could list the colours they, or the people around them, wear most often.

2   The Philip Green picture packs, especially the one on *Colours*, offer ample opportunity for creative writing—or even matching colours in the classroom.

3   Red is for danger, but what else does red mean? When do we use red in painting?
   Green means go, but what else is green?

4   Special Days:
a   **Rastafarians** wear white on holy days. Their special colours are red, yellow and green, which are the colours of the Ethiopian flag. *Our Culture: Rastafarian* by Jeremy Wood (Franklin Watts 1988) has a picture book account of Rastafarianism.

b   **Baisakhi** is a very happy Sikh festival which marks the New Year, celebrated on 13 April. Everyone wears bright, colourful and when possible new clothes; people worship in the gurdwara and then hold a celebration. Dancing is very popular, *bhangra* in particular. Teachers can find out more in *Religions through Festivals: Sikhism* by Davinder Kaur Babraa (Longman 1989) and in *Religions* by Alan Brown, John Rankin and Angela Wood (Longman 1988).

Festivals and seasons

In India white is for mourning, in China too.

Chinese New Year
Chinese New Year is a time for bright clothes, garlands, highly coloured dragons and the very popular little red envelopes that children receive (they contain money).

Dat's New Year by Linda Smith (Black 1985) tells us all about it. Children may enjoy making dragons for themselves in exciting colours.

Holi
The following is a description of Holi, from *Hindu Festivals* by Swasti Mitter (Wayland 1985).

Holi is a famous and very popular spring festival in northern India. It is celebrated for five days and provides an excuse for everyone to have great fun. Although the festival is meant to be in honour of the minor goddess, Holika, it is more a celebration of the spring wheat harvest. Bonfires are built, people play outdoor games and everybody is encouraged to be boisterous. They throw red powders and coloured water at each other, not just over their friends but over strangers too, so it's wise to wear old clothes!

The Holi bonfire is considered sacred. When it is being built, all the families in the neighbourhood contribute fuel for it. The ashes of the fire are streaked on the forehead to bring good luck in the year ahead.

This Hindu spring festival can be compared with the harvest festivals of ancient Europe, and even more with the riotous Roman

A highlight of the Chinese New Year — usually celebrated in February — is the colourful Dragon Dance. This photograph was taken in London but the festival is celebrated in every Chinese community.

festival of Saturnalia. This took place in December and everyone was allowed to make fun of many things normally respected and held sacred throughout the rest of the year.

Holi is celebrated in a different way in the rice-growing area of eastern India. There, on the day of the full moon, the legendary love of the god Krishna (an incarnation of Vishnu) and his beloved Radha is re-enacted to the accompaniment of traditional songs. Swings are made of flowers, as Radha and Krishna are supposed to have played together in a swing on that day.

Throwing coloured powders at each other is also seen as a remembrance of the playful frolics of Radha and Krishna. In some parts of India, in fact, the festival is first and foremost a celebration of their love.

Mrs Lodhia remembers Holi

'Holi is my favourite festival. We had a holiday from school on Holi day and the festival lasted one day in Uganda. We'd get together with our friends and mix coloured water and then we'd throw it over each other! Sometimes we'd throw glasses of coloured water. Other times we'd use syringes. We'd wear old clothes and start playing at about two and go on 'til six. We even threw colours over the Headteacher! We used to use a plant that coloured the water orange. After playing Holi we'd shower, put on new clothes and go to the temple. There'd be a bonfire and we'd put coconuts, popcorn and channa (chick peas) on it. Later we'd eat some of the roasted coconut as prasad—that's food that's been offered to God. We'd carry small children and babies around the fire. But throwing paint was the best part. When I went to India two years ago I played Holi for the first time for 18 years, since I came to England. Even old people were playing. But it's too cold to do it here!'

(from *Religions through Festivals: Hinduism* by Robert Jackson, Longman 1989)

British Hindu children on Holi

Chetan: 'We go to the temple and pray and sing songs called "bhajans". At home we throw colour on each other—mostly dry, but we can squirt as well. We sometimes use washing-up liquid bottles as squirters. We squirt colour on everybody so people don't wear their best clothes on that day. We go to the temple and throw coconuts on the bonfire. Then we take them off and eat them.'

Sejal: 'I went to India two years ago, and we played colours at Holi. We wore old clothes—I wore my cousin's nightie—and we threw water balloons and sprayed people. We got up early in the morning and it went on all day.'

(from *Religions through Festivals: Hinduism* by Robert Jackson)

Holi, Festival of Colour
by Punitha Perinparaja

Throw the waters, coloured waters,
Holi Festival's here.

Musicians playing, drummers beating,
Processions leading through the streets.

Joyfully children dance and sing,
Holi the colourful Festival of Spring.

Friends and relations all will meet,
Sweetmeats, balloons, for when they greet.

Throw the waters, coloured waters.
For Holi Festival's here.

(from *What a Wonderful Day* chosen by Tony Bradman, Blackie 1988)

These Hindus are covered in powder thrown during the festival of Holi. There is a bonfire and coloured powder is normally thrown by all those who attend.

In Christianity there are liturgical colours which accord with the season; green is used when there is no other colour allocated.

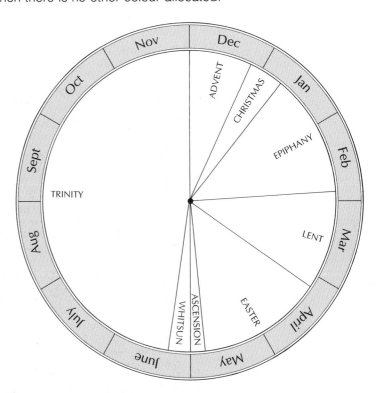

The Church year

Liturgical colours

Advent	*Purple*
Christmas	*White/Gold*
Epiphany	*White/Gold*
*Lent	*Purple*
Easter	*White/Gold*
Whitsun	*Red*
Trinity	*White*

* Some churches follow an ancient English tradition and use the colour of unbleached linen in Lent—a buff colour. This represents the 'austerity' of Lent—with cloth that has been neither whitened nor dyed.

Note that some branches of the Christian Church do not use 'liturgical' colours, and some consider their use as contrary to Christ's teaching, being too much concerned with outward appearances.

Activities

1   Tell the story of Holi and celebrate in ways that are possible in the classroom. (The Shap Calendar will tell you the date of it for the current year. The calendar is obtainable from the Shap Working Party, National Society's RE Centre, 23 Kensington Square, London W5 8HN.) The class could share some *raita* (see recipe on page 19)—or coconut or popcorn. Coloured balloons and music would add to the sense of festival. For one of the stories told at Holi, see section 3, page 156. Perhaps it would be possible to throw coloured confetti.

2   Ask an Anglican or Roman Catholic priest to bring some coloured vestments to school and explain their colours, OR make a prepared visit to a church for the same purpose.

3   Listen to some pieces of music with the class—do they suggest a colour? Paint while listening to music—eg the Colour Symphony by Arthur Bliss.

Resources

Books
L Lionni, *Frederick*, Andersen Press 1986
(Story of a reflective fieldmouse who stores colours in his mind for sustenance in hard times!)

About festivals
O Bennett, *Holi: Hindu Festival of Spring*, Hamish Hamilton 1987
L Smith, *Dat's New Year*, Black 1985
Ming Tsow, *Chinese Spring Festival*, Hamish Hamilton 1988
P Polacco, *Rechenka's Eggs*, Collins 1988
(Story of spring and Easter and Rechenka's wonderfully coloured eggs)

For Teachers
If these books can be obtained from a library they might be enjoyed with children for their colours:
B Lloyd, *The Colours of India*, Thames & Hudson 1988
Prisse D'Avennes (Ed), *Arabic Art in Colour*, Dover 1978

AVA
A13 *Colours*, Philip Green Educational
(Set of 12 poems and pictures)
P40 *Colours 1 Nature* }
P50 *Colours 2* } Philip Green Educational
(Sets of A4 colour photos (12 in each) with teacher's notes)

6 Patterns and Seasons

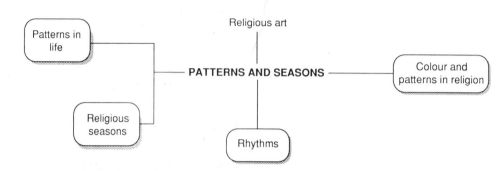

Patterns in life — Religious art — PATTERNS AND SEASONS — Colour and patterns in religion

Religious seasons

Rhythms

Aims

The aims of this unit are:
- to help pupils develop an awareness of the rhythm and pattern of life;
- to enable pupils to recognise the seasons of nature and the 'seasons' in the religious calendar;
- to help pupils become more aware of pattern in the natural, as well as in the humanly created, world.

Patterns in life

To put 'Patterns' and 'Seasons' together is to recognise that there is a pattern in life—days of the week, months of the year, and so on—and that seasons have a regularity and familiarity about them also. Most pupils will be familiar with the natural seasons. The following is a collection of words associated with a particular time of year.

Spring is   birds nesting, pigs rooting, lambs playing, ducks dabbling and flowers.

Summer is   ripening corn, holidays, buzzing insects, heat waves and thunderstorms.

Autumn is   leaves flying, squirrels hoarding, tractors ploughing, bonfires and geese soaring, longer nights.

Winter is   foggy days, frost at night, ice and snow and endless rain.

Then it's Spring!

(from *Seasons* by John Burningham, Jonathan Cape 1969)

This pattern, so important for the religious festivals associated with the seasons of nature, offers food for discussion and creative work. Seasons can link with colour, trees, nature. They link with birthdays, religious festivals, Lent, Harvest Festival, Passover etc. What do you remember, what do you look forward to? What comes after winter, or before the autumn?

Puddle Splashing
by Frank Flynn

I'm fed up
With dry sunny days
Because I've got this pair
Of brilliant, bright, brand-new
Yellow wellingtons
That shine like a new car
And come right up to my knee
The next time it rains
I'm going puddle splashing.

(from *Four Seasons Poetry Book: Summer* compiled by J Wilson, Macdonald 1987)

There are special seasons for special things:

First Day at School
by Roger McGough

... What does a lessin look like?
Sounds small and slimy.
They keep them in glassrooms
Whole rooms made out of glass. Imagine.
I wish I could remember my name.
Mummy said it would come in useful
Like wellies. When there's puddles.
Lellowwellies. I wish she was here.
I think my name is sewn on somewhere
Perhaps the teacher will read it for me.
Tea-cher. The one who makes the tea.

(from *Four Seasons Poetry Book: Autumn*, compiled by J Wilson, Macdonald 1987)

These poems, and others suggest something of the associations with a time of the year—or the weather. 'First Day at School' is an adult poem but it does show a way to approach new experiences—every school year is new but the first day at a new school is special.

Activities

1   Help the pupils make a list of patterns in their day—getting up, going to school, etc.

2   Investigate the classroom for patterns—on the floor, the walls, how the tables are arranged. What about the patterns on clothes and curtains? What other parts of the school have patterns?

3   At home, are there patterns on the floor?—bathroom tiles, etc? Pupils can design their own patterns by painting, by using potato printing (or hand and foot printing) or by using play-dough.

Time and nature

A chart like the one below sets out a range of possibilities for Patterns and Seasons.

Patterns in Daily/Human Life

Day and night	School timetable
Ticking clocks	Meal routine
Rhythm of music	Calendars/Diaries
Sleeping and walking	Rhythm of heartbeat
Footsteps/Clapping	Rhythm of respiration
Birthdays	Marching/Dancing
Patterns on fabrics/prints	Tiles/Windows/Bricks

Patterns in the Natural World

Fruit segments	Skeletal patterns of leaves
Fir cones	Bark patterns
Shells	Ears of corn
Animal species	Peapods
(ie what do all dogs/cats	Spider's webs
have in common?)	Frogspawn

Seasons

Animal camouflage
Hibernation/Migration
Fish scales
Snake skin
Rainbow/Spectrum
The tides
Seed dispersal

Colour and Patterns in Religion

Festivals (within the child's experience), eg Rangoli patterns for Divali, Mehndi patterns for Hindu weddings	Patterns of worship — daily/weekly, festivals, call to prayer	Stained glass Calligraphy of Islam

Activities

1   Choose some examples from each section and ask the pupils to bring in what they can collect. Some will lend themselves to a collage, or a table display.

2   Some will link patterns and seasons, for the natural things like fir cones, ears of corn and so on only come at certain times of the year. Pupils can do rubbings on trees or use seeds to make sticky patterns on paper.

3   Colours also reveal patterns—when the time of year for them comes, large leaves could be looked at.

Pattern-making

Most cultures design patterns which are distinctive. The picture shows an American Indian Sand Circle. It is made with various dusts, chalk and earth, and probably represents a prayer for rain. Of course this is only one example of the many manifestations of patterns. There are patterns on leaves, ears of corn, spiders' webs, shells; the rainbow is a pattern, as are the wheel spokes of a bicycle; and then there are tiles, windows and bricks. The pupils could explore the regularity of pattern.

There are patterns on churches, mosques and temples. In the Islamic tradition the representation of nature was forbidden, so Muslim artists turned to a mathematical form of decoration. Even calligraphy took on a rhythmic mathematical pattern. Geometry and rhythm reflected the glory and oneness of God.

A sand circle made by American Indians with various dusts, chalk, black earth, berries or grain. This design could represent 'High Mountain — River Deep' — or a pictorial rain dance, the clouds returning water to the inner centre. The centre is usually a threshold into which a person enters trans-personal realms.

Activities

1 Pattern-making is a natural activity for infants. Painting, printing, jigsaws, discovering tessellated shapes, or the simple lines of symmetry in natural objects, all contribute to their understanding of its variety.

2 Visiting a place of worship can begin with a search for the mathematics of the building based on the experience of **1** above. Look for repeating patterns in wood, stone, paint and fabric. How do they repeat? How many different patterns are there?

3 Hindu and Buddhist art produce **mandalas**—patterns within a circle, the painting of which is part of the development of a person's spiritual life. The sand painting of North American Indians follow the same idea of the sacred pattern (see illustration).

A mandala in the Buddhist religion is a means to aid meditation and insight. This one is made from sand.

A diagram of the maze on the floor of
Chartres Cathedral in France.
Note it is in the form of pilgrimage — the
walker walks all four quarters of the maze
before arriving at the centre — the New
Jerusalem (ie heaven).

Celtic Christians decorated their crosses and manuscripts with elaborate
coiled designs. Pilgrims at Chartres Cathedral went on their knees round a maze
in the shape of a circle, physically finding their way to the centre. All these
patterns have helped individuals to gain a sense of spiritual wholeness, either by
looking at them or by creating them. Encourage the pupils to examine some
mandala patterns and comment on them—ask them to pick out shapes.

Resources

Books
A and R Cartwright, *The Winter Hedgehog*, Hutchinson 1989
(Story book on a hedgehog's experience of winter)
K McLeish, *Let's Celebrate: Spring*, Ginn 1987
(See *Seasonal Projects* series, Wayland, for details)
Seasonal Projects (series), Wayland:
J Jones, *Projects for Autumn*, 1989
C McInnes { *Projects for Winter*, 1988
          { *Projects for Spring*, 1988
          { *Projects for Summer*, 1989
(A wide range of projects and activities relating to the seasons)

J Wilson, *Four Seasons Poetry Books* { *Spring* *Summer* *Autumn* *Winter* } Macdonald 1987

For 'patterns' used in religion, Islam offers much scope. See for example:
J Bourgoin, *Islamic Patterns: an infinite design colouring book*, Dover 1977
(45 designs; limited photocopying permissible)
J Mayled, *Religious Art*, Wayland 1987
(Primary topic/information book)
E Wilson, *British Museum Pattern Books: Islamic Designs*, British Museum Press 1988
(A visual anthology of 280 designs, adult text)

AVA

Patterns in Nature } Pictorial Charts Educational Trust
Symmetry in Nature
(Poster packs of good quality photographs exploring these themes)
E722 *Religion in Art* } Pictorial Charts Educational Trust
E723 *Religion in Art*
(Posters drawn from a variety of traditions, some offering exploration of pattern)
P36 *Spring*
P43 *Autumn* } Philip Green Educational
P52 *Summer*
P57 *Winter*
(Packs of 12 A4 colour photographs with notes)

7 Places

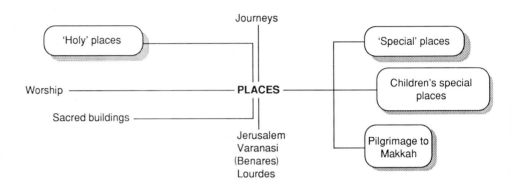

Journeys

'Holy' places

'Special' places

Worship —————— **PLACES** ——— Children's special places

Sacred buildings ————

Jerusalem
Varanasi
(Benares)
Lourdes

Pilgrimage to Makkah

| Aims |

This unit seeks:

- to enable pupils to understand what makes a place special;
- to help pupils be aware that some places are particularly important in some religious traditions;
- to introduce pupils to the idea that places that are special to us may not only be those with which we are familiar but may also be cities and countries we have never visited.

Places

Most children of 5–7 have a special place which is of great importance to them—it may be their bedroom or a particular place in the house, garden or nearby play area. It is also likely that many of them will be aware of special places to visit—relatives, friends, shops, the mosque, church, etc.

Read this short passage from *The Wind in the Willows* by Kenneth Grahame, where Mole comes back *home* (his special place). He sniffs the air, digs and scrapes, then is overcome when he finally discovers his own front door.

Home! That was what they meant, those caressing appeals, those soft touches wafted through the air, those invisible little hands pulling and tugging, all one way! Why, it must be quite close by him at the moment, his old home that he had hurriedly forsaken and never sought again, that day when he first found the river! And now it was sending out its scouts and its messengers to capture him and bring him in. Since his escape on that bright morning he had hardly given it a thought, so absorbed had he been in his new life, in all its pleasures, its surprises, its fresh and captivating experiences. Now, with a rush of old memories, how clearly it stood up before him, in the darkness! Shabby indeed, and small and poorly furnished, and yet his, the home he had made for himself, the home he had been so happy to get back to after his day's work. And the home had been happy with him, too, evidently, and was missing him, and wanted him back, and was telling him so, through his nose, sorrowfully, reproachfully, but with no bitterness or anger; only with plaintive reminder that it was there, and wanted him.

The call was clear, the summons was plain. He must obey it instantly, and go. 'Ratty!' he called, full of joyful excitement, 'Hold on! Come back! I want you, quick!'

'O, *come* along, Mole, do!' replied the Rat cheerfully, still plodding along.

Please stop, Ratty!' pleaded the poor Mole, in anguish of heart. 'You don't understand! It's my home, my old home! I've just come across the smell of it, I must, I must! O, come back, Ratty! Please, please come back!'

The Rat was by this time very far ahead, too far to hear clearly what Mole was calling, too far to catch the sharp note of painful appeal in his voice. And he was much taken up with the weather, for he too could smell something—something suspiciously like approaching snow.

'Mole, we mustn't stop now, really!' he called back. 'We'll come for it tomorrow, whatever it is you've found. But I daren't stop now—it's late, and the snow's coming on again, and I'm not sure of the way! And I want your nose, Mole, so come quick, there's a good fellow!' And the Rat pressed forward on his way without waiting for an answer.

Poor Mole stood alone in the road, his heart torn asunder and a big sob gathering, somewhere low down inside him, to leap up to the surface presently, he knew, in passionate escape. But even under such a test as this his loyalty to his friend stood firm. Never for a moment did he dream of abandoning him... With a wrench that tore his very heartstrings he set his face down the road and followed submissively in the track of Rat, while faint, thin smells, still dogging his retreating nose, reproached him for his new friendship and his callous forgetfulness.

Another well-known story about places—in this case a garden—is *The Selfish Giant* by Oscar Wilde. It is very suitable for this topic, and there are many children's versions of it. Or you might read a poem:

Our House
by Dorothy Brown Thompson

Our House is small —
The lawn and all
Can scarcely hold the flowers,
Yet every bit,
The whole of it,
Is precious, for it's ours!

From door to door,
From roof to roof,
From wall to wall we love it;
We wouldn't change
For something strange
One shabby corner of it!

The space complete
In cubic feet
From cellar floor to rafter
Just measures right,
And not too tight,
For us, and friends, and laughter.

Activities

1 If a holiday is coming up soon, the pupils could be encouraged to think about 'places' where they are going. These may be holiday places, or the homes of friends or relatives.

2 Is there a special place in the children's house? Where do they play most of the time? Is there a special place in school—a place to sit, a place to play?

3 Special events happen in special places. What happens in the school hall, a netball pitch, a football pitch, the library, a mosque, a church, a special place in the home?

4 When they are returning home after having been away, what do the pupils most look forward to? What do they like *most* about their home?

5 Some people have gardens, some don't. What is special about a garden? What things do pupils want in a garden?

6 'My bedroom'—what is in it? Do the children have special things in their bedroom—photographs, toys, a teddy bear?

7 Is there a special place in the town (or city) which they like to visit? Why?

Religious places

There may even be special places overseas that the children have heard of and think they would like to visit — or perhaps a parent or relative has made a long trip — or maybe even lives abroad. In this approach the horizon is extended from the home, to include the world of travel — the world of religious pilgrimage and also some special religious places in the world.

Special places to visit

Some people visit a special place — in this country it may be Iona (Scotland), Walsingham (East Anglia), or Glastonbury (West Country) — because they believe it is important. Some Christians want to visit Israel because of its association with Jesus' life and death; many Jews visit Israel because of its historical association with the people of Israel. Muslims go on a pilgrimage to Makkah in Saudi Arabia, but Jerusalem is also special for them because of its association with the Prophet Muhammad.

Here the statue of 'Our Lady of Walsingham' is being carried in procession. The shrine of Our Lady in Walsingham, Norfolk, is visited by both Anglican and Roman Catholic pilgrims.

Hajj — a visit to Makkah

The fifth pillar of Islam is called Hajj. Hajj is the name given to the journey, made by Muslims, to the Ka'aba at Makkah in Arabia. This journey, also called pilgrimage, should be made by all Muslims at least once during their lifetime if they are able. Inside the courtyard of the great mosque at Makkah is the Ka'aba. The Ka'aba is a cube-shaped building which Muslims believe was built by Abraham for the worship of One God. It is generally covered by a black cloth called a kiswah, and a new one is made every year. Muslims all over the world turn to face the direction of the Ka'aba when they offer their daily prayers.

Before reaching Makkah, each pilgrim puts on special clothes. Men wear two sheets of unsewn material and women wear plain clean clothes. This is all called putting on ihram, and it shows that all men and women are equal before Allah. When arriving at Makkah the pilgrim enters the courtyard of the great mosque and walks around the Ka'aba seven times. There is a black stone set in one corner of the Ka'aba built by Abraham, and every pilgrim tries to kiss or touch this stone as he passes. As they walk round the Ka'aba, pilgrims recite from the Qu'ran and praise Allah.

After the pilgrims have walked around the Ka'aba seven times they make their way towards two small hills a short distance apart. Pilgrims walk or run the distance between these hills, Safa and Marwah, seven times. As they do this they remember Abraham's wife, Hagar, and son, Ishmael. Hagar ran up and down between the two hills looking for water. Water appeared from the ground where Ishmael stood. The spring, known as the well of Zamzam, has been there ever since, and many pilgrims take a bottle of the water home to relatives.

(from *Teaching about Islam*, Westhill Project RE 5–16, Mary Glasgow)

Note: the pilgrims all wear white clothes, to show that all men and women are equal before Allah.

Mr Rashid packs his bags

One evening when Razwan was getting ready for bed, Mr Ahmed called to see his father. They went into the front room and talked alone. Razwan could hear their voices, and he wanted to know what they were saying. He tiptoed downstairs and listened at the door.

His father and Mr Ahmed were talking about going on a long journey. It sounded exciting. Razwan hoped that he could go too. They were talking about a place called Makkah. Just then, a door opened and Razwan had to scamper back upstairs to bed.

The next day, at tea time, Mr Rashid told Razwan and Shanaz that he was going on a journey to Makkah with Mr Ahmed. 'I'm going to be away for two weeks,' he said.

Shanaz thought, 'I'll be able to stay up later while Daddy's away!'

Razwan asked, 'Can I come too?'

'I'm afraid not,' said his father. 'This is a very special journey. It's only for grown-ups. When you are older, you will be able to make this journey. All Muslims must try to go on this journey once in their lifetime!' Razwan was very disappointed. He had been lying awake in bed thinking about it.

Two weeks later, Razwan woke up early. It was dark, but he could hear his father moving about in the next room. He got up and went in, rubbing his eyes in the bright light. 'Daddy is packing and ready to go on his pilgrimage,' said his mother. 'Would you like to help?'

'Yes, please,' said Razwan.

They were putting things into a case. 'What's that?' Razwan asked, pointing to some long white clothes he hadn't seen before.

'It's called an ihram,' said his mother. 'Daddy will wear it when he arrives in Arabia. 'All the pilgrims will wear an ihram.'

After prayers they had breakfast, and then Mr Ahmed arrived. Razwan was sad. He would miss his father. He still wanted to go. 'Will you bring me something back?' he asked.

His father gave him a big hug. I hope you will think about me while I'm away,' he said. 'This is a very special journey for me. I will tell you all about it when I get back.'

(Westhill Project on Muslims, Book 1, edited by Garth Read and John Rudge, Mary Glasgow 1988, pp 61–65)

Activities

1 Information and activities about *hajj* can be found in *RE Topics for the Primary School*, pp 156–161.

2 Using slides or posters of Makkah, discuss what the pupils can see.

3 Imagine the pupils were going to Makkah. What would they need for the journey? How would they make the journey? How would they feel about it?

The Ka'aba in Makkah, Saudi Arabia, is the place all Muslims try to visit. Millions of Muslims pilgrimage to Makkah each year and worship and kiss the black stone housed in the shrouded building.

4 Using a world map, pick out two or three special places—Makkah, Lourdes, Varanasi (Benares), Jerusalem ... Talk with the pupils about the numbers of people who go. What is the temperature? (A daily paper will give a rough guide.) Discuss the preparations for any particular journey. Ask the children to talk about any journey they take.

5 See *RE Topics for the Primary School*, pp 80–83, for Christian places in Britain, and other activities. Also pp 148–155 for information on Palestine and pp 84–87 for Varanasi.

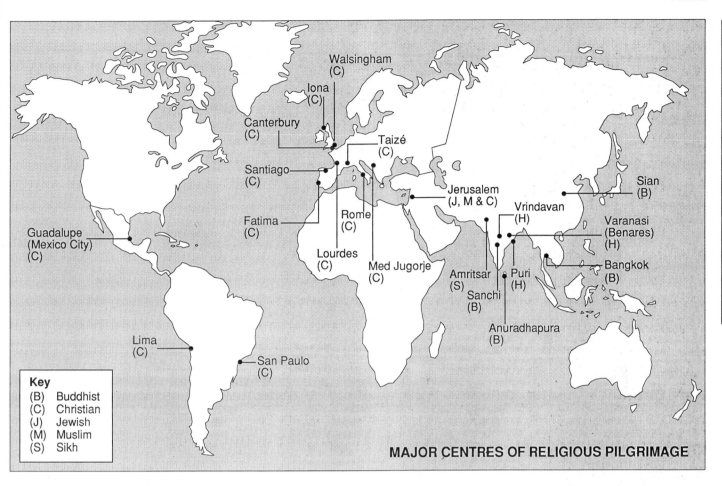

Walsingham (C)

Iona (C)

Canterbury (C)

Taizé (C)

Santiago (C)

Jerusalem (J, M & C)

Sian (B)

Vrindavan (H)

Varanasi (Benares) (H)

Rome (C)

Fatima (C)

Guadalupe (Mexico City) (C)

Lourdes (C)

Med Jugorje (C)

Amritsar (S)

Puri (H)

Bangkok (B)

Sanchi (B)

Anuradhapura (B)

Lima (C)

San Paulo (C)

Key
(B) Buddhist
(C) Christian
(J) Jewish
(M) Muslim
(S) Sikh

MAJOR CENTRES OF RELIGIOUS PILGRIMAGE

Resources

Books
BBC, *Cathedrals*, Heritage Books 1989
(Book accompanying BBC's series *Zig Zag*, picks up pilgrimage to cathedrals)
C Collinson and C Miller, *Pilgrimages*, Hodder & Stoughton 1990
(Book for secondary level, but useful for information on special places)
M Davies, *The Three Holy Places of Islam*, The Muslim Institute 1984
(Pamphlet for children about Makkah, Madinah and Jerusalem)
D Self, *Stories from the Christian World*, Macdonald 1986
(Contains the story of the origins of Walsingham as an important place for some Christians)
Shadiya Sugich, *Living in Makkah*, Macdonald 1987
(For older children, but a useful source of information for teachers)

AVA
E724 *Holy Places*, Pictorial Charts Educational Trust
(4 wall charts and teacher's notes relating to Christianity, Hinduism, Islam, Sikhism)
Our Jerusalem
(8 mini magazines for young (Jewish) children; colour photos and activities. Available from the Jewish Education Bureau (address on p 25)
Primary RE Materials: Islam Wallet: Fasting & Pilgrimage, Centre for Study of Islam and Muslim Christian Relations and the Regional RE Centre (Midlands)
(Resource wallet; details of series and address on p 31).

8 Homes

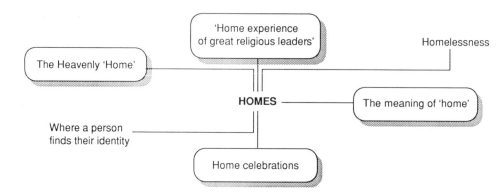

The Heavenly 'Home'

'Home experience of great religious leaders'

Homelessness

HOMES — The meaning of 'home'

Where a person finds their identity

Home celebrations

| Aims |

The two senses of home that are useful for RE are: (1) the place where people are brought up and find their identity; (2) the symbol of the goal in life which they desire.

The aims of this unit are to help children develop in their understanding of the part 'home' plays in people's lives and to assist in the children's own personal coming to terms with 'home'.

What does home mean?

Teachers of course recognise that the happiness which children find at home varies greatly, but home is nevertheless the key experience for them all and so a positive exploration will be rewarding.

This approach aims at drawing out from the pupils their own feelings and perceptions of home. There are some universal elements, such as parental care, physical needs, leisure activities, relationships with other people. From these move on to 'home' celebrations, such as birthdays and weddings and funerals. These will, incidentally, reveal differences in religious practice and perhaps the rituals of secular non-religious contexts. If the composition of the class allows, the teacher could begin to record a selection of religious practices as these emerge from the children's accounts. In some situations it may be necessary to feed in deliberately some missing features.

Religious ceremonies marked at home might be, for example:

Christian   Baptism. Wedding. Grace at meals. Night prayers

Muslim   Naming ceremony. Wedding. Prayer times

Hindu   Home shrine (see under 'Senses'). Prayers. Wedding

Sikh   Naming ceremony. Wedding. Morning and evening prayers

(See pages 28–31, 'Birth' customs)

These lists are by no means exhaustive and care should be taken not to exclude the account of any particular customs reported of any other religion.

Activities   1 Encourage the children to express their feelings about home. Perhaps they could be stimulated by the following poems (both from the *Walker Book of Poetry*.

Home! You're where it's warm inside
by Jack Prelutsky

Home! You're where it's warm inside
Home! You're a special place,
You're where I wake and wash my face,
Brush my teeth and comb my hair,
Change my socks and underwear,
Clean my ears and blow my nose,
Try on all my parents' clothes.

Home! You're where it's warm inside,
Where my toes are gently dried,
Where I'm comforted and fed,
Where I'm forced to go bed,
Where there's always love to spare,
Home, I'm glad you're always there.

What someone said when he was punished on the day before his birthday
by John Ciardi

Some day
I may
Pack my bag and run away
Some day
I may
— But not today.

Some night I might
Slip away in the moonlight
Some night
— But not tonight

Some night
Some day
I might
I may
— But right now I think I'll stay.

---

2 Discuss special occasions the children have experienced and ask each pupil to describe one of them in detail. Perhaps this could be recorded on audiotape and then edited to a short 'radio' style presentation.

3 Make a class 'Wedding' book in which several different types of wedding are described — with pictures if possible.

Homes of key religious figures — Jesus

There is not much description of the home of Jesus in the gospels. However, there is a consensus that he lived with his family in Nazareth; that his mother was Mary and his earthly father, Joseph, was a carpenter; that the family observed the Jewish festivals and could well have owned some scrolls of the Torah. Jesus' obvious knowledge of the scriptures demonstrates early training in this field. When taken together with what is known from other sources about life in first-century Palestine, it is possible to build up a picture of life in a carpenter's home in Nazareth.

Opinion is divided about whether Jesus had any brothers or sisters. Although reference is made to them in the gospels (see Mark 6:3), some would argue that these are relatives in a wider sense, eg cousins. In some Christian opinion, the idea of the unique birth of Jesus would cut out any possibility of Jesus having any first-hand brothers or sisters.

Emphasise the positive aspects of Jesus' childhood upbringing, and relate his experience to the metaphors which he used in his teaching. The indication of his higher vocation as revealed during the visit to Jerusalem will also be important. 'Did you not know that I must be in my Father's house? (Luke 2:49)

Activities

Houses in Palestine at the time of Jesus

1 Ask the children, 'If you wanted to know what the home of Jesus was like, what kind of questions would you ask?'

It is important to form the list from their answers, but it will probably include the following:

What kind of house did he live in?
What sort of food did he eat?
What kind of job did his parents have?
Did he go to school?

In dialogue with the children, establish that houses in Palestine at the time of Jesus had:

- flat roofs with a parapet all the way round (flat roofs in mainly dry countries): the roof was used for drying corn flax and fruit — often also for eating and sleeping out on hot nights;

- a stone staircase on the outside wall;

- a *mezuzah* fastened to the doorpost. The mezuzah is a small box containing a piece of parchment with the words in Hebrew from Deuteronomy 6:4–5:
    Hear, O Israel: The Lord our God is one Lord; and you shall love the Lord your God with all your heart, and with all your soul, and with all your might.
Fastening them to the doorpost fulfils the command in Deuteronomy 6:9, 'You shall write them on the doorposts of your house.' The mezuzah is touched on entering and leaving the house.

2   The children could be encouraged to make, in plasticine or other materials, models of houses in Palestine at the time of Jesus. Perhaps a whole village could be made by the class.

3   Most houses were just one large room with a raised platform at one end where the family sat and slept and had their meals. The bed rolls, the lamp and other possessions were kept in niches cut in the wall. On ground level were the farming implements and the grain and oil stored in large jars. Here too was the manger for the animals stabled for the night — most commonly goats and sheep. A small grindstone was used to grind flour for bread.

If the man in the house was a craftsman, then part of the ground floor would also be a workshop.

Joseph, Mary's husband, was a carpenter. A carpenter would make yokes for the oxen which pulled the plough or cart, wooden ploughs, tables, chairs, benches, chests, doors and doorposts, wooden locks and beams for the roofs of houses.

Jesus said:

Come to me all who labour and are heavy laden, and I will give you rest. Take my yoke upon you and learn of me...for my yoke is easy and my burden is light.

Discuss with the children what Jesus meant by 'my yoke is easy'.

4   The children might like to create a model interior to the Palestinian house. If available, some corn could be ground with pestle and mortar and subsequently made into a flat cake mixed with olive oil and cooked on a griddle. Alternatively, part of the classroom could be turned into the interior of a Palestinian house 2,000 years ago.

Perhaps some children could make a model of a mezuzah.

5   Reference to the infancy of Jesus will be made in teaching about Christmas.

Other features of his boyhood can be suggested, such as helping Joseph in the workshop, learning to read Hebrew from the family scrolls and at the synagogue school.

6   Read the story of the visit to Jerusalem at the age of twelve.

SECTION 2: FOR 7–9 YEAR OLDS

A story from Jesus' childhood

Now Jesus' parents went to Jerusalem at the feast of the Passover. And when he was twelve years old, they went up as usual; and when the celebration was over, as they were on their way back home, the boy Jesus stayed behind in Jerusalem. His parents did not know this but thought he was with the rest of the group returning to Galilee. They travelled for a day and then went looking for him among their relations and friends. When they could not find him they went all the way back to Jerusalem in search of him. After three days they found him in the temple, sitting among the teachers, listening to them and asking them questions. Everyone who heard him was amazed at how much understanding he showed and how well he spoke. When they saw him they were really surprised and his mother said to him, 'Son, why have you treated us like this? Your Father and I have been very anxious about you, looking everywhere.' And he said to them, 'Why were you looking for me? Did you not know that I must be in my Father's house?' And they did not understand the words he spoke to them. And he went down with them to Nazareth, and was obedient to them; and his mother kept all these things in her heart.

(Luke 2:41–51, slightly adapted)

Discuss with the children the meaning of 'Did you not know that I must be in my Father's house?'

Perhaps this incident could be re-enacted. For some information about the feast of the Passover today see *RE Topics for the Primary School* pp 76–79.

Homes of key religious figures — Krishna

Krishna is probably the best known of the incarnations of Vishnu in the Hindu tradition. For many Hindus he is not thought of in his relation to any pantheon, but is for them simply God himself. The earthly life of Krishna is a manifestation of the divine in human form. There are many stories about his childhood which show his divine origin. Many of these portray him as a mischievous child and having supernatural powers from an early age.

Activities

The Hindu tradition has many stories of Krishna. He was born in India, at Mathura between Delhi and Agra.

1   Read the following story of his birth.

Krishna's Birth

Krishna's mother was called Devaki and his father was Vasudeva. At the time of his birth his parents were in prison where they were kept by the wicked king Kamsa. He had been told in a dream that the son of Devaki and Vasudeva would be responsible for his death. So the king was waiting to kill the baby as soon as he was born.

At the moment of his birth, the prison was filled with a soft light streaming from the baby himself. As he lay in his mother's lap, they saw shining out from him four arms. One hand held the Shankha or battle trumpet; another held the discus; another the mace; and in the fourth hand was a lotus on a stem. Devaki and Vasudeva recognised all these as the signs of the god Vishnu. Then the vision faded and they saw him just as their own baby again.

The childhood of Krishna.

Vasudeva then heard a voice telling him to take the baby to the house of Nanda, in the village of Gokula, and to bring from there the girl-child which had just been born there. Vasudeva wondered how he could do this as he was in prison! But he lifted up the child and went to the prison entrance. To his amazement the bolts slid back, the locks turned, the chains fell softly, and the heavy door swung outwards. Outside, the guards and soldiers were asleep, and no one woke as Vasudeva passed by with the baby Krishna.

There was a terrible storm raging, with heavy rain and wind. Vasudeva was very worried because to obey the voice he had to cross the Jumna river. In the darkness a jackal appeared and walked before him, leading the way until they came to the riverside. The jackal plunged in and Vasudeva followed, discovering that this was a ford.

At last Vasudeva came to Gokula and to the house of Nanda. He came inside. The lamp stood by the bedside of a sleeping mother and a new-born child. Very quietly, Vasudeva bent down and exchanged the children. Then without a word, he turned and went back by the way he had come, to the dungeons of Kamsa, in the city of Mathura, and gave the girl-child of Nanda to his own wife Devaki. King Kamsa was astonished to discover that the baby born in the prison was a girl and could not be the boy that was to kill him.

The exact period of Krishna's earthly life is not known, but his early years were spent in simple but idyllic surroundings with the cowherds.

2   There are many beautiful Indian paintings portraying Krishna in the pleasant fields and forests of Vrindaban. Show a selection of these pictures in slide projection and play some sitar music. Ask the children to talk about what they see. (Note that Krishna and some other Hindu gods are traditionally depicted as deep blue or even black.)

Homes of key religious figures — Muhammad

It was through Muhammad that the message of the Qur'an was revealed. The Qur'an is the book of the Muslims and it contains guidance for the whole of life. Muhammad is revered as the *messenger* or *prophet* of God and is in no sense seen as God himself. The very idea that any person should claim to be God is abhorrent to Muslims. Nevertheless, Muhammad is held in such esteem that his life is believed to provide a model for living. On every mention of his name, Muslims will always add the words 'Peace be upon Him'. His childhood helps us to see the context in which the message of the Qur'an was delivered.

Muhammad was born in Makkah (Mecca) in 570 CE. Note that Islamic dates are counted from Muhammad's migration from Makkah to Madinah (Medina) and so this will not be the date in Islamic reckoning. His father died before he was born and for the first six years of his life he was brought up by foster parents with nomadic shepherds in the desert. So Muhammad's early home was in the black tents woven from goats' hair. These nomadic tribes moved through the desert with camels for transport, from one pasture to another. Their everyday food was dates, bread and porridge made from flour, and rice. On special occasions, and when receiving guests, there would be mutton and rice. People served themselves from a huge dish, using their right hand to roll a ball of rice and meat before popping it into their mouths. The nomads obtained their supplies from merchants who travelled among them changing their goods for wool and butter and livestock.

More important merchants travelled in great caravans from oasis to oasis across the desert to trade in Syria, Iran and Egypt. At the age of six Muhammad returned to the city of Makkah. Soon afterwards his mother died and he went to live with his grandfather. Two years later he also died and Muhammad was adopted by his uncle, Abu Talib. Abu Talib was a wealthy merchant and the young boy accompanied his uncle on his trading missions. As he grew older Muhammad gained a reputation as an honest and reliable trader. His nickname in Makkah was *al-Amin*, 'the trustworthy one'. So the childhood of Muhammad fell into two main parts: his infancy in the tents of the nomadic shepherds in the desert; and his later childhood mostly spent travelling the great caravan routes as his uncle's assistant. Once when travelling north to Syria, they stopped near a place where a Christian monk called Bahira had his cell (in those days most monks lived in separate cells). Bahira recognised that Muhammad was a special person and told his uncle that he was 'the greatest prophet'.

(For more information on the life of Muhammad, see *RE Topics for the Primary School*, pp 132–139.)

Black Bedouin tents in the Israeli desert near Beersheba. Muhammad would have had his home in tents like these during his infancy — and during his period as a trader.

Activities

1 Talk to the children about nomadic life in the desert and, with the use of some black material, make a model of a tent or a small nomadic encampment. This could be expanded with model date-palm trees and simulated water at an oasis. Ask the children what effect life in the desert might have had on the prophet. It is felt that the simple rigorous life made him strong and able to withstand the temptations of wealth and corruption of the city.

2 With the help of a scale map, work out the land distances from Makkah to Cairo, Damascus and Baghdad. Show illustrations of Arab dress and laden camels. Ask the children to paint a caravan scene as a frieze. How would Muhammad's experience as a traveller help him in his later calling as a prophet?

'Home' as a metaphor

There is a Christian hymn which begins, 'Jerusalem, my happy home'. *Two* metaphors are involved here. Very early in Christian history 'Jerusalem' became a symbol for heaven—or rather a 'heavenly' Jerusalem was thought of as complementing the earthly Jerusalem. The second metaphor is 'home'. A similar symbolism is attached to Makkah (Mecca) in Islam. Indeed the metaphor of Makkah as the ultimate goal of life has passed into many languages (but not, of course, as symbol of heaven). The Ka'aba in Makkah is a sacred shrine, a house of God.

Activities

These can grow out of the explorations in 'What does home mean?' (page 64). The purpose of activities suggested below is to encourage the metaphorical understanding of the word 'home'.

1 Talk about being away from home. Have the children ever been homesick? What did they miss most? If any of the children have never felt homesick, can these *imagine* what sort of things they would miss? Talk through this quite thoroughly. Try to bring out the meaning of 'home' as: being wanted, feeling safe, knowing where you are, knowing your way about, being with friends, etc.

2 Ask the children to write a poem about what they would miss if they were away from home. They should try to use colourful phrases as in 'Favourite things' from *The Sound of Music*, or in Rupert Brooke's 'The Great Lover':

White plates and cups, clean gleaming,
Ringed with blue lines; and feathery faery dust;
Wet roofs beneath the lamplight; The strong crust
Of friendly bread; and many-tasting food;
Rainbows; and the blue bitter smoke of wood

OR the topic could be 'The Perfect Home'.

Resources

Books

M Keene, *Life in the Time of Jesus*, Oliver & Boyd 1987
(Intended for lower secondary pupils — but useful background for this topic)
J A Thompson, *Handbook of Life in Bible Times*, IVP 1986
(Large reference book (adult) giving comprehensive coverage)

B Roy Chowdhury, *The Story of Krishna*, Hemkunt Press 1977
(Indian story book about Krishna including sections on his childhood)
A range of other (large-format story and colouring) books written from within a Hindu tradition
and about Krishna's childhood are available from the Bhaktivedanta Books Ltd, PO Box 324,
Borehamwood, Herts WD6 1NB. See for example:
Childhood Pastimes of Krishna: Krishna master of all Mystics
Childhood Pastimes of Krishna: Kaliya king of serpents
Damodara
P Mitchell, *Dance of Shiva*, Hamish Hamilton 1982
(An introduction to Bharata Natayam, school of Indian dance. Two friends learn how to dance
and how to tell some of the story of Krishna's childhood. In *The Way We Live* series)

M Davies, *The Life of Muhammad*, Wayland 1987
(Stories about the life of the Prophet — 2 about his childhood)
Khurram Murad, *Love at Home*, Islamic Foundation 1983
(11 stories from the life of Muhammad told for Muslim children to foster concern for family life
and the home. Would need adaptation for school)
Muhammad Alotaibi, *Bedouin: the Nomads of the Desert*, Wayland 1986
S Peters, *Bedouin*, Macdonald Educational 1980
(2 books which look at Bedouin life past and present)

9 Remembering

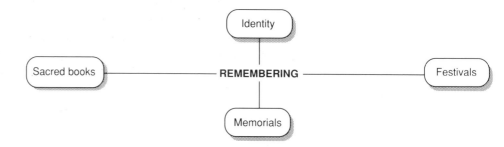

Identity

Sacred books — **REMEMBERING** — Festivals

Memorials

Aims

'Remembering' plays an extremely important part in the practice of religion. RE can help children move towards an understanding of:

- how religious tradition 'passes on' a set of values in sacred scriptures;
- the importance of memory for a person's identity, ie for having a sense of 'who I am';
- how 'collective remembering' of important events in a people's past is the basis of most festivals.

Who am I?

When someone is faced with this question the only way he or she can answer is to recount their individual 'story'. If some essential element in the story of the past is forgotten the person suffers some loss of identity. One of the most essential elements is a person's 'name'. This raises an interesting question about the importance of names in identifying *anything*, but is probably too difficult to pursue at this stage. The children could, nevertheless, investigate the history and meaning of their own names.

Activities

1 As a class activity, make a list of the things you need to know to answer the question 'who are you?' Try to draw out the following:

a name, address, age, occupation, family, previous addresses;

b likes, dislikes, hobbies, things you do well.

2 Play a version of the game popularised by the TV programme *Tele Addicts*, where one team prepares information about a television character in three sets of clues. If the other team guess after being given the first set, they win three points. If they need the second, they win two points, and so on.
Example
Clue 1: She wears big earrings and serves in a pub.
Clue 2: She has a husband called Alec and wears a lot of make-up.
Clue 3: Her name before she was married was Lynch.

3 The children could be asked to write down information of a similar kind about themselves. The teacher can then use this to play a game in class in

which they have to guess who you are talking about. *Note that physical descriptions should be left out in the first two clues.* These are too easy in a small group! Outward appearance can be used, however, as a last resort when someone is not identified from other information.

4   Now ask the children to imagine that they have lost their memory. (This takes a big effort of concentration!) Then ask them to think what difference it would make. This could be done as a class activity or as individual written work. What you are trying to help the children to realise is the importance of memory, which we take for granted. Ask them to imagine 'not remembering the way home', or 'being lost and not being able to say who you are', or 'not remembering brothers or sisters', and so on. Perhaps they could draw a picture or write a poem to say how they might feel.

Sacred books

Almost every religion has sacred writings, eg the Bible for Christians, the Qur'an for Muslims, the Torah for Jews. They have to do with memory in two ways. In some, the emphasis is on 'sacred history'. That is, they recount a part of the history of a people in which events took place which are considered to be specially important as containing a divine intervention which gives a meaning for all time. In others, the emphasis is on *reminding* followers about important truths or values. Examples of the first are the stories of the Exodus of the Hebrews from Egypt, the crucifixion of Jesus, or the revelation of the words of the Qur'an to Muhammad. Examples of the second are the Ten Commandments, the Sermon on the Mount, and the *suras* of the Qur'an.

SECTION 2: FOR 7–9 YEAR OLDS

Activities

The scroll of the Law is held up in the synagogue. Behind is the Ark in which the scrolls of the Law are kept.

1   Describe with the help of pictures (or transparencies, or a visit) the service in a synagogue, and draw attention to the ark with the sacred scrolls of the Torah. At each service, a scroll of the Torah is taken with ceremony from the ark and a portion is read. Explain that the Torah has the same words as the first five books of the Christians' Old Testament. With the help of Bibles, read Exodus 2:1–10 and 20:1–7. Ask the children if they can say what the book is about. All that is expected is that the children should recognise the book as being about the history of the Jews and see that there are laws given in it. The books of the Torah are read all the time in the synagogue. They remind the Jews constantly of their history as the people of God. (See *RE Topics in the Primary School*, pp 64–75.)

2   Now try the same sort of exercise with the gospels. You could direct the pupils to particular passages, but you could try allowing them to read any part of the gospels at all. They are all about Jesus and they are always read in church. Why? For Christians the story of Jesus is the most important knowledge there is. (See 'Life Stories' on page 106 below, and *RE Topics for the Primary School*, pp 60–63.)

3   Other exercises could be devised with the help of the chapter on 'Sacred Writings' in *RE Topics for the Primary School*, p 66. Keep in mind that you want the children to understand that, in most religions, it is by the reading of sacred scriptures that the religion's history and teaching are kept alive in the minds of the followers, and handed on from one generation to another.

Festivals as remembrance

Religious festivals are usually a commemoration of some part of the sacred story of a religion, or celebrated to commemorate the life of an outstanding member of a religion.

Activities

1   Make a list of the festivals known to the children. They may think of some Christian festivals such as Christmas and perhaps Easter. Depending on the composition of the class, they may also suggest Passover, Hanukah, Sukkot from the Jewish festivals, Divali from Indian ones, Eid ul Fitr from Muslim ones, Baisakhi from Sikh ones, and so on. With the help of the chapter on 'The Christian Calendar' in *RE Topics for the Primary School* (p 54) and the *Shap Calendar of Religious Festivals*, discover with the children the story behind each of the festivals, and make a simple display with captions like: 'Christmas celebrates Jesus' birth', 'The story of Rama is often told at Divali', and so on. Explore some of the ways in which festivals are actually celebrated, so that the children can see that the idea of a festival is to try to make a past event alive in the present. (Note that Harvest festivals are not in this category.)

2   Make a *short* study of the Holy Communion, with emphasis on the words 'Do this in remembrance of me', and tell the children the mysterious story of Jesus' words at the Last Supper. (See 1 Corinthians 11:23–26). The point to be understood is that this celebration, which takes place in almost all Christian churches, is an act of remembering. This study can be taken further by considering the things used at the Eucharist — such as the paten (plate) and chalice (cup) which can be viewed in a local church, and the symbolism of bread and wine. (Some useful ideas could be adapted from *The Eucharist* by John Rankin, Lutterworth Press 1985).

Memorials

The best-known memorial in Great Britain is probably the annual Remembrance Day (Sunday nearest 11 November) marked at the Cenotaph in London, commemorating the dead of two world wars. But there are other commemorations which may occasionally come within a child's knowledge, such as the Battle of Britain, D Day and so on. These events are usually commemorated in some solemn manner, and Remembrance Day is distinguished by the sale of red artificial poppies made in British Legion workshops. There are also individual memorials that are observed.

The Cenotaph in London where Remembrance Sunday is celebrated each year.

Activities

1   Children of this age do not usually have the inhibitions acquired later in talking about death, and some teachers have built interesting projects around a visit to a cemetery or churchyard. With careful preparation, the teacher can find one which has a sufficient variety of gravestones and memorials to raise interesting questions. Remember to make arrangements and obtain permissions. It is important to try to allow the children to find their own points of interest. Sometimes an analysis of the dates can indicate when the burial ground was most used. On most gravestones the age of the person at death is given. Can any conclusions be drawn from these? (For example a higher number of child deaths in Victorian times and earlier.) There are often pious religious expressions on the stones. Perhaps useful discussions can take place about these. The visit

could be the substance of a classroom display of children's writing and photographs, perhaps some rubbings from designs on stones (obtain permission) and some drawings.

2   Make a study of Remembrance Sunday. Interviews with old people will elicit a great deal of information which the children can note down or record on tape. Pay a visit to the local war memorial. Is the list of names longer for 1914–18 or for 1939–45? It would be appropriate if this were done around the end of October / beginning of November, so that the event itself would complete their study. Key topics to explore are:

the eleventh hour of the eleventh day of the eleventh month
two minutes' silence
the Flanders poppy
the Last Post
Reveille
medals
'remembrance' poem

Make a display or a class book.

Notes

In the period between the two world wars, Remembrance Day was always on 11 November, the day on which the armistice for the First World War was signed (it was usually called 'Armistice Day'). At eleven o'clock everything which could, stopped for two minutes. Buses would draw into the side of the road, and people stood where they were. Men removed their hats and bowed their heads.

The last verse of the 'remembrance' poem composed by Laurence Binyon is used all over the United Kingdom at Remembrance Day parades and services. After it is read, all those present repeat the last line — 'We will remember them'.

They shall grow not old, as we that are left grow old:
Age shall not weary them, nor the years condemn.
At the going down of the sun and in the morning
We will remember them.

(from 'For the Fallen', *Oxford Book of 20th Century Verse*, ed. Philip Larkin, 1973)

SECTION 2: FOR 7–9 YEAR OLDS

Resources

Books

C Brighton, *Cathy's Story*, Evans 1980
(Large picture story book about a growing relationship between an old lady and a young girl, Cathy. Cathy hears all about Mrs Slinger's childhood memories)
A Fletcher, *Abrar's Holiday*, CUP 1987
(One of the *Allsorts* readers series: Abrar returns from his holiday in Pakistan and his class want to hear what he remembers; they go on to bring Pakistan and India alive in the classroom)
J Paton Walsh, *Babylon*, André Deutsch 1982
(A story of three West Indian children, two of whom have a memory of their country of origin; the other, a girl, has no such memory . . .)

J Mayled, *Commemorative Festivals*, Wayland 1987
(Information book which picks up a variety of days which are not necessarily directly linked with religious traditions. Arranged thematically around Freedom, Birthdays and Families, Dates from the Past, and the Sun and the Moon)
A Vincent, *All the days of the Year*, Young Library Ltd 1987
(A calendar of events — historical, religious, festive, seasonal for each of 366 days. Choice of events varied and variable, but the book illustrates human concern with 'remembering')

Shap Calendar of Religious Festivals, Hobsons Publishing
(Annual publication covering 18 months and drawing on some 12 religious traditions represented in Britain.)

AVA

Sacred Books, BBC Publications 1982
(One of the *Quest* series of programmes — originally produced as filmstrip and notes to accompany broadcast. Emphasises idea of books communicating values, ways of life important to a faith. Best used as slides; transcript could be pre-recorded on cassette)

Note: resources on holy books listed under 'Communication' (see p 93) will also be useful here.

Celebration Meals, BBC Publications 1984
(Also a programme for the *Quest* series; looks at how meals and sharing food can recall past events.)

10 Senses

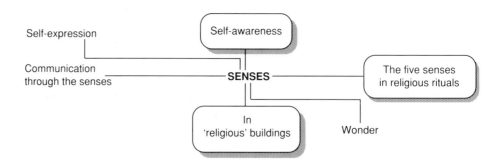

Self-expression

Communication
through the senses

Self-awareness

SENSES

The five senses
in religious rituals

In
'religious' buildings

Wonder

Aims

The aims of this unit are:
- to help children recognise the 'sights and sounds and actions' of religion;
- to encourage the children's awareness of their capacities, their own identity, and the complexity of human life.

Minarets at the Blue Mosque in Instanbul.
The Muezzin is making the call to prayer.

The five senses

Explore the five senses—sight, hearing, touch, smell and taste. Games can be played which heighten awareness of these senses, such as identifying objects blindfold, and identifying tastes, smells, or (recorded) sounds.

Then explore the specific 'feel' of particular religions. Visits are best, asking the pupils to record what they see and hear—and smell (See Activities below). It may not be possible to achieve everything in a visit, and some simulations—such as scripture reading or playing recordings of, for example, the Muslim call to prayer—may have to be arranged in the classroom.

Activities

1 **Experience of a church**, explored through:
Sight—shape of the building, distinguishing marks, stained glass (stories in the glass?), paintings, statues. Remember to look up!
Sound—bells?, organ playing (try to arrange that this happens), the echo of voices?, silence?, footsteps, hymns, reading.
Smell—musty?, incense?, candle smoke?
Touch—be careful not to encourage fingering of everything! Touch is not only by the hands—eg bottoms on seats, feet on floor, wind on face.
Taste—needs to be set up separately; see below.
   Try to allow the pupils to make their own personal discoveries and encourage discussion in the classroom.

2 **Experience of a mosque** would produce another set of perceptions.

Note that it is important not to use these visits in the same way that you would in learning about the history of the building or exploring buildings generally. The pupils must be encouraged just to think about their senses and try to record what comes through these senses.
   Responses back in the classroom could be in paint or verbal description. The children should be encouraged to express their feelings freely.

Taste

A special exploration of tastes can be arranged. Consider some or all of the following:

Salt on the tongue at a Roman Catholic baptism. The symbolic purifying meaning of salt comes into play here.

The bread and wine used at a Christian Eucharist. The bread and wine represent the Body and Blood of Jesus for Christians. He gave these to his disciples at the Last Supper, saying 'Do this in remembrance of me.'

Karah parshad (see page 17 for the recipe) in the Sikh gurdwara. Guru Nanak taught his disciples that to share in the worship of God, his followers must not make caste or class distinctions and must be prepared to eat together in the Guru's kitchen. *Parshad*, in Indian religion, is received in temples with God's blessing and represents a sharing with the god. It can be of any kind of food. In Sikhism it is always made from semolina, milk and sugar, and always prepared in the same way. All receive this sign, *together* in the gurdwara.

Latkes at Jewish Hanukah, or the **maror** and **haroset** at Passover.

The actual taste of some of these is important symbolically. For example, the salt is a symbol of purification, the sweet rich taste of the karah parshad symbolises the richness of God's blessing in which all are invited to share. Latkes are cooked in deep oil, associated with the oil which miraculousiy continued to be provided in the temple at Jerusalem (See *RE Topics for the Primary School*, pp 110–111). The taste of the haroset represents God's mercy to the Jews in contrast to the taste of the 'bitter herbs' which stand for the suffering of captivity in Egypt.

See *RE Topics for the Primary School* (p 165 for *Karah parshad*; p 114 for *latkes*; pp 78–79 for *haroset*).

Activities

1 Discuss with the children pleasant and unpleasant tastes.

2 Experiment with very small quantities of some of the foods mentioned above. It may be possible to prepare one or two of them as a class activity.

3 Encourage some writing about tastes, finding expressive words.

4 If appropriate, the whole area of special foods related to religious festivals could be pursued.

Mindfulness (Buddhist)

An exploration of the senses could lead specifically to arousal of awareness of the problems of the blind or deaf.

The efforts of concentration required to imagine oneself in the position of a deaf person or a blind person could in turn lead to an examination of the practice of 'mindfulness' in Buddhism. 'Mindfulness' is a manner of meditation in Buddhism. The ultimate aim is *nibanna* (nirvana), involving the suspension of all attachment to sense experiences. Initial exercises are designed simply to discipline the mind by an effort of concentration—to prevent thoughts from wandering all over the place in an undisciplined way. 'Mindfulness' is a technique of concentration in which the meditator deliberately concentrates on his or her own physical sensations. In Sri Lanka, monks sometimes practise a 'walking meditation', placing each foot down in turn with total concentration aware of the every tiny shape in the ground on which they tread.

Activities

An experience of 'meditation'

Note that although this is the first part of a particular kind of meditation, it does not imply any commitment, nor is there any danger for the children. Indeed it is a refreshing activity.

Ask the pupils to sit up straight but comfortably, then to close or half-close their eyes (this is just to prevent distraction from other people). Then ask them to think quite slowly and deliberately about their breathing out and in, what they can hear, the feel of the chair they are sitting on, the feel of the floor under their feet. How long you can spend will depend on the particular class, but there should be no feeling of 'rush'. Afterwards the children should be encouraged to talk about their experience.

A Hindu shrine.

Hindu puja

Puja is a general word for worship in Hindu, and it can be applied to quite a number of activities, including the offering of a single flower petal to a god. What is described below are very common elements in puja—although there will be variations.

Another element usual in puja is the careful preparation of the image at the shrine. That is to say the god is honoured by being served in the way that an important person might be served by a personal servant. The image is washed carefully with scented water, dried with a precious cloth, perhaps also anointed with scented oil and dressed in specially made clothes. Images in Hinduism are a way of making worshippers vividly aware of the divine presence. The senses are used to convey a spiritual reality. God is felt to be present in the image while it is used in this way, but is not identified with the image in itself.

Activities

Set up a simple Hindu shrine (or go and see one). All you need is an image (a picture will do), it may be of Krishna or Shiva or some other god. Set a small table before it, covered with a bright colourful cloth and place upon it some fruit, some flowers, a fan, some sticks of incense in a holder, a lamp or candle, a bowl of water and a small bell.

Ask the pupils what senses are involved with each of the objects there. Explain that these things actually represent the *elements of the world*:

Earth—fruit and flowers
Air—fan
Fire—candle or lamp
Water—bowl of water

Explain that the bell, at least the sound of the bell, represents what is called the 'ether' or 'outer space'.

All these things are offered to the god in worship. Ask the pupils to say why they think each one is offered. Incense brings a sweet smell although it is not an 'element'. Thus all the senses are involved in the worship.

Note that what is proposed is not an actual act of worship but simply a study of the elements used.

SECTION 2: FOR 7–9 YEAR OLDS

Resources

Books
V P (Hemant) Kanitkar, *Indian Food and Drink*, Wayland 1986
C Osborne, *Middle Eastern Food and Drink*, Wayland 1988
A Paraiso, *Jewish Food and Drink*, Wayland 1988
(An attractive series giving much scope for exploring taste)
More orientated to religious traditions, but less interesting is:
A Paraiso and J Mayled, *Soul Cakes and Shish kebabs*, RMEP 1987
The following books, intended for middle years and above, all offer helpful material on Hindu worship:
R Jackson, *Religion through Festivals: Hinduism*, Longman 1989
R Jackson and E Nesbitt, *Listening to Hindus*, Unwin Hyman 1990
J Hirst and G Pandey, *Growing up in Hinduism*, Longman 1990
The following is a simple story book about Hindu worship for this age-group:
J Jones, *To the Temple for Arti*, Blackie 1987
A Bancroft, *The Buddhist World*, Macdonald 1984
(This information book includes a section which gives a very simple introduction to Buddhist meditation)

AVA
S38 *Our Senses*, Philip Green Educational
(24 slides of excellent quality to explore senses. Includes some frames relating to animal and plant life)
CEM video *Hinduism through the eyes of Hindu children*, Pergamon Educational Productions
(Although best for an older age range, short sections of this could probably be used with children of this age group to illustrate Hindu puja. Worth borrowing from a resources centre or hiring)
R744 *Indian Musical Instruments*, Pictorial Charts Educational Trust
(Set of excellent small posters which could be used in extending this topic)

11 Imagination

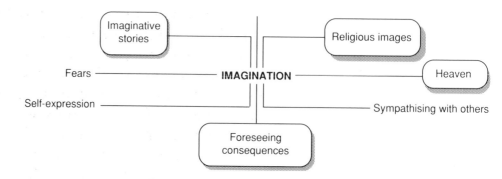

Imaginative stories — Religious images

Fears —— **IMAGINATION** —— Heaven

Self-expression —— Sympathising with others

Foreseeing consequences

Aims

This unit aims:

- to lay foundations for understanding those beliefs in religion which go beyond sense experience;
- to help the development of a moral sense and the capacity to reflect on the quality of human actions.

Using imaginative stories

For example, the Narnia stories by C S Lewis (*Complete Chronicles of Narnia*, Collins–Lions paperback, seven volumes, 23rd impression 1989) provide very good material.

These stories have an immediate appeal to most children because the children in the stories can do things normally impossible and the moral idealism is one which they appreciate.

At the same time the stories have a deeper level of meaning which is often spontaneously understood, for example the correspondence between Aslan and Jesus. However, it is important *not* to *suggest* interpretations to the pupils.

The stories are very good for reading aloud and there is real value in simply allowing the pupils to enjoy them in an immediate way.

It is interesting to look further into the mythical beasts which C S Lewis uses to provide characters for the stories. While the author borrowed freely from Greek mythology, there are many other beautifully described characters such as Reepicheep the mouse (*The Voyage of the Dawntreader*), Nikabrik the dwarf (*Prince Caspian*) and Puddleglum (*The Silver Chair*). The pupils could be asked to create their own animal (or other) character and give it a suitable name. It could be drawn or painted or modelled or described in writing—or just talked about.

Discussion of the moral dilemmas in the stories could be valuable. It is important not to use them simply to back up conventional ideas of behaviour but to let the pupils explore their own feelings where they can identify with the feelings of different characters.

Activities

1 Read or allow the children to read the following extract:

'Oh! Ugh! What on earth's *that*! Take it away, the horrid thing.'

Eustace had some excuse this time for feeling a little surprised. Something very curious indeed had come out of the cabin in the poop and was slowly approaching them. You might call it — and indeed it was — a Mouse. But then it was a mouse on its hind legs and stood about two feet high. A thin band of gold passed round its head under one ear and over the other and in this was stuck a long crimson feather. (As the Mouse's fur was very dark, almost black, the effect was bold and striking.) Its left paw rested on the hilt of a sword very nearly as long as its tail. Its balance, as it paced gravely along the swaying deck, was perfect, and its manners courtly. Lucy and Edmund recognised it at once — Reepicheep, the most valiant of all the Talking Beasts of Narnia, and the Chief Mouse. It had won undying glory in the second Battle of Beruna. Lucy longed, as she had always done, to take Reepicheep up in her arms and cuddle him. But this as she well knew, was a pleasure she could never have: it would have offended him deeply. Instead, she went down on one knee to talk to him.

Reepicheep put forward his left leg, drew back his right, bowed, kissed her hand, straightened himself, twirled his whiskers, and said in his shrill piping voice:

'My humble duty to your Majesty. And to King Edmund, too.' (Here he bowed again.) 'Nothing except your Majesties' presence was lacking to this glorious venture.'

'Ugh, take it away,' wailed Eustace. 'I hate mice. And I never could bear performing animals. They're silly and vulgar and — and sentimental.'

'Am I to understand', said Reepicheep to Lucy after a long stare at Eustace, 'that this singularly discourteous person is under your Majesty's protection? Because if not —'

At this moment Lucy and Edmund both sneezed.

(*The Voyage of the Dawntreader*, Collins 1980, pp 16–17)

SECTION 2: FOR 7–9 YEAR OLDS

2 Ask the children to describe Reepicheep (they could be asked to paint him too) and then to say what kind of person he was and what kind of clothes he might wear. Ask them to make up a 'Talking Beast' of their own — so that we can tell what kind of person it is.

An alternative is to invent a 'Talking Beast' as a class activity.

3 Read out this second extract:

...Caspian had nearly dropped off to sleep when he thought he heard a faint musical sound from the depth of the woods at his back. Then he thought it was only a dream and he turned over again; but as soon as his ear touched the ground he felt or heard (it was hard to tell which) a faint beating or drumming. He raised his head. The beating noise at once became fainter, but the music returned, clearer this time. It was like flutes. The moon was bright; Caspian had been asleep longer than he thought. Nearer and nearer came the music, a tune wild and yet dreamy, and the noise of many light feet, till at last, out from the wood into the moonlight, came dancing shapes such as Caspian had been thinking of all his life. They were not much taller than dwarfs, but far slighter and more graceful. Their curly heads had little horns, the upper part of their bodies gleamed naked in the pale light, but their legs and feet were those of goats. 'Fauns!' cried Caspian, jumping up, and in a moment they were all round him. It took next to no time to explain the whole situation to them and they accepted Caspian at once. Before he knew what he was doing he found himself joining in the dance.... The Fauns footed it all round Caspian to their reedy pipes. Their strange faces, which seemed mournful and merry all at once, looked into his; dozens of Fauns, Mentius and Obentius and Dumnus, Voluns, Voluntinus, Girbius, Nimienus, Nausus, and Oscuns .... When Caspian awoke next morning he could hardly believe that it had not all been a dream; but the grass was covered with little cloven hoofmarks.

(*Prince Caspian*, pp 74–75)

4 If the children have access to the Narnia books, ask them to find some more special creatures in the texts—such as Centaurs and Unicorns. Research on the origins of these creatures in classical mythology can be brief or extended.

A faun — one of the creatures C. S. Lewis took from classical mythology.

5 Ask the children to compose some music which is 'wild yet dreamy' with whatever resources are available.

Consequences

One of the most important uses of imagination is in being able to foresee what the possible results of any particular actions might be. It is the basic ability in 'responsible' behaviour. The purpose of this approach is to encourage children to reflect on the quality of particular actions and on the possible options. This lays the foundations for consideration of an ordered or 'moral' universe, or of human beings as creatures in whom certain kinds of behaviour are more valued than others. At this stage it is sufficient to foster the capacity to reflect imaginatively on actions, whether their own or others'.

Activities

1 Describe an incident or ask the children to describe an incident in which they felt happy or sad or uncertain. Then ask them to think about what happened next or what they would have done. Here are two examples.

'Will you play?'

I went to call for my friend. When I knocked on the door, her Mum opened it and I asked her if Julie could come out to play. Her Mum said yes and told me that Julie was in the garden with some other girls and that I could go and join them. I went into the garden but Julie was hiding with the others, behind a bush. They were whispering and giggling but they would not come out. I did not know what I could do so I started to cry and went away.

Questions:

1 What else could this girl have done? What would *you* have done?
2 EITHER write a story as if you were Julie, OR alter the story to include things which have happened to you.
3 The next day these girls played happily together. Do you and your friends behave like this?

(from Schools Council Moral Education 8–13 Project 'Startline', *Choosing Book 1 'What shall I do?'*, p 5)

Lost Property

I forgot my football boots when I went home. I left them beside the desk. The caretaker comes in to sweep the classroom every evening and so I asked him if he had seen them. He said they were lost. I believed him and told my mother and she bought me some new ones the next day. That same day I met the caretaker when he was walking down the steps at school. He said, 'Have you found your boots?' I replied, no. He then added, 'They're at my place in the lost property, because you are not allowed to leave things on the floor.'

Questions

1 What do you think about what the caretaker did?
2 What would you have done if you had been the boy or girl in the story?
3 What do you think the mother said when she was told what had happened?

('Startline', *Choosing Book 3*, p 24)

There are many variations of this kind of exercise.

2   Invite the children to dramatise, in any way they like, situations in which people are: angry, wanting something, not liking each other, loving and being pleasant. If they get the hang of this, they could also be encouraged to act out more situations of their own choosing (eg when they feel frightened). This can be elaborated to include making scenery, or a puppet theatre. (Adapted from 'Startline'.)

A better vision

The ability of human beings to think of a better world or a better destination which follows death is the source of much of the strength which people show in working for good.

Activities   1   Ask the children to describe their idea of heaven or 'the kind of country you would most like to live in'.

Perhaps they could also express their feelings about heaven in paint.

2   Ask the children to describe what changes they would like to make in the world. This could be a class or individual activity. They should be helped to think through the consequences of the changes they suggest (as in 'Consequences', above). Perhaps the class could be encouraged to list the most important changes in the form of a solemn charter or declaration to be signed by everyone and decorated in an impressive and suitable way. It could be a Bill of Rights for example, but it is important that the outcome should be from the children themselves.

Imagination and religion

Religions present their followers with information and inspiration in the form of pictures and artefacts which are the products of artists. For example: Orthodox Christians have constantly before them 'icons' of Jesus and the saints; Hindu shrines have images of the gods; Buddhist shrines have images of the Buddha; Islam forbids images but uses intricate patterns in tiles or mosaic and beautiful calligraphy; Sikhs strictly do not allow pictures in the gurdwara, but every home has a picture representing the gurus and especially Guru Nanak and Guru Gobind Singh. A good visual introduction to the use of the imagination in religion is to show some of these artefacts and to discuss with the children what kind of message is received from them. One discovery they will probably make is that if a particular artefact comes from one's own culture it does not seem strange and is readily accepted. Pieces from cultures other than one's own take some time to understand.

Activities   1   Looking at and talking about a particular picture is a useful exercise in itself. Discover how much the children can see in a picture of Guru Nanak, for example, before telling them who it is. A study of the John Piper tapestry in Chichester Cathedral, concentrating on the use of conventional Christian symbols in a modern work of art, is another possibility.

2   The beautiful tessellations which often appear in Islamic art, and which are meant to reflect the divine order, can be carefully studied and the children can be encouraged to develop their own.

Typical Islamic decoration from an old house in Madinah.

3 Encourage the children to produce a painting out of their own tradition (if they have one), saying something important about it. Children with a Christian background might be invited to design a cross or paint an Easter garden scene of the empty tomb, for example. Children from a Muslim background could write and decorate some words from the Qur'an. Sikh children might like to draw the Khanda or one of the gurus. In all cases, there must be a dialogue with the pupils to discover what kind of religious idea they would like to apply their visual imagination to. If any of the children have no clear tradition to draw on, they can be helped to choose an artefact or invent a design of their own.

Buddha image from Thailand.

Above: an icon of the Virgin Mary and the child Jesus in a Greek Orthodox Church in Hackney.

Opposite: Rama, an incarnation of the Hindu god Vishnu, with his wife Sita and brother Lahksmana.

Resources

Books

The following stories allow the theme of 'imagination' to be taken up in different ways:

M Foreman, *Panda's Puzzle*, Puffin 1977
('Who or what am I, really?' is the problem facing Panda. His journey takes him to many places in search of an answer)

C Garrison, *The Dream Eater*, Collier Macmillan 1986
(A story set in Japan. Yukio has bad dreams; so has everyone else . . . until he meets a creature called the baku, which devours bad dreams, and leaves everyone to dream of things which really matter to them)

T Jones, *Fairytales*, Puffin 1983
(30 new tales intended for *telling*, offering fantasy, morality, humour and suspense)

H Larson, *What are you scared of?*, A & C Black 1977
(Children share their fears)

R and N Thomson, *Whatever next?*, A & C Black 1988
(A story set in Trinidad; Aisha imagines all the problems and the disaster which lies round the corner as she prepares for her dance show)

L Shanson, *Journey with the Gods*, Mantra 1987
(Vinita and Deepak are awoken by the light of a magical moon, and set out on an amazing adventure with gods and heroes from Indian mythology)

C Keeping, *Adam and Paradise Island*, OUP 1989
(Different kinds of imagination! A council breaks up a community for a fine new flyover; but Adam and the local people fight back in a creative way)

Three books which may encourage children to listen to others' hopes and explore the kind of world *they* would like:

R and H Exley (Eds), *Dear World*, Exley Publications 1978
H Exley (Ed), *Cry for our beautiful world*, Exley Publications, 1985
J Zim (Ed), *My Shalom My Peace*, New English Library 1975
(Collection of writing by Jewish and Arab children)

AVA

CEM produce the following poster sets which may be found helpful:
Christianity: Artefacts
Hinduism: Artefacts
Islam: Artefacts
(Available from CEM, Royal Buildings, Victoria Street, Derby DE1 1GW)
For teachers or teachers' centres wanting to build up their own collection of artefacts, see 'Teaching by Touching — with £100 to spend, or less!' in *Religions and Education* edited by A Wood (Shap Working Party 1989).

12 Communication

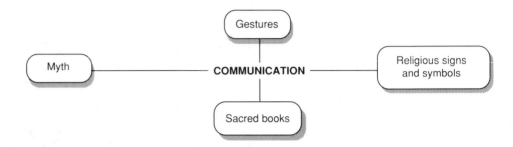

Aims

Religions are in one sense sets of symbols by which the world is interpreted. Religions also provide a way in which each person can feel they have an identity. They give a context in which a child growing up can have a sense of belonging, of knowing 'who they are'. So communication is the lifeblood of a religion—communication in passing on the historical accumulated tradition (see under 'Remembering'), and communication in the practice of a religion.

This topic aims to help children:

- discover that religions have a special vocabulary, which frequently uses metaphor;
- meet the use of mythical narrative in religion;
- begin to understand how symbols go beyond the level of simple information;
- understand the use of gesture to give or add meaning.

The meaning of gestures

Beginning from everyday gestures, move on to other actions and gestures, asking the children to say what they communicate. (See below.) Then consider a number of specifically religious positions and gestures, such as kneeling in prayer, the sequence of positions in Islamic prayer, the gesture of blessing and the hand mudras, specifically in Buddhism.

Activities

1 Begin by demonstrating certain gestures to the class: shaking a fist; thumbs up; hunched shoulders; open palms.
  Ask for interpretations.

2 Consider other gestures. Are they all easily understood? Would they be easily understood by people from other countries or cultures (eg Maoris, who rub noses as a greeting)?

3 Explore a collection of pictures of people 'praying' or engaged in some religious ritual. Consider the prayer positions in Islamic prayer; a Christian priest giving a blessing; a Buddhist meditating; a Sikh paying homage to the Guru Granth Sahib; the 'Peace' in an Anglican or Roman Catholic Eucharist; kissing an icon in an Orthodox church; Indian dancing.

A Sikh worshipper prostrates himself before the sacred book (Guru Granth Sahib) before taking his place in the gurdwara.

A father and son show their devotion by kissing an icon in an Orthodox church.

Hindus dancing at Divali.

SECTION 2: FOR 7–9 YEAR OLDS

Produce a display of gestures and postures in a religious context and let the children write captions for them after they have thought about them together. The pictures could perhaps be drawn by the children, or a sequence of photographs taken by them could be used.

Religious symbols

This is a very important aspect of the study of religion and needs to be followed up in later years. Here the aim would be to heighten awareness of the role of symbols in religion. It could be done by visiting places of worship with the specific intention of finding symbols and subsequently discussing their meaning. There could be a specific concentration on the meanings of 'water' in baptism. The task is to help the children distinguish between 'literal' meaning and symbolic meaning.

Another approach is to introduce a range of artefacts in the classroom and to talk about their meaning. For example, some Hindu images, a crucifix, a copy of an icon, communion breads. It is important for the children to discover that all these things are used to tell people about something else.

Activities

Lakshmi standing on a stylised lotus flower.

Hindu OM symbol.

Allah written in Arabic.

1 Visit a church and/or another religious building accessible to the school. Remember to make arrangements and to brief anyone who may be helping you about the exact nature of your topic. Help the children to identify the symbols being used and make a list (even of ones not understood, for later research).

A church may produce:
- images of Christ and saints (these will have their own symbols too, such as bishops' mitres and croziers, St Peter's keys etc.),
- the cross in varying forms,
- perhaps other emblems such as the lamb, the Alpha and Omega letters intertwined, the Chi-Rho, and so on.

A Hindu temple may produce:
- images of the gods with their distinctive emblems,
- the OM sign.

A mosque will impress with its space, but one can discuss the meaning of it having almost no furniture inside.

The *mihrab* indicates the direction of Makkah. The decoration will include calligraphy. This may be the time to explore what Arabic writing looks like and how it has developed as an art form in Islamic culture.

A synagogue will have:
- an ark with scrolls of the Torah inside,
- a platform (*bimah*) for the reading of the scriptures.

It is not suggested that *all* these should be explored, but the field is very rich and the teacher will need to make good preparation to respond to the particular discoveries in particular localities. Make a display of what has been found out.

2 Some specific religious symbols can be examined carefully in the classroom. Try to choose ones that have some importance in the religion to which they belong and that are generally recognised.

Here is a possible selection:

The lotus flower is a universal symbol in **Hinduism** and **Buddhism**. It is always an indication of divine origin and all images of gods and goddesses and of the Buddha are presented standing or sitting on a lotus (which is often very stylised).

The OM symbol is found everywhere in **Hinduism**. It consists of three letters which are approximately AUM. It is said to be the sound of the universe itself and is the sign of the ultimate. It is pronounced before every prayer and is sometimes used by itself in meditation.

The Arabic word for Allah (God)
Islam forbids the use of the images of anything in God's creation, and so the beautiful decoration found in mosques is either abstract pattern or writing. The word for Allah is often repeated and frequently hangs on the walls of Muslim homes as a reminder of God's sovereignty over all things.

The Cross has long been a symbol in **Christianity** and a study of its many forms can be of great interest. (See *RE Topics for the Primary School*, p 184.)

All these can be reproduced in the classroom. Take care, however, not to use the word for Allah at the same time as the other symbols as this could be offensive to Muslims, suggesting as it does that it is one among many.

3 Examine the 'five Ks' of Sikhism. (See p 13 of this book and also *RE Topics for the Primary School*, pp 38 and 164.)

Myth

The concept of myth is too abstract and difficult for this age range, but the children can come to see that much religious truth is passed on in the form of *stories*, without worrying about the definitions of myth.

Activities Read the creation story from the Bible—Genesis 1:1—2:3.
Talk about the seven days of creation.

Ask the children to draw a circle and divide it into seven segments and, in each segment, draw or paint something to represent what happened on that day in the seven-day creation. The children could also be asked to draw the picture of the universe represented by this creation story.

Draw out from the children what they think the most important message of the story is. The point for emphasis is that one should be asking what the story *means*, and not be treating it as a scientific account of the beginning of the world. The (Jewish/Christian) message conveyed is that this world is God's creation, and that people are therefore responsible to God for the care of his creation. This activity could be extended to include also other creation stories from different religious sources; or even further—into other myth topics.

Resources

Books

O Bennett { *Buildings* / *Signs and Symbols* } Bell & Hyman 1984
(2 books in the *Exploring Religion* series: both draw on Christian, Jewish and Hindu traditions)

J Mayled { *Holy Books*, Wayland / *Religious Dress*, Wayland 1987 / *Religious Symbols*, Wayland
(In the *Religious Topics* series; colour illustrations; text not always acceptable)

C and P Morgan, *Buddhist Iconography*
(Useful introductory handbook, available from the authors at Westminster College, N. Hinksey, Oxford OX2 9AT)

Y H Safadi, *Islamic Calligraphy*, Thames & Hudson 1978
(Adult and detailed book, worth obtaining from a library for reference)

AVA

The following sets are available from Pictorial Charts Educational Trust:
E726 *Holy Books 1*
E727 *Holy Books 2*
(2 sets of picture charts with notes, drawing on Buddhist, Christian, Hindu, Jewish, Muslim, Sikh traditions and others)
R748 *Indian Dance: Holi*
(Set of 7 pictures showing how dance can express the meaning of story. Mudras (hand gestures) are explored on each picture)
E728 *Places of Worship*
(Set of 4 charts which look at an Anglican Church, a Mosque, a Synagogue and a Gurdwara.)
Primary RE Materials: Islam Wallets — Mosque — Prayer & Almsgiving, Centre for Study of Islam & Muslim Christian Relations/Regional RE Centre (Midlands)
(See p 31 for address)
The Westhill Project RE 5–16: Muslim Photopack, MGP 1988
(20 pictures on stiff card with notes; examples of prayer and calligraphy included; now available from Stanley Thornes)

13 Difference

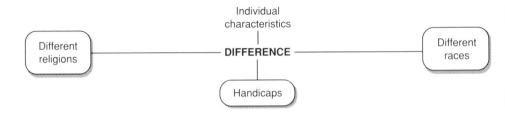

Individual characteristics

Different religions — **DIFFERENCE** — Different races

Handicaps

Aims

Seeing differences is the first step in any kind of investigation and is fundamental to any kind of reasoning. RE can contribute to children's understanding and development by encouraging positive attitudes and tolerance, and by fostering recognition:

- that individuals differ;
- that there are different races and cultures which makes life richer for everyone;
- that people have different religions and some have none; and that they can learn from each other.

The human family

Children can be encouraged and helped to form an idea of belonging to a large human family whose members have more in common with each other than they have differences. The location of some schools ensures that teachers and

children have direct encounters with children from many races, countries and cultures. Elsewhere, some classes exchange letters (and perhaps visits) with classes in another school in another town, sometimes in another country. Even if permanent links are not formed, it is worth engaging in activities of this kind. Affirming a shared humanity is a necessary first step towards appreciating difference.

Activities

1   Using a picture like the one opposite (of people from many races), EITHER discuss with the children what differences they can see OR first ask them to write down the differences they can see, and then ask 'In what ways do these people look like each other?'

2   Follow this with a discussion of why people look like they do, stressing the fact that people inherit their physical appearance from their parents. If you have the resources, this could be combined with a lesson on basic genetic inheritance. The reason for different skin colour is not certain, although there are many theories. (For example, that over a long period of time races made adaptations to the climate in which they lived. Black skin appears to act as a shield against the rays of the sun in hot climates, while white skin allows the sun to reach a layer in the skin which permits the production of the important vitamin, Vitamin D.) There is a need to make it clear that human beings share the same basic characteristics and that colour difference is simply a superficial difference in skin pigmentation. The reason for whole races sharing characteristics which have remained constant is that until recently people moved around the world relatively little.

The story of slaves from Africa

It is important that children learn about the extremes to which prejudice can drive human beings. The story of the enslavement of black people for the new colonies in America from the seventeenth century onwards is a good example of how prejudice fed by greed can bring unbelievable suffering. This piece of history is also useful to study because it explains the existence of large populations of coloured people in America and the Caribbean. When Britain annexed the islands of the West Indies, there was a shortage of labour to work the sugar plantations. Traders solved the problem by seizing black people in Africa or buying them from Arab slavers who rounded them up from the villages and brought them to the West African seaports to sell as slaves.

They were then shipped to the West Indies packed in the ships like cargo. Many died on the sea voyage to the Caribbean, where the survivors were sold to the plantation owners. The vessels would then load sugar to be shipped back to Britain. In Britain the sea captains would stock up on weapons and iron chains ready for the next slave raid in Africa. This trade continued over a period of almost 300 years until slavery was abolished in the British Empire in 1833. Slaves were treated abominably. Families were broken up and beatings were frequent. Those who carried out the trade, or did nothing to prevent it, often excused themselves by saying that black people were quite different and had none of the finer feelings of white people. Ever since that time black people have had to struggle for equal treatment with whites. Most of the inhabitants of the West Indies are descendants of these slaves. In the 1950s and after, there were immigrations of workers from the West Indies to fill a labour shortage in Britain.

Activities

1 Tell the story of the seizure of slaves from Africa by British merchants.

2 Tell a shortened version of the story of William Wilberforce and the end of slavery in Britain.

3 Use paintings and Negro spirituals to help conjure up the feeling of slaves at the time.

4 Discuss with the children the reasons why black people were so badly maltreated.

If desired, the study could be continued by looking at some selected parts of the Civil Rights campaigns in the United States in more recent times (eg Martin Luther King).

A plan of a slaveship, showing how to pack in the slaves in the hold.

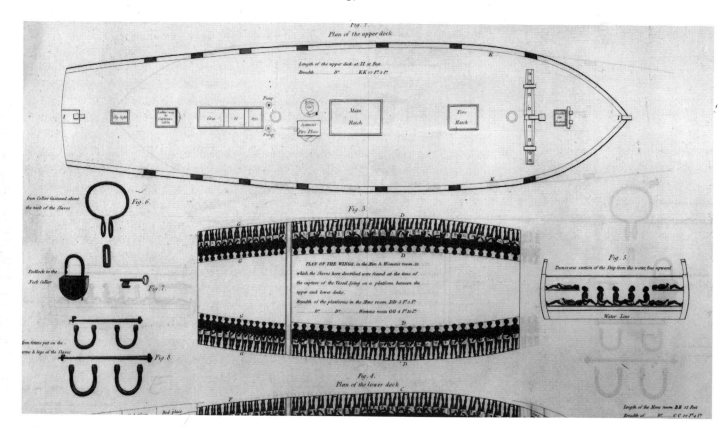

Religions in Britain

This approach involves the children in identifying the main religions which are practised in Britain today, not so much to provide detailed knowledge of religions at this stage, but to talk through the children's perception of them and to discuss the reasons for their particular feelings.

Activities

1 Present a stimulus—such as a picture (or refer to an example that they all know)—of a mosque or a church and ask the children to talk about it. It will be important to find a starting stimulus which you know, from your knowledge of the children, that they will be able to recognise.

OR

Plan a 'walkabout' in your area, identifying religious buildings. Make a big map and put them on it.

2 Move on to less familiar buildings, and gradually identify Christian, Jewish, Islamic, Hindu, Sikh, and perhaps also Buddhist ones. Teachers will find useful outlines for their own use in *Religions* by A Brown, J Rankin and A Wood (Longman 1989).

3 Help the children to identify the key symbol of a number of religions and to make their own copies.

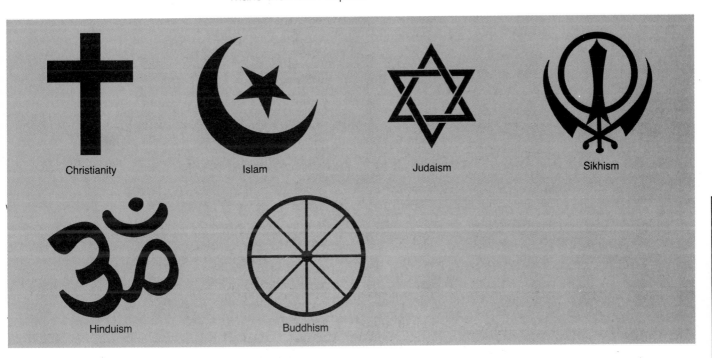

Christianity

Islam

Judaism

Sikhism

Hinduism

Buddhism

4 Prepare a class collage, showing people practising each of these religions. Label them, in each case inserting the word 'British', eg: 'a *British* Muslim at prayer'; '*British* Sikhs in their gurdwara'; '*British* Christians praying together'. You could also add the location, eg 'in Leeds' or 'in Crawley'.

Children with special needs

Children are sometimes different because they are blind or deaf or suffer some permanent physical handicap or have long-term ailments such as asthma. Learning about these takes away the fear that children sometimes feel when faced with things which are out of the ordinary. Children with handicaps also need to feel that they are accepted and understood.

Maria

My name is Maria. I use my ears and my hands and my nose to see the world because I am blind.

Every day when I wake up, Bumper is there. Bumper is my secret friend. She is hundreds of years old and I tell her everything I do because she likes to know. In the morning, when my sister Anna is getting ready for school, Bumper and I sit by the window out of the way. Over Christmas, Anna will be at home with us. I show Bumper how I put my hands against the glass to tell the weather. 'In the summer,' I say, 'the glass is warm, in winter it is freezing. And when it rains the air feels damp.'

When Anna has said goodbye and gone, Mummy starts her work. She is a dressmaker and all day long her machine whirrs and the backs of the chairs get covered with clothes.

Bumper watches when I stand on the chair and Mummy pulls clothes stuck with prickly pins over my head. The dress feels cold and smooth. I trace with my fingers round and round like a giant puzzle.

The first communion dress feels cold too next to my skin. Mummy has sewn on crinkly flowers that smell of paper. Bumper makes me pull the petals out and the flowers unwind. Then I get scolded.

I show Bumper my pet birds and how they cling to my finger with their little claws. I stroke the tops of their heads and I let them wriggle in my hands. Their hearts beat very fast.

When Anna comes home from school she tells me what's on television, so I can laugh too. They don't have television where Bumper comes from.

When Daddy comes home from work we fight to get on his knee. I can tell what sort of work he has been doing by the dirt on his overalls. Cement is powdery when I rub it, but earth is cracked and hard, and the smell is different too. He gives Bumper and me his bus tickets and we keep them in a match box.

After my bath I smell of talcum powder. It's supposed to be roses. Daddy puts Bumper and me in between the smooth sheets next to my bald teddy and the cold hard doll that once belonged to Mummy. I sing to Bumper and then she tells me a story about long ago.

When we lie in bed I know the door is open because I can smell cooking. Bumper stays with me until I go to sleep and then I think she goes away.

(*Maria* by Catherine Brighton, Faber and Faber 1984)

Activities

1 Read Maria's story and ask the children to say what they found most interesting. Perhaps they could try guessing what the weather is like by touching the window. What part is Bumper playing? Is it because Maria is blind that she has this 'friend'? Play some games of being blind — like trying to identify objects or finding your way round the classroom blindfold.

2 Tell the children about individual handicaps children sometimes suffer from and explain them. There is a useful series published by Franklin Watts called *One World*, in which individual children tell of their particular handicap — for

example diabetes, spina bifida, deafness, asthma, and Down's syndrome. Make a choice of one or two.

This boy, who has a physical disability and often has to use a wheelchair, is gaining the confidence to ski through the use of a pole. He will progress to skiing without a pole. Blind people are also taught to ski in the same way.

Resources

Books

B Birch, *A Question of Race*, Macdonald 1985
J Kuper, *Race and Race Relations*, Batsford Educational 1984
(Whilst this unit is not on race issues as such, these 2 books for secondary schools provide some background on the issue of differing appearance and on slavery)

M Pollard, *My World*, Macdonald/UNICEF 1979
(A book about 7 children, each growing up in a different part of the world; recognises difference, but also the ways in which the children are alike; aims to encourage children to grow up knowing more about others and understanding their feelings. Worth obtaining via a library or resources centre)
C Barker, *The United Nations: Its work in the world*, Macdonald 1986
(Attractive information book (top juniors) illustrating the work of the UN and affirming a shared humanity)
J Bradley, *Human Rights*, Franklin Watts 1987
(Information book (top juniors) raising issues of human rights around the world)
M Hayward (Ed), *World Religions in Education 1986: Religion in Britain*, Shap/CRE
(Material on world faiths in Britain — useful background reading for teachers)
Communities in Britain series, Batsford Academic & Educational
(A series for teenage readers, providing useful background information on Britain's minority communities. Series covers West Indian, Chinese, Jewish, Hindu and Sikh communities)
My Belief series, Franklin Watts
(10 titles focus on religious belief and practice, each through the eyes of a child living in Britain today. Series includes, for example, Rastafarian, Pentecostal, Greek Orthodox, Muslim. Usually the book gives a history of the child's family showing patterns of migration)
See also Resources for 'Journeys', p 133.

H Exley (Ed), *What it's like to be me*, Exley 1984
(A book written and illustrated entirely by disabled children who tell of their experiences)
E Musty (Comp.), *Special People and Books*
(A list of books relating to and about children with special needs, giving some indication of reading age. Available from Special RE Network, 7 Elyham, Purley on Thames, Berks RG8 8EN)

AVA

I'm Special Myself, ILEA/ACER
(See Resources for 'Myself', p 17 for details. The posters from this set would be useful for this topic)
Ourselves, ILEA/ACER
(Teaching pack based on stories of children from different backgrounds; includes worksheets and teacher's notes. Address on p 17)
E728 *Places of Worship*, Pictorial Charts Educational Trust
(Set of 4 charts (Christian, Muslim, Jewish and Sikh))
'Myself'
'Communities' } CEM
(2 posters accompanying CEM *Exploring a Theme* booklets on these topics)

14 Light

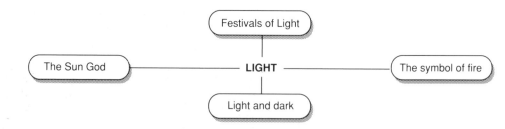

Festivals of Light

The Sun God — **LIGHT** — The symbol of fire

Light and dark

| Aims |

The symbol of Light is universal in religion and this unit aims to help children come to understand the symbolic and metaphorical use of light and fire and sun.

Lights of various kinds are used in many religious festivals. Experience of some of these will help to extend children's awareness of what part religion plays in people's lives.

Festivals of light

Observing, preparing, celebrating, simulating festivals in which light plays a predominant part is probably the most productive and exciting way of tackling the religious dimension of this topic.

Activities

Consider the use of light in the following celebrations.

Advent

An Advent crown, with the white candle lit on Christmas Day.

Advent is the period of preparation for Christmas observed in most Christian churches. The custom of the Advent crown is particularly typical of Continental (especially German) Protestant churches. Four candles, evenly spaced, are placed in a crown of holly and other evergreens (usually supported by wire mesh or some other medium — plasticine is useful in making the candle holders). One candle is lit on each of the four Sundays in Advent. On Christmas Day a fifth candle is added in the centre to represent the coming of Jesus. The four are usually red and the fifth one white.

In school the class could make an Advent crown and a candle could be lit at the same convenient time in each of the four weeks before Christmas. Alternatively, smaller-scale crowns could be made by each child, to take home at the end of term with a white candle for Christmas Day. (See *RE Topics for the Primary School*, pp 9–10 and 43.)

Christmas

A Scandinavian custom at Christmas is making 'Christingles'. An orange represents the world. A candle is inserted into it to represent Christ, in Christian belief the Light of the world. The Christingle is then decorated with pieces of crystallised fruit on wooden sticks to represent all the fruits of the earth. This custom developed in Scandinavia in the eighteenth century. Christingles are quite easy to make. Christmas, being a winter festival, is also generally associated with the warmth of candlelight and the light of the star which is said to have led the wise men to Bethelemen. (See *RE Topics for the Primary School*, pp 42–43.)

Divali
Many customs attach to Divali, but the custom which gives this Indian festival its name is the use of *divas*, ie lamps. Divali comes at the end of the rainy season and these lamps are used to decorate the outside of houses. Celebration is very much a public event. Children can make diva lamps with clay, shaped, dried and painted. Light is obtained with oil and a cotton-wool wick. 'Night lights' are a good substitute. These can be placed in a row in front of an image or picture of Lakshmi, who is the goddess especially revered at this time. (See *RE Topics for the Primary School*, pp 14–15.)

Divas — lamps used at the celebration of Divali.

Hanukah
Hanukah is a Jewish festival in which the lighting of lights is the central act. The story is told how when the Jews regained their temple from the Greek–Syrian occupiers, they could find only one jar of oil for the lamp, enough for one day.

Miraculously, the lamp burned for eight days. The commemoration of this is celebrated by lighting, on the first day, one light, on the second, two, and so on for eight days. A special candelabra is used called a *hanukiah*. It has places for eight candles and one extra, called the *shammas* or servant candle, from which

A Hanukah menorah. Note the eight candles (one for each day of the festival), together with the *shammas* or 'servant' candle.

the others are lit. This is because the Hanukah lights are for pure rejoicing only and must not be used for utilitarian purposes. Children can make a class hanukiah of a simple kind, or one can be brought into the classroom and the celebratory lighting demonstrated. It is intended to signify the joy of freedom. (See *RE Topics for the Primary School*, pp 110–115.)

The Paschal candle

Easter candle, showing the Alpha and Omega, and the 'nails'.

The ceremony of the Paschal candle, performed on the eve of Easter, is one of great antiquity and is full of symbolic meaning. 'New fire' is lit outside the church and from it is lit a very large candle which is carried into the darkened church. Three times the minister carrying the candle calls 'Christ the Light'; the congregation respond 'Thanks be to God'. The congregation light their own candle from the Paschal candle, which is placed in its own stand before the performance of other ceremonies. The Paschal candle represents the coming of Christ the light. On it are impressed five grains of incense, standing for the five wounds of Christ, and the letters Alpha and Omega—the beginning and the end of the Greek alphabet—symbolising God; the calendar year is also inscribed on the candle. It is possible to demonstrate the use of the Paschal candle in class. (If appropriate a local member of the Anglican or Roman Catholic church may be invited to speak about it.) Smaller Paschal candles can be purchased for demonstration purposes if necessary. (See *RE Topics for the Primary School*, p 44.)

The sun

The sun has been a very frequent symbol for deity in many civilisations: Aztec, Egyptian, Greek, Chinese and Indian, for example. An exploration of any of these would be stimulating and have plenty of visual examples. Children would recognise the awe and wonder felt by humankind before the most potent force in nature, and how, although with greater knowledge perhaps we no longer think of the sun as a god, it still remains a powerful sign.

Activities

The consideration of the sun as divine would best take place in a topic study which included a study of the sun in relation to the earth and other planets.

1 In **ancient Greek mythology**, Apollo is the god of solar light, but the Sun God himself was Helios.

Every morning Helios rose up in the East from a swamp. He had a golden chariot. Harnessed to the chariot were nine winged horses. They were dazzling white and their nostrils breathed out flame. Their names were Lampon, Phaeton, Chronos, Aethon, Astrope, Bronte, Pyroeis, Eous and Phlegon.

The god then took the reins and climbed up into the sky.

'Drawn in his swift chariot, he sheds light on gods and men alike; his eyes flash and sparkling rays glint from his breast; his brilliant helmet gives forth a dazzling splendour; his body is draped in shining gauze whipped by the wind.' At midday Helios reaches the highest point of his course and begins to

The ancient god Helios with his chariot depicted on a vase.

descend towards the West. At the end of the day he arrives in the land of Hesperides where he seems to plunge into the ocean. There a barque is waiting with his family. He would sail all night and in the morning get back to where he started.

The island of Rhodes was sacred to Helios and there, it is said, was a huge statue of him — about 30 metres high — and ships in full sail could pass between his legs. This statue is known as the 'Colossus' of Rhodes, one of the wonders of the ancient world.

Ask the children to say what Helios' chariot journey represented. Discuss whether they like this way of thinking of the sun's rising and setting. Can they suggest other ways of describing the passing of the sun over a day? How can they tell from the story that the ancient Greeks did not know that the world was round or that the earth moved round the sun?

2 In **ancient Egyptian mythology** the Sun God is called 'Ra'. He is shown seated, with the head of a falcon. Above his head is a disc representing the sun and this is surrounded by an asp which spits fire in defence of the god. Ra is often represented holding in his hand the *ankh*, symbol of life (see *RE Topics for the Primary School*, pp 74–75).

Ra in his ship shown on a wall painting.

During the daylight hours Ra rode his boat across his Kingdom from East to West. He took care to avoid the attack of his enemy Apep, the great serpent who lived in the depths of the heavenly Nile. Sometimes Apep succeeded in swallowing the Sun God's boat and there would be an eclipse of the sun. But in the end, Ra's defenders were always victorious.

In the hours of darkness Ra sailed on in the caverns of the underworld where many more dangers awaited. However the inhabitants were pleased to see him for he brought a momentary period of light. After he passed they fell back into the agony of darkness.

The children can be invited to compare the two stories of Helios and Ra.
The rulers of Egypt (the Pharaohs) called themselves 'sons of Ra'.

Fire

For Zoroastrians (mostly represented by the Parsees of India), the one God is Ahura Mazda, the 'Lord of Wisdom'. His name develops into *Ohrmazd*. The Spirit of Evil is Angra Mainyu, later *Ahriman*. Fire is especially important in their religious observance. It signifies the power by which evil is overcome. In the middle of winter a festival is kept called *Sada* (the 'hundredth day' festival, so called because it falls 100 days before the main New Year festival). Sada is celebrated principally with a huge bonfire built by the whole community. It is to blaze up against the darkness of winter. Darkness represents evil. Sadness and melancholy too are brought on by Ahriman, and so should be countered with joy and laughter.

A bonfire, in many European countries, celebrates the feast of John the Baptist on 24 June. Tradition has it that this is because John said, 'I baptise you with water for repentance, but he who is coming after me...will baptise you with the Holy Spirit and with fire' (Matthew 3: 11). However it is probable that a bonfire marked the summer solstice in pre-Christian times.

Note too the lighting of the new fire which forms part of the celebrations of the Paschal candle (see above).

See also 'Fire' pages 152–161 below.

Activities

1 A celebration of St John's Fire in the summer term, with all joining hands and moving round the bonfire, can be fun. Of course it is not always possible to have events like this, but it may be possible to do it on a small scale with a special metal container.

2 Children can be invited to respond at several levels and modes to the ideas of 'Light and Darkness'. They can be asked to:

a create a sequence of movements relating dark and light;

b compose a piece of music with whatever resources there are in the school;

c make a pictorial representation either individually or as a planned and discussed larger picture;

d experiment with 'light and dark' words in a piece of writing.

Resources

Books
The festivals mentioned above are covered in many series from a number of publishers. The following series are worth following up according to your interests:
Celebrations, Black (Divali)
Celebrations, Wayland (Christmas, Easter)
Festival!, Macmillan & Commonwealth Institute (Divali)
The way we live, Hamish Hamilton (Holi, Divali)
Living Festivals (Middle/Secondary), RMEP (Advent, Christmas, Easter; Divali; Holi; Hanukah)
See also:

O Bennett $\left\{ \begin{array}{l} \textit{Signs \& Symbols} \\ \textit{Festivals} \end{array} \right\}$ *Bell & Hyman 1984*

J Foster, *Let's Celebrate: festival poems*, OUP 1989
(Contains a number of poems relating to festivals where light is a symbol; many poems really capture the mood of the festivals they 'describe')
Y and S Wurtzel, *Lights: a fable about Hanukah*, Rossel Books 1984
(Also available as a video; obtainable from the Jewish Education Bureau—see p 25)
The series *Seasonal Projects* from Wayland (volumes covering each season, Christmas, and Easter) also offers activities relating to light and darkness.

AVA
The following poster sets from Pictorial Charts Educational Trust contain relevant pictures:
E745 *Christian Festivals* (Christmas), E746 *Jewish Festivals* (Hanukah), E748 *Hindu Festivals* (Divali, Holi)
See also:
R745 *Indian Dance: Divali*

See also Resource lists under 'Christmas', 'Easter', 'Divali', 'Hanukah' and 'Wesak' in *RE Topics for the Primary School*.

15 Life Stories

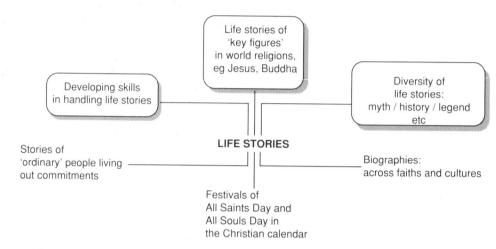

- Life stories of 'key figures' in world religions, eg Jesus, Buddha
- Developing skills in handling life stories
- Diversity of life stories: myth / history / legend etc

LIFE STORIES

- Stories of 'ordinary' people living out commitments
- Biographies: across faiths and cultures
- Festivals of All Saints Day and All Souls Day in the Christian calendar

---

| Aims |

Biographies of 'famous people' have enjoyed considerable popularity in RE. Very often their focus has been on Christians 'doing good'; the range of people introduced has been fairly predictable and a chronological overview of a person's life the most common pattern: these features certainly prevail in many of the books available for this age range. Here 'life stories' is used to break away from this mould and highlight a broader approach. This topic has clear connections with those on 'Remembering' and 'Time' and aims to help children:

- begin to acquire skills in thinking about and handling life stories;
- recognise something of the diversity of life stories;
- engage thoughtfully with some life stories from world religions.

Thinking about life stories

Children in this age range are *beginning* to acquire skills in identifying and handling different kinds of evidence; they are likely to be doing this across the humanities as well as in science; RE should be no exception here. In RE children may be involved in thinking about:

- how we can find out about people from the past;
- the types of evidence available to us if we are writing about a person or event in the twentieth century;
- the kinds of things for which people are remembered — their sayings, key moments or events in their lives, achievements and so on, but also their qualities, *who* they are;
- how you decide what to include in a life story — a question about the perspective of the person or community telling a life story.

Here the concern is mainly with the last two issues; they are questions children might explore in relation to their experience of life (see Activities) and in relation to others' life stories. This approach is explored in relation to two key figures, Jesus and the Buddha (also known as Gautama and Prince Siddhartha).

Example one: Jesus

Children at the end of primary school can be quite sceptical about the *existence* of Jesus; some consideration of how he is known about might be appropriate. Children may be able to suggest some ways — written records in the gospels, Christians celebrating his life — but the focus here could be on non-Christian evidence:

Josephus 38–100+ CE Jewish soldier, settled in Rome	He wrote the *Antiquities of the Jews*	In his *Antiquities* Josephus wrote about the Jewish high priest Ananias. In passing, he referred to Ananias' trying of James, *the brother of Jesus*.
Tacitus 58–116 CE Roman historian	He wrote the *Annals*	In the *Annals*, writing of the burning of Rome in 64 CE, and of the ensuing persecution of Christians, Tacitus speaks of Christus who suffered the extreme penalty during the rule of Tiberius at the hand of the procurator, Pontius Pilate.
Suetonius 75-140 CE Secretary to the emperor Hadrian	He wrote the *Life of Claudius*	In this book he wrote of the emperor expelling the Jews from Rome in 49 CE as a result of disturbance over 'Chrestus'. This is probably a misprint for 'Christus' and refers to quarrels between Christians and Jews.
Pliny the Younger 62–113 CE Governor of Bithynia	He wrote a letter to the emperor Trajan in about 112 CE	Pliny asked Trajan for advice on how to deal with cases of Christians charged before him. While we learn much from the letter of his view of Christians, obliquely he assumes that *Christ* existed. Christians, he says, sang hymns to Christ, 'as to a god' . . .

Another approach might be to imagine how Jesus' followers have kept his memory alive and how the writings Christians have about his life came about. As background it will be useful to have a broad summary in mind of what may have happened:

- People *remembered* and *told* stories about Jesus' life and teaching.
- Such stories and sayings were probably shared on occasions when groups of his followers *met for worship*.
- These small communities thought about what they knew and heard of Jesus and *related it to their lives*.
- Collections of, for example, Jesus' sayings were made and written down probably before the gospels came into existence.
- These collections of stories and sayings were used by individual writers, who used their own understanding to 'shape' each gospel.
- The gospels were thus written by people *with faith, for the purpose of helping other people's faith*.

The four gospels Christians know today were only officially recognised in 367 CE. Before that time others circulated; Christians also had other ways of remembering Jesus, eg in breaking bread as he had commanded them and in

The Annunciation to Mary.

The Birth of Jesus.

The Presentation in the Temple.

The Baptism of Jesus.

The Transfiguration of Jesus.

The Raising of Lazarus.

The Entry of Jesus into Jerusalem.

The Crucifixion of Jesus.

The Resurrection and Harrowing of Hell.

Twelve festivals of the Christian year according to Orthodox tradition: this cycle of themes based on the Bible and Church tradition was a popular series from the eleventh century onwards. The events remembered are identified (rather than the names of the festivals) below each illustration.

The Ascension of Jesus.

The Beginning of the Church at Pentecost.

The 'Dormition' of Mary.

celebrating important events of his life each year, eg his death and resurrection. An annual cycle of festivals is still an important way of recalling and telling Jesus' story.

Example two: the Buddha

The story of the Buddha gives children a chance to see that some events in a life story come to have great importance for a community; they can sum up what a whole life was about.

The story might by approached initially through a series of pictures like those shown here, supplemented by one or two *rupas* (images) of the Buddha (see page 110).

The story of the four signs—old age, sickness, death and then a holy man—which Prince Siddhartha saw is told in many books. *Prince Siddhartha* by J Landaw and J Brooke (Wisdom Publications 1984) is an attractive publication

Siddhartha's mother dreams of a white elephant. She learns that the meaning of this dream is that she will give birth to a great and noble son.

Siddhartha grows up to be a gentle and thoughtful man. He proved how skilled he was in such war-like arts as archery but he would not fight or hurt others.

Siddhartha marries his beautiful cousin, Yasodhara. They live together in the palaces his father built to protect Siddhartha from ever discovering that suffering and sorrow exist in the world.

One day, Siddhartha leaves the palace grounds. He comes across an old man, a sick man and a dead man – for the first time in his life. He also sees a holy man.

Siddhartha decides he must find a cure for this suffering. He leaves his family, cuts off his hair, and orders his heart-broken servant and horse back to the palace.

Siddhartha searches for the truth about life by studying and meditating. He takes very little food and rest. He grows thin and weak but he finds no answers.

He decides neither a life of luxury nor one of hardship are the right way to live. He starts to follow the Middle Way. After some time he achieves enlightenment and becomes the Buddha. He passes on his teaching to others.

The Buddha dies. His teachings about giving up greed and selfishness and being kind and thoughtful to others are spread all over the world. Today there are about 500 million Buddhists.

An outline life of the Buddha.

SECTION 3: FOR 9–11 YEAR OLDS

which picks up this and other key moments in the story, including the Buddha's first sermon at Varanasi. The sermon is known as the 'Setting in Motion of the Wheel of the Law'. Buddha claimed to teach the truth about 'the way things are': this is summarised in the **Four Noble Truths** (opposite) and the **Eightfold Path** (see page 132).

The Buddha preaches his first sermon. Notice his hands in the *mudra* indicating the Turning of the Wheel of the Law. Below the Buddha image the scene shows Buddha teaching five disciples in the deer park at Varanasi; the Buddha is seen turning the wheel for the first time.

THE FOUR NOBLE TRUTHS
1 **Dukkha**
   Life is changeable, impermanent; all things are unsatisfactory.
2 **Samudaya**
   Life's unsatisfactoriness arises from thirst, craving or attachment (*tanha*) which burns within people like a flame.
3 **Nirodha**
   This unsatisfactoriness will cease (*nirodha*) when tanha is extinguished by magga.
4 **Magga**
   Following the middle way, a path (*magga*) leading to the cessation of dukkha and comprising eight practical ways of daily living.

Activities

1 Children might explore their 'life story so far' by making a 'programme of life', selecting key moments or events to go inside the programme. They might also add a few key events which they think *might* occur in the future. Each child can go on to design a symbol which 'says' something distinctive about him/her for the cover of the programme.

OR

After discussion with parents or relatives children might identify an important event, experience or achievement for each year of their lives and record it for display.

2 Read with the children over a period of time a book about the life of the Buddha (see above and Resources).

a Discuss which parts of the story seem to share 'everyone's' experience of life.

b Which are those which seem 'special' to the Buddha and distinguish him from others?

3 The festival of Wesak recalls the Buddha's birth and enlightenment. Buddhists send cards at this time which sometimes show both his birth and enlightenment. Using some of the symbols often associated with the Buddha, or ideas of their own, children might design cards which communicate ideas from the Buddha's teaching.

4 Through the school library service, for example, bring together as many children's books as you can about Jesus. Involve children in a survey of the books. Make a chart to indicate which stories are most frequently told in the 'sample' you have. Distinguish between those which are 'events' and those which are 'teachings'.

5 Children might be asked to imagine they are first-century 'reporters' who want to find out about this man called Jesus. Where will they look for evidence and information? What kinds of questions will they want to ask?

6 Older children might use, for example, Mark's gospel (individual and inexpensive copies are available from the Bible Society, Stonehill Green, Westlea, Swindon SN5 7DG) and work in groups to find out the kinds of things which were remembered and recorded about Jesus by Mark. A Good News Bible version of Mark would be most helpful for children because it divides the gospel into sections, each with headings.

SECTION 3: FOR 9–11 YEAR OLDS

A window typical of many parish churches in Britain showing five key events in the 'story' Christians tell of Jesus. From left to right: his birth, baptism, and crucifixion, the Last Supper and his ascension.

7   According to local circumstance, children might explore a church, asking the question 'Which events in the life of Jesus are recorded in this building?' (eg in stone, carvings, glass), so that they become familiar with events Christians have particularly remembered.

OR

Using, for example, the annual *Shap Calendar of Religious Festivals* (see page 77) draw up a list of Christian festivals which are associated with the life of Jesus. If you can find 'visuals' (eg postcards of paintings) to match with them, this will be useful. Use Bibles to find the story which matches each festival. Notice which events are of particular interest.

A Wesak card depicting the Buddha's enlightenment.

Life stories told with a purpose

This approach offers the opportunity to think about telling life stories with a particular purpose or purposes in mind; the diversity of life stories can also be seen from the examples given here.

The story of Joseph — Genesis chapters 37–50

This is a perennial favourite in many schools, not least because of its musical associations!

It is succinctly told in *The Bible Story* by Philip Turner (OUP 1989). Many other books are available, but tend to focus on just one part of the story (see Resources). When telling the story to children engage them in thinking what the story is about, why it is *there* and remembered at all. Here are some things to think about:

- It is a story about family relationships and sibling rivalry and jealousy, but also about how these things were resolved after many years.

- It is a story about an insignificant person who becomes important, who shows magnanimity to those who ill-used him.

- It is there for a reason. It tells how the Hebrews came to be in Egypt and thus it is a prelude to the story of Moses.

So far we have said something about its human appeal. What of its 'religious' purpose?

- It is a story which seems to have the purpose of sharing with its hearers a conviction something like this: look at this unpromising series of events; even through these, God is working out his purposes for his people.

**Jataka tales
(Buddhist)**

A *Jataka* is literally a 'birth story'. These are stories about Gautama Buddha's *previous* births or lives. Clearly they are not open to historical or objective investigation, but they are stories with a purpose and children can think why they are told. In effect these stories, often about animals, put forward Buddhist ideals and qualities such as those listed in the ten 'Perfections' (page 120). Some sources of these stories are listed under Resources.

**Janam Sakhis
(Sikh)**

These are literally 'birth evidences' or 'life evidences' and are stories about Guru Nanak. Scholars discuss their historical value and debate their religious importance, but meanwhile they continue to be told by Sikhs and offer insight into the ideals of Guru Nanak's teaching. Two suitable story books for school include examples: *Stories from the Sikh World* by R and J Singh (Macdonald 1987), and *Guru Nanak and the Sikh Gurus* by R Arora (Wayland 1987).

A set of line drawings suitable for colouring (also available as overhead transparencies) and ten stories under the title *The Janam Sakhi of Sri Guru Nanak* is available from the Minority Group Support Service, Coventry LEA.

Again in exploring these stories with children, discuss questions like these: What does this story want people to understand about Guru Nanak? What kinds of things did Guru Nanak think were important / not important; of value / not of value?

Activities

1 Ask the children to make a list of up to five people they know well: against the name of each person write down a list of positive characteristics of the person. Write a short 'life story' to illustrate an occasion when the person has really *shown* a particular characteristic.

OR Share experience of this kind in discussion.

OR Present the 'life story' in a comic strip.

2 Share with the children the story of Joseph.

a Explore why the story is remembered and told.

b Work on a serialised version of it, different groups covering different parts of the story in a suitable form, eg: plays, poems, pictures, wall newspaper, diary entry.

c In the light of the 'serialisation', discuss what is known / not known about Joseph. Pupils can begin to understand that events are chosen which suit the writer's purpose.

d Make a list of the 'good happenings' in the story and the 'bad events'. Why might it be important to have both 'sides' in?

3 Tell the children some of the Jataka tales. Talk about the ten 'Perfections' (page 120). Which of these are explored in the stories?

4 Explore some of the Janam Sakhi stories (see above for resources). Let children present them as radio news items OR newspaper articles including discussion of what Guru Nanak wanted people to understand by his actions/ words.

5 This topic could obviously be extended to look at 'biographies' of people for whom religious faith has been a significant factor in their lives. In planning work on such people it might be helpful to ask, with regard to RE:

- Is it possible to include people who are Muslims, Sikhs etc. as well as those who are Christian?

- Are there people of non-European cultures and races who we can include?

- Can children have a variety of source materials/evidence to use in building up 'their' picture of the person?

6 Schools might also think how they can make contacts with people in their local community who will be willing to be interviewed by children—so that children can build a picture of individuals' and communities' life stories. For thinking about this, see 'Religious Education: From "Ethnographic Research to Curriculum Development"' by R Jackson, in *Humanities in the Primary School* edited by J Campbell and V Little (Falmer Press 1989) and also the *Listening to...* series of books (see below).

Resources

In addition to those noted above:
O Bennett *Listening to Sikhs*
R Jackson and E Nesbitt *Listening to Hindus* } Unwin Hyman 1990, available from Collins
(A series aimed at secondary school students, focusing on discovering lives of those who belong to a faith community; other titles forthcoming)
P Curtis, *Exploring the Bible*, Lutterworth Educational 1984
T Shannon, *Jesus*, Lutterworth Educational 1982
(2 books in the Chichester Project series on Christianity for secondary schools. Useful background for this unit—for teachers)
P Morgan } *Buddhist Iconography*
Buddhist Stories
(Useful presentation of symbols and stories, including information about and examples of the Jatakas. Available from Westminster College, N Hinksey, Oxford OX2 9AT)
Jataka Tales
(Inexpensive paperback available from Independent Publishing Co Ltd, 38 Kennington Lane, London SE11)
C Storr { *Joseph and his Brothers,* } Franklin Watts 1984
{ *Joseph the Dream Teller,* }
(Retelling of parts of the Joseph saga)

SECTION 3: FOR 9–11 YEAR OLDS

16 Community

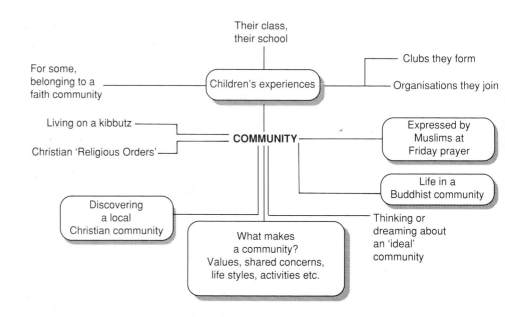

Their class, their school

For some, belonging to a faith community

Children's experiences

Clubs they form

Organisations they join

Living on a kibbutz

Christian 'Religious Orders'

COMMUNITY

Expressed by Muslims at Friday prayer

Life in a Buddhist community

Discovering a local Christian community

What makes a community? Values, shared concerns, life styles, activities etc.

Thinking or dreaming about an 'ideal' community

Aims

This units aims to develop children's understanding of what it means to belong to a community and to identify different ways in which people express belonging.

Starting with the children

Families, Belonging, Homes and Myself are all popular topics which seek to draw firstly on children's self-discovery and then on their experience of relating to others. 'Community' builds on and extends this experience. You may wish to start with the community all the children have in common — school.

Activities

For example, starting with 'their school' or 'their class':

1   Identify its immediate members; what do they do individually and communally? What does the school do *together?* For example: it celebrates important events in its life and the lives of its members and the wider community; supports special causes, eg charities; shares common concerns. Each school will have its own community identity: what makes it a community? Make a school brochure or wall display to provide a picture of *your* school or *your* class.

2   Some children will have the experience of belonging to other groups which have specific purposes and ideals that can be explored, eg cubs/scouts, brownies/guides, sports teams, choirs, orchestras. Children of this age may also have formed their own clubs and be willing to talk about 'What you have to do to belong'. Provide opportunities for children to share experiences of belonging.

Exploring 'community' in religions

Most religions place some emphasis on being part of a community. 'Community' is expressed in different ways by religions, and three contrasting expressions are suggested here: Buddhist, Christian, Muslim. In the case of Buddhism, living in a community is the focus; in the case of Christianity, a local church community might be the focus, illustrating a wide range of activities and involvement; a look at a community's newsletter might be a useful starting point. In the case of Islam the focus is on how community is expressed through the Friday congregational prayers. Try to use at least two of the examples in exploring the concept of community.

Living in a Buddhist community

There are now many Buddhist communities in Britain. As Buddhism is not such a widely practised religion here, people who have a deep interest in the Buddhist teaching often come together to live in communities, where a sense of spiritual companionship and mutual help can be cultivated. In countries where Buddhism is the dominant religion, there is no widespread need to form such special communities, as the ordinary life of village or town is often permeated by the religion.

However, in Buddhist countries — as is the case just about everywhere and for all religions — those who have a particular 'calling' to the spiritual life are to be found in intentional communities such as monasteries.

Here we have a glimpse of life in a particular community which serves both of the needs expressed above. It is primarily a monastery, but it also affords ample accommodation for lay people who wish to spend some time in a quiet place where Buddhist teaching is a part of the ordinary day-to-day life.

Here is the 'Daily Routine' taken from the monastery's brochure for guests. (Apart from this and 'The Eight Precepts' which follows, the other extracts in this section come from a small magazine prepared for children by members of the monastic community.)

THE DAILY ROUTINE

Guests are expected to observe the monastic precepts and conventions, and to participate in the community's activities as far as they are able. The structure of a typical day is given below; note that the specific times for some activities (marked *) can vary at different times of the year.

4 am	*Rising bell*
5	*Morning chanting and meditation*
6.30 to 8.30	**Domestic chores* and **Morning community meeting.* A hot drink and porridge are usually served; often ends with a reading and short period of meditation.
before meal	*Free time.* Useful for sorting our personal things, or for helping with the meal preparations.
10.30	*The meal.* The Theravada Buddhist tradition of one meal a day is observed here. Afterwards there is time for a rest.
12.30 pm	*Tea break.* Afternoon work is assigned.
1	*Afternoon work begins.*
5 or 6	**Tea break* (work ends). An opportunity for informal contact with members of the community and other lay guests.
7.30 or 8	**Evening chanting and meditation.* Often followed by a talk by the abbot or one of the senior monks.

This cartoon presentation gives one person's view of the daily routine:

Notice the variety of activities in Anne's day at the monastery. How can you tell that this is a Buddhist community?

Tim, like Anne in the pictures, is an Anagarika. At this monastery, time as an Anagarika constitutes the period of postulancy. Here Tim explains more simply what this means:

'Anagarika' is the word in the ancient Pali language which means 'Homeless One'. Our main purpose is to study and train ourselves in order to become monks or nuns after two years. We shave our heads and our eyebrows like the monks and nuns, but we have fewer rules to follow than the monks and nuns have. Because of our fewer rules we are able to help look after the monks and nuns by doing things that they are not allowed to do — just as you help your brothers and sisters as best you can. We cook, use money to buy things and drive cars, in addition to many other small jobs. Looking after the monks and nuns allows us to develop the qualities of the *Paramitas*, or 'Perfections' like generosity, patience, truthfulness, kindness and acceptance. These are not things we do because we have to, or because someone tells us to, but because being kind and gentle and friendly makes us happy and is good for everyone around.

Following are two lists of the 'Promises' (or Precepts) and the 'Paramitas' (also called the 'Perfections') to which Anagarika Tim refers. The Eight Precepts are the basic standard of conduct within Buddhist monasteries (and full monks and nuns in fact have quite a few more rules to follow), while the Five Precepts/Promises are the standard for lay Buddhists in ordinary life.

THE EIGHT PRECEPTS
1 *Harmlessness:*
   not intentionally taking the life of any living creature.
2 *Trustworthiness:*
   not taking anything which is not given.
3 *Chastity:*
   refraining from any sexual activity.
4 *Right Speech:*
   avoiding false, abusive or malicious speech.
5 *Sobriety:*
   not taking any intoxicating drink or drug.
6 *Renunciation:*
   not eating after mid-day.
7 *Restraint:*
   refraining from attending games and shows, and from self-adornment.
   (Guests are asked to dress modestly, and not to play radios, musical tapes or instruments.)
8 *Alertness:*
   to refrain from over-indulgence in sleep.

THE FIVE PROMISES (The Five Precepts, as expressed for children.)

1   I promise to try not to harm any living beings.

2   I promise to try not to take that which does not belong to me.

3   I promise to try not to take more from life than I really need.
    (*Editorial comment*: This is a special wording which has the child's limits of understanding in mind. The precept is generally — and accurately — expressed as the promise 'to refrain from sexual misconduct'.)

4   I promise to try not to use my speech in harmful ways.

5   I promise to try not to take harmful drinks or drugs which cloud my mind.

THE TEN POWERS OF GOODNESS (Paramitas)

1   Generosity
    Giving or sharing what we have with others.

2   Virtue
    Doing good and not doing harm.

3   Unselfishness
    Giving up things which we don't need.

4   Enthusiasm/energy
    Putting effort into developing goodness.

5   Wisdom
    Understanding things and people, knowing for yourself the difference between good and bad.

6   Honesty
    Being truthful.

7   Determination
    Being determined to do good no matter how difficult it is.

8   Patience
    Being patient with life.

9   Kindness
    Being kind and helpful to all beings.

10 Even-mindedness
    Being quiet inside yourself, accepting whatever happens in life calmly.

Other examples of the teachings which Buddhists follow can be found on page 111 (The Four Noble Truths) and page 132 (The Eightfold Path).

Discovering a local Christian community

Contact with a local church whose members are willing to meet with children, talk with them and be interviewed is ideal and should be a possibility for most schools. The focus here is indicated in the kind of activities children might be engaged in, rather than information. It will be useful to focus on *one* Christian group to build up your picture of a community.

Meeting at the mosque

This exploration of community might be done mainly through using pictures like those shown opposite and on page 122.

Muslims meet on Friday at midday for the Jum'ah prayers: doing this goes right back to the time of Muhammad when Friday was a day when everyone was in town for trade and there was a chance for the Muslim community from a big area to gather for prayers.

Pictures like those on pages 121 and 122 provide an opportunity for exploring the concept of community.

Salatul Jum'ah: Friday prayer. Muslims pray together facing in the direction (qiblah) of Makkah. The qiblah wall in the mosque indicates the direction for the community. In what other ways are unity and community expressed here?

Midday prayer on Friday is the occasion for a weekly sermon. Why might this be important for a community?

Muslims complete *salah* (prescribed prayer) by turning to the right and saying 'Peace and mercy of Allah be on you', and then by turning to the left and repeating the greeting.

They may also greet each other informally and socialise outside the mosque after prayer. Friday prayer is an occasion for the gathering of Muslims from an area, it helps to draw them together as a community.

Activities

Anagarika Anne

1   Let children make programmes of their own day, noting the fixed times in it to help discussion of the pattern of the day. Discuss the daily programme at the monastery (page 118), when does it begin/end? Notice special times for different activities; discuss the importance of different activities and special times.

2   Build on children's experiences of 'rules'. Look at 'The Five Promises' ('Precepts') and 'The Ten Powers of Goodness' (*Paramitas*/'Perfections').

a   Discuss things children might do such as:
help a new member of the class to feel 'at home',
share crisps with a friend,
care for an injured pet,
refuse to 'gang up' on someone.

Which 'power' would they be using?

b   Discuss ways in which keeping the five promises would help create a harmonious community.

3   Discuss with the children whether they think it would be easy or difficult to belong to a community like Anagarika Anne's.

The local Christian community

4   Explore for example: important events in the life of the community — how are they marked and celebrated?; individual events celebrated in community — birth, marriage, death.

5   Interview the oldest member and build up a 'time-line' of the community.

6   Draw up a plan of a typical week or month in the life of the community. Identify different kinds of events and activities which occur and think why they are important.

7   Look at a 'cameo' of an early Christian community in the Acts of the Apostles (see for example Acts 2:42–47). What are its features? Does it 'match' a Christian community today at all?

Providing food, warmth and shelter for those in need has always been part of the Salvation Army's 'living out' the Christian gospel.

The mosque

8 Explore midday Friday prayers at a mosque today in Britain, through video or slide material.

a Discover with the children how:

the building helps to give the community identity (orientation towards Makkah, room for many people to come together and stand side by side as one united body) (See *RE Topics for the Primary School*, pp 92–95);

the community expresses its identity in the form of prayer (words/posture), language (Arabic), exchange of the greeting of peace which ends prayers.

b Where appropriate, identify the countries from which the Muslims present have come — an example of the brother/sisterhood in this community, and of religious faith overriding nationality.

2 Extend the study by looking at the Hajj (pilgrimage to Makkah) and the coming together of Muslims from all over the world as one community. (See *RE Topics for the Primary School*, pp 156–161)

Reflecting on community

When you have worked with material from the approaches above, children might undertake work which brings together what they have learnt about communities and offers opportunity for reflection. This might be done by engaging children in a variety of activities; for example:

1 Children might present:

a record of a week or day in the life of a community they have studied,

OR

an imaginative piece of work in which they tell of 'their' life in a particular community,

OR

for those who belong to a faith community, a short project on the community in which they share.

2 Present children with a series of pictures illustrative of 'community' or of specific communities they have studied for which they can provide brief explanatory captions.

3 Ask children to think of 5 ways of completing the sentence 'Community is . . .'.

4 Discuss with the children the ways in which the communities you have studied are similar, and the ways in which they are different. Build up the concept of 'community', listing children's ideas arising from their work.

Resources

Books

O Bennett, *Exploring Religion: Worship*, Bell & Hyman 1984
(Useful material on Islam, Christianity and Buddhism as background to this topic)
P Morgan, *Being a Buddhist*, Batsford 1989
(Secondary level series, but useful background for teachers)
D and U Samaraskera, *I am a Buddhist*, Franklin Watts 1986
A Wood, *Being a Muslim*, Batsford 1987
M Aggarwal, *I am a Muslim*, Franklin Watts 1984
A Brown, *Christian Communities*, Lutterworth Educational 1982
(Part of Chichester Project secondary series, useful background for teachers)
The Buddhist Directory The Buddhist Society 1987
Directory of Buddhist groups and centres in the UK and Ireland. Available from
58 Eccleston Square, London SW1V 1PH)

AVA

The Westhill Project RE 5–16 { *Christians Photopack,* MGP 1986
{ *Muslims Photopack,* MGP 1988
(20 pictures in each case, with detailed notes. Both now available from Stanley Thornes)
BBC Radiovision, *Christians in Britain*, BBC Enterprises 1989
(54 slides from *Quest* series trying to give a picture of Christianity in one town)
ILEA, *Islam: A Guide to the Mosque/Eid ul Fitr*, available from Educational Media International,
235 Imperial Drive, Harrow, Mddx HA2 7HE
(29 minutes video for children of 12+, but extracts could be used with younger children)

SECTION 3: FOR 9–11 YEAR OLDS

17 Journeys

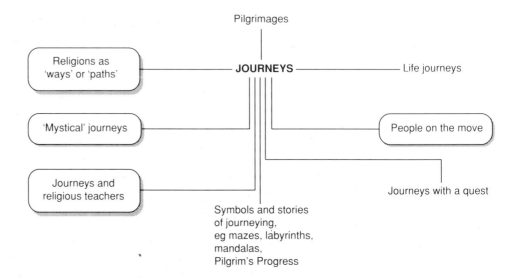

Pilgrimages

JOURNEYS ———— Life journeys

Religions as 'ways' or 'paths'

'Mystical' journeys

People on the move

Journeys and religious teachers

Journeys with a quest

Symbols and stories of journeying, eg mazes, labyrinths, mandalas, Pilgrim's Progress

Aims

Religious Education has a lot to offer to a topic on journeys. Some journeys are made in the name of religion to sacred places (see 'Journeys', 'Sacred Places', 'The Holy Land' and 'Pilgrimage to Mecca' in *RE Topics for the Primary School*). Others have *had* to be undertaken by religious groups because of persecution, or political and economic factors. But 'journey' is also used in a metaphorical way: so life itself may be seen as a journey. There are stories which tell of miraculous journeys, quests and discoveries; others speak of 'mystical' journeys which defy time and space and stretch the imagination. Some religions speak of themselves as a 'path' or 'way'. This unit offers a variety of approaches and aims:

- to help children move towards understanding 'journey' as a symbol or metaphor;
- to let children meet religions as a *way* of life, which may provide meaning and identity for a person's 'life journey'.

People 'on the move'

This approach has *two* perspectives. It recognises that throughout history groups of people have often *had to move* because of religious, economic and political factors, sometimes manifested in persecution. When they have moved, their religion has travelled with them. Judaism for example is sometimes described as having a 'portable culture' with its focus on the home and family in the celebration of festivals and Shabbat.

At a simpler level many children will have experienced *moving house*, and for some this may have been marked by some kind of religious ceremony. Children might explore the *mezuzah* (see Activities) in a Jewish home; Rumer Godden's *The Kitchen Madonna* (Macmillan 1967) could help children understand the importance of an *Icon* (picture of a saint or Jesus) in the home for some

Christians; Olivia Bennett's *Our New Home* (Hamish Hamilton 1990) is the story of a Sikh family moving house, and of the importance of the Guru Granth Sahib (the Sikhs' holy book) being brought to their new house to be read.

Activities

1   Share experiences in the class of moving house. Think about any 'precious' possessions that had to be carefully looked after and not lost in the move. Discuss feelings about leaving the familiar place and arriving in the new. When did children begin to feel the new home was '*their* home'?

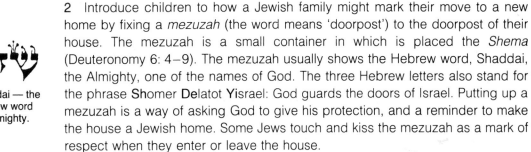

Shaddai — the Hebrew word for Almighty.

2   Introduce children to how a Jewish family might mark their move to a new home by fixing a *mezuzah* (the word means 'doorpost') to the doorpost of their house. The mezuzah is a small container in which is placed the *Shema* (Deuteronomy 6: 4–9). The mezuzah usually shows the Hebrew word, Shaddai, the Almighty, one of the names of God. The three Hebrew letters also stand for the phrase **Sh**omer **D**elatot **Yi**srael: God guards the doors of Israel. Putting up a mezuzah is a way of asking God to give his protection, and a reminder to make the house a Jewish home. Some Jews touch and kiss the mezuzah as a mark of respect when they enter or leave the house.

   a Discuss with children why the mezuzah is important and the significance of the verses in it for the family as they 'journey' to and from the house each day.

   b Children might try making mezuzot (plural) in different materials and carefully writing out the correct verses to put in them.

3   If possible, obtain some postcard reproductions of icons for the children to look at and enjoy. A useful background booklet for teachers is T Holden's *Explaining Icons* (1985), available from Stylite Publishing Ltd, 37 Salop Road, Welshpool.

   Picture 7 of the Westhill Project RE 5–16: *Christians Photopack* (see page 125) shows a family gathered to pray before the icons in their home, and provides information about this. Children might:

   a Mount some postcards on card and varnish them OR try painting some pictures in the style of icons OR produce some in mosaic work.

   b Display the icons in school—possibly as an icon corner in an appropriate place.

4   If you can, share *Our New Home* with children, they might follow this up with an imaginative exercise in which they think about the preparations they would have to make in *their* home before the Guru Granth Sahib could be brought in. They might design suitable invitations to invite friends to the reading from the holy book.

5   a The *My Belief* books (Franklin Watts) listed under Resources each give a history of two generations of the family in the book, showing how families move and where the family came from. Children might if appropriate draw diagrams to show where *their* families came from (you will of course need to be sensitive to the circumstances of children in your class).

   b To extend this, but with due sensitivity to children and circumstance, it may be possible to invite someone who has come to live in Britain from another country to talk to the children about their experiences.
   OR
   It may be possible to visit, for example, a mosque or synagogue and meet

SECTION 3: FOR 9–11 YEAR OLDS

with a small group who are willing to be interviewed by the children. Prepare the questions before you go, eg, Were there special reasons for coming to England? Does following 'their way of life' help them to feel 'at home' in Britain? Is it sometimes difficult to follow it here? Obviously the intention is simply to explore such questions at a very simple level.

6   The theme of journeying because of persecution is found in the story of the Exodus, which might be explored through Passover (see *RE Topics for the Primary School*, p 76), and the subsequent journeying through the wilderness is recalled particularly during Sukkot (ibid, p 16).

Try sharing a contemporary story of 'exodus' and 'journeying': that of the Jews of Ethiopia, who in 'Operation Moses' in 1984 were air-lifted to Israel is a good example. At children's level the story is told in J P Kendall's *My Name is Rachamim*, illustrated by a young Ethiopian artist (available from the Jewish Education Bureau — address on page 25). Rachamim, a young Jewish boy, tells his family's story. This is a story to be shared and discussed. It would offer the chance to think about why people sometimes *have to move*, about how they value their religious heritage, and about settling in a new place.

'Mystical' journeys

'Mystical' is used here simply to point to stories about which there is a sense of 'mystery'; such stories often tell of an important experience for a person which may make a great difference to their way of understanding, eg themselves, others, God, the nature of life. Such stories often transcend the boundaries of time and place; the element of mystery is integral to them. Asking 'What does the story say?' and letting children's imaginations 'play' with its meanings are therefore more important than asking 'What actually happened?' These stories are often key ones in religious traditions and this approach simply provides children with an opportunity to extend their understanding of 'journey'. There *is* a 'literal' journey in each story, but the journey works as a symbol too: the person 'moves' to a new understanding.

Activities

Having an opportunity to hear and reflect on the story is probably sufficient here: you might tell some of the following stories.

Guru Nanak and the River Experience

Guru Nanak was the first of the Sikh gurus. Like others, he bathed each morning in the river...

ONE DAY AS USUAL HE SET OUT FOR THE STREAM, TO BATHE.

Muhammad: The Night Journey and Ascension

The year 619 CE (?620) was the 'Year of Sorrow' in Muhammad's life. His uncle and protector Abu Talib died, and so did his wife Khadijah who had been his constant support. The people of Makkah were opposed to him but at this sad time Muslims believe Muhammad made a journey, by night, to Jerusalem and thence through the seven heavens into the presence of God. Muslims throughout the world commemorate this story on the 26th day of the month Rajab in their calendar; mosques and minarets may be lit in honour of the night journey, and Muslims may spend the night telling traditions about the event, reading the Qur'an and praying. (The story can be found in *RE Topics for the Primary School*, p 150.)

Jesus: His Baptism and the Temptations (Luke 3:21 and 4:1–13)

Both Matthew's gospel and Luke's tell of Jesus' 40 days and nights in the wilderness. Christians interpret the story in different ways, but in the telling of the story both writers are probably recalling the period of Israel's wandering in the wilderness (40 years), and thinking of the wilderness as a place for communing with God. In some Christian churches the story is traditionally told at the beginning of Lent.

Elijah: The Storm at Horeb

Many stories are told of Elijah; they are important to both Jews and Christians. This one tells literally of a journey he made—running away because his life was threatened; but Elijah also made a journey in understanding. The story can be found in 1 Kings 19: 1–18 (especially verses 11–13) and needs to be well read to children. The cycle of stories about Elijah are helpfully told in *Winding Quest* by A Dale (OUP 1972).

In each of these stories the central figure comes to important new understanding which leads him on to action. Guru Nanak begins to make many journeys to share what he has understood; Muhammad and his few faithful followers make a journey (*hijrah*—migration) to Madinah (Medina) (see *RE Topics for the Primary School*, pp 134–136); Elijah returns to face the difficulties from which he has run away; and Jesus, according to Luke, announces his 'mission' in the synagogue in Nazareth (Luke 4:14–22).

Journeys and religious teachers: Jesus

This approach could be used with particular reference to the Buddha, to Guru Nanak and to Jesus. Its importance of course is *not* in making maps. Travelling to share a message says something about the importance of the message; also it is an invitation to *follow* the message, to 'travel' with it, so 'journey' can be a *symbol of discipleship*, and of *growing in understanding*.

The journey is an important theme in St Luke's gospel and in its sequel, the Acts of the Apostles, where 'Christianity' is first known as 'the Way'. The 'shape' of Luke's books may be seen as a Journey *to* Jerusalem and then as a Journey *from* Jerusalem (see Acts 1:8). Within this framework are many 'smaller' journeys. Some you might consider with children are suggested here. This approach might build on that of 'The Life of Jesus', p 60 in *RE Topics for the Primary School*, and on 'Life Stories' above, page 106.

Activities

1 Tell Luke's story of Jesus in Nazareth (Luke 4:14–21): Jesus reads out the words of Isaiah and they become a kind of 'manifesto' for his work; Alan Dale's *New World* (OUP 1967) provides a readable version for children. This story offers a framework for looking at Jesus' teaching and deeds. Perhaps children can design 'charters' declaring this message.

2   Two stories Jesus told are based on the theme of a journey.

Explore the **Good Samaritan** (Luke 10:25–37) with the children. Notice, it's an 'answer' to a question and ends with a question! Children might try writing a story with this kind of beginning and ending—and in no more words than this one.

When you handle the story be careful not to distort it: it is *not* a story told against *Jewish* officials as such! As one Jewish writer put it: the priest and the Levite, people of stature in society, were too selfish and fearful (the robbers being not far away) to help their neighbour. The Samaritan, a person of low rank, did help his neighbour—each person should be prized for what he does, not for what he is or seems to be!

Discuss the story of the **Forgiving Father** (Luke 15:11–32), whose son travels far from home and ultimately makes the journey back. Note who the story is told to (Luke 15:1). How would the different people respond to the story? Who do the children sympathise with? Notice, this is a 'journey in understanding' as well as a literal journey.

How does the message of these stories connect with Jesus' 'manifesto'?

3   Find out about the twelve disciples' journey (Luke 9:1–6). What instructions are they given for the journey? Ask the children to think of reasons for such instructions: it might help if they think first of the kind of preparations they make for journeys—clearly those given to the disciples are very different. Discuss why this might be.

4   **The journey to Emmaus**: (Luke 24:13–35)
Approaches to this story can also be found in *RE Topics for the Primary School*, page 107. Let the children hear the story and ask their own questions about it; explore these. Discuss with the children how the disciples are at the beginning and end of the story. Why might Christians who follow 'the Way' today like this story?

Religions as 'ways' or paths

This approach offers an opportunity to discover some of the teaching which religions give to their followers, and to help children understand that religions are 'ways' of life—in fact this is how they may speak of themselves. Islam is sometimes described as 'The Straight Path', a phrase from the *Fatihah*, the opening *surah* (section) of the Qur'an. The Qur'an speaks of itself as guidance given for humankind from Allah. Buddha taught his disciples the Eightfold Path, represented in the wheel with eight spokes, and Hinduism offers four *margas* (paths or ways) of travelling through this life to *moksha* (release from rebirth). Christianity was first known as 'the Way'. Examples from two faiths are given below, but this approach could be extended to include others.

Activities

1   a   Discuss with children their ideas of how they would 'like to be known'— the kind of person they would like to be, rather than 'what' they would like to be. Make individual lists, then a composite class list. Identify possible practical examples of each characteristic.

b   Balance this individual approach by building with the children a picture of the kind of world they would and would not like to live in. Children might do some creative writing, or art work about this. One book of interest here might be *Dear World* by R and H Exley (Eds) (Exley Publications 1978).

2 The above tasks might provide a context for discovering some of the 'ways for living' suggested by religions. For example the Eightfold Path (Buddhism) and the Straight Path (Islam), below.

The Eightfold Path

Children might think about these questions; they are the kind of questions Buddhist children might be encouraged to answer when they are learning about the Eightfold Path, and are adapted from a magazine for Buddhist children (*Rainbows*, Summer 1989).

- Write down 5 jobs which follow Right Livelihood and 5 jobs which don't. If you can think of more than 5, write these down too.
- Write down which step of the Path you would find most difficult to follow, and say why. Which would you find the easiest, and why?
- Can you see how the steps of the Path are linked together? Can you write about this?
- Can you draw your own Dhamma wheel to show the Eightfold Path?
- How do you think meditation might help in someone's ordinary life? Give some examples of times when it would be helpful.

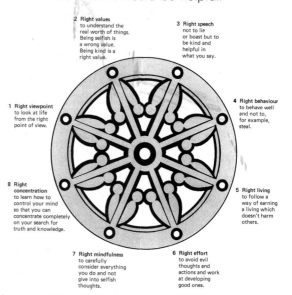

The Straight Path

Here is the **Fatihah**; this is repeated in Arabic each time a Muslim prays.

> Praise be to Allah,
> Lord of the Universe
> Most Compassionate, Most Merciful
> Master of the Day of Judgement
> You alone do we worship
> And to You alone do we pray for help.
> Show us the Straight Way
> The Way of those whom You have blessed
> With whom You are not angry
> And who have not gone astray.

(from *The Essential Teachings of Islam* by K Brown and M Palmer (Eds), Rider 1987).

Muslims believe that the Qur'an is the best guidance for life and to follow its path will lead to a life beyond this one, in paradise. *The Qur'an: Basic Teachings* (see Resources) would provide short extracts for exploring the theme of guidance.

One way in which Muslims follow the Straight Path is by keeping the Five Pillars. Children might look at *Salah* (prayer five times a day) and think about why Muslims might find it important to them as they follow the Straight Path. Information about prayer is available in many books, and children might do research on:

the times
the direction of prayer
praying in a prepared place (carpet, mosque)
wudu: washing for prayer
the language of prayer
the body positions in prayer

How might these aspects of prayer help a Muslim to keep on the Straight Path?

Here is an example of *one* Muslim explaining what prayer means to her. Think about how prayer helps to remind her that there are Muslims all over the world following the Straight Path:

Salah is a celebration of God. By repeating the prayers five times each day it helps me to remember the importance of Allah. Before I pray I wash my hands, arms, face and feet to make sure they are clean. This helps me to prepare my mind before I begin. I usually pray on a prayer mat which I turn towards Makkah which is our Holy City. I then repeat some simple movements of standing, bowing, kneeling and sitting while I say my prayers. The most important moment is when I am kneeling and I touch the ground with my forehead. That is the moment when I realise how important Allah is to me.

The idea behind the prayer is to show my devotion and obedience to God. What is very exciting about the prayer is knowing that Muslims all over the world are performing the same movements and saying the same prayers. It makes me feel close to my fellow Muslims, even when I pray alone. The prayers are short. They only last a few minutes—but afterwards I feel quite different. I am more relaxed and peaceful. When I go back to what I was doing, I feel more enthusiastic—even if it is work!

(from *Religion through Festivals: Islam* by A Brine, Longman 1990, p 11)

Resources

Books
The Qur'an: Basic Teachings, Islamic Foundation
The following titles in the *My Belief* series published by Franklin Watts:
I am a Jew, I am a Muslim, I am a Sikh (see pages 99 and 171)
P Morgan, *Buddhist Stories* and *Buddhist Iconography* (see page 93)

Visuals
Westhill Project RE 5–16, *Muslims Photopack* (see page 125)
(Pictures 9, 10, 11 & 12 relate to prayer—'Salah')

SECTION 3: FOR 9–11 YEAR OLDS

18 The Natural World

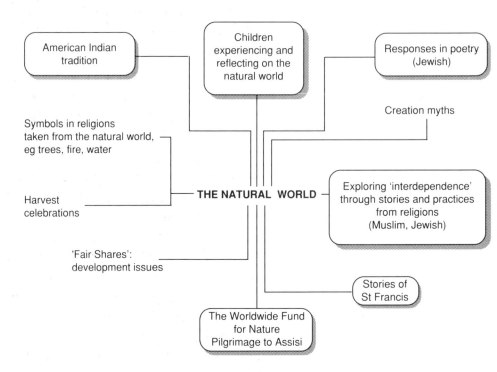

| Aims | Awareness of the natural environment, the recognition of humankind's dependence on it and a consequent concern for the development of positive and responsible attitudes towards it are encouraged in many areas of the primary curriculum. RE offers an opportunity for children: |

- to reflect on the order, shape, pattern, usefulness, beauty and mystery humankind finds in the world;
- to explore the interrelatedness of humankind and the natural world, often expressed in myth and poetry in religious traditions;
- to begin to discover how religions are rediscovering and affirming their ancient insights about the environment.

Reflecting on the natural world

Encourage exploration and observation of the natural world, explore its moods and allow children to make their own creative responses to what they discover (see Activities). Alongside their explorations introduce some of the words and experiences of religious traditions.

The North American Indians   The feelings and reverence of the North American Indians for the land are well documented, as is their dismay at the White Man's exploitation of the land. The story is told clearly in 'The Rainbow Warrior', a song for children (pages 136–138).

The Indians' respect for the land, for animals, and for objects; recognition of their dependence on the land and their relation with it — recognition, too, that no one 'owned' it — are all themes to be explored. These extracts come from a book which has resources for doing this.

In the following passage, an old holy Wintu woman speaks sadly about the needless destruction of the land in which she lived — a place where gold mining and particularly hydraulic mining had torn up the earth:

THE WHITE PEOPLE NEVER CARED FOR LAND OR DEER OR BEAR. When we Indians kill meat, we eat it all up. When we dig roots we make little holes. When we built houses, we make little holes. When we burn grass for grasshoppers, we don't ruin things. We shake down acorns and pinenuts. We don't chop down the trees. We only use dead wood. But the White people plow up the ground, pull down the trees, kill everything. The tree says, 'Don't. I am sore. Don't hurt me.' But they chop it down and cut it up. The spirit of the land hates them. They blast out trees and stir it up to its depths. They saw up the trees. That hurts them. The Indians never hurt anything, but the White people destroy all. They blast rocks and scatter them on the ground. The rock says, 'Don't. You are hurting me.' But the White people pay no attention. When the Indians use rocks, they take little round ones for their cooking... How can the spirit of the earth like the White man?... Everywhere the White man has touched it, it is sore.

These words were spoken by one Indian as he was confronted with selling land on which he and his ancestors had lived for generations:

I WONDER IF THE GROUND HAS ANYTHING TO SAY? I WONDER if the ground is listening to what is said? I wonder if the ground would come alive and what is on it? Though I hear what the ground says. The ground says, It is the Great Spirit that placed me here. The Great Spirit tells me to take care of the Indians, to feed them aright The Great Spirit appointed the roots to feed the Indians on. The water says the same thing. The Great Spirit directs me, Feed the Indians well. The grass says the same thing. Feed the Indians well. The ground, water and grass say, The Great Spirit has given us our names We have these names and hold these names. The ground says, The Great Spirit has placed me here to produce all that grows on me, trees and fruit. The same way the ground says, It was from me man was made. The Great Spirit, in placing men on the earth, desired them to take good care of the ground and to do each other no harm...

(from *Touch The Earth* compiled by T C McLuhan, Abacus 1973, pp 8 and 15)

SECTION 3: FOR 9–11 YEAR OLDS

Jewish tradition

Jewish scriptures, shared also by Christians, may be drawn on to provide examples of writing which 'rejoices' in the natural world. Psalm 148 shows close observation of the natural environment by the writer, and his belief that everything is within the providence of God. Another example of a similar kind, this time written as it were from God's perspective, can be found in Job chapter 8; this chapter points to the mystery of the natural world and to how little humankind grasps or comprehends this.

The Song of the Three Holy Children, illustrated by Pauline Baynes (Methuen 1986), offers another example of this kind of writing from Jewish tradition and this is a beautiful presentation of it. Details about the story of the 'three holy children' can be found in the topic on 'Fire' (page 154).

Activities

1   Encourage children to explore their local environment. Are there places which are very special to them, where they like to be? Distinguish between 'natural' and 'manmade' environment as appropriate. If the school is in an urban area, what evidence of the natural world can they find?

2   Involve children in preparing and documenting a trail in your school's locality which will highlight 'discovering the natural world'. Other curriculum areas might be involved in this; let RE encourage its exploration by touch, smell, observing colour, shade and shape. An extension of this might be to plan such a trail for someone who cannot see.

3   Look at some living organisms under a microscope. Explore shapes and colours seen there in art work. Where this is not possible, pictures might be used instead. Pictorial Charts Educational Trust poster sets on *Patterns in Nature* (W735) and *Symmetry in Nature* (W737) would offer scope here.

4   Write short reflective pieces to explore answers to the question, What is life? Here is an American Indian example:

> WHAT IS LIFE? It is the flash of a firefly in the night. It is the breath of a buffalo in the winter time. It is the shadow which runs across the grass and loses itself in the sunset!

> (from *Touch the Earth*, op. cit., p 12)

5   Learn 'The Rainbow Warrior' song and plan a dramatic presentation of it.

The Rainbow Warrior

'When the earth is sick, the animals will begin to disappear. When that happens the Warriors of the Rainbow will come to save them.'

(from *a North American Indian prophecy*)

Long ago when the world was new
The grass waved green and the sky was blue;
The sun shone warm and the air was sweet,

Long ago when the world was new The
grass waved green and the sky was blue; The
sun shone warm and the air was sweet, And the
people all had food to eat. Then the

Rainbow Warrior smiled to see That the
earth was strong and the people free.
Drum, drum, beat the drum, And the
Rainbow Warrior, he will come.

And the people all had food to eat.
Then the Rainbow Warrior smiled to see
That the earth was strong and the people free.

Drum, drum, beat the drum,
And the Rainbow Warrior, he will come.

Soon the pines grew tall and the hawk flew high,
The cold moon glowed in the midnight sky;
And the fishes swam in the silver stream,
And the earth spun round in a timeless dream.
Then the Rainbow Warrior smiled to see
That the earth stayed strong and the people free.

Drum, drum, beat the drum...

Then the white man came and his gun brought fear,
He seized the land and he slew the deer;
And he killed the braves and the widows cried,
And without the hunters the children died.
Then the Rainbow Warrior frowned; he saw
That man would live in peace no more.

Drum, drum, beat the drum...

Next the white man laid the railroad down,
Where tepees stood there grew a town;
And he felled the trees and he trapped the bear,
And the homeless birds took to the air.
Then the Rainbow Warrior grieved to see
The earth grow sick and the creatures flee.

    Drum, drum, beat the drum . . .

Last the factories rose, breathing flame and smoke;
Now the air grows thick and the cities choke;
And the giant tankers spill their waste
And the water now has a bitter taste.
Now the seabirds die upon the shore
And the great whale soon will be no more.

    Drum, drum, beat the drum . . .

(words by Patricia Middleton, music by Douglas Dimm; from *Sing for your Life*,
A & C Black)

6   Share stories which relate to human involvement and care in creation: eg
Charles Keeping's *Joseph's Yard* (OUP 1969); Ruskin Bond's *The Cherry Tree*
(Hamish Hamilton 1980).

Interdependence

The Muslim story of Adam

The story of Adam, the first human, is told by Muslims as well as by Jews and
Christians; it can be found in full in *Worlds of Difference* by M Palmer and E
Bissett (Blackie 2nd Edition 1989). Allah, it is said, created Paradise, a wonderful garden where all living things dwelt in harmony. Adam himself was created
from clay of seven colours — in this way he is seen to be one with the earth and
is symbolic of the oneness of humankind. Adam and Eve, succumbing to the
tempting of Iblis (Satan), have to leave the garden; but Allah places them on
earth, which is wholesome and good, offering all that they need; on earth Adam
and Eve are *khalifa*, caretakers, responsible for 'care-taking' of Allah's creation.
Moreover, the Qur'an tells that earth is full of signs (*ayat*) which point humankind
God-wards, reminding men and women — ever forgetful — that God provides for
them abundantly.

Jewish blessings

In Jewish tradition recognition that the earth is good and given for humankind's
enjoyment and pleasure is recalled in the custom of saying blessings over food.
To say a blessing is to give thanks for what is given and to be aware of all that is
experienced and enjoyed in life. Here are two traditional blessings, offered over
the wine and bread which is shared in *Kiddush*, the ceremony marking the
beginning of Shabbat in a Jewish home.

> Blessed are You, Lord our God, Ruler of the
> universe, Who creates the fruit of the vine
>
> Blessed are You, O Lord our God, Ruler of
> the universe, Who brings forth bread from
> the earth.

A selection of *Berakhot* (blessings) relating to things one can taste, smell, see and touch can be found in *The First Jewish Catalogue* by R Siegel and S & M Strassfield, Eds (available from the Jewish Education Bureau—see page 25 above for address).

Kiddush in a Jewish home. Notice the kiddush cup and the two plaited loaves (*challot*).

Building a sukkah.

Sukkot

Recognition of humankind's dependence on the earth and God is also expressed in the Jewish festival of *Sukkot* (or 'Tabernacles'). This is both a harvest-time in Israel and a recalling of the time when the Israelites were in the wilderness after God had delivered them from their slavery in Egypt. At Sukkot families will share in the building of a 'shelter'/'hut' in their gardens. It must be temporary and it must allow those in it to glimpse the stars through the roof. It will be decorated with greenery and fruits—especially fruits from Israel. For a whole week, meals will be eaten in the *Sukkah*—a reminder not only of history, but of humanity and its dependence on the natural world. (cf *RE Topics for the Primary School*, p 16).

Activities

1   EITHER make a list of the different foods you eat in a week; OR plan a menu for a special meal. Try to write 'blessings' which would be appropriate for use before eating each kind of food in your list/menu. Try to relate the blessing closely to the nature of the food—eg: look at its colour, shape; think of its taste.

SECTION 3: FOR 9–11 YEAR OLDS

2 EITHER draw a table for class pets, indicating the care they require from humans and what they provide for humans; OR take some other aspect of the natural world, eg: trees or water, and explore all the different ways in which it might be used, appreciated or experienced by humankind. Pictorial Charts Educational Trust, *Ways of Seeing* (E20) would be useful here with regard to trees.

3 Using paint or collage, create a 'paradise garden': think about the relation of plants and creatures, about colour, sun, shade, water. This could be extended into Environmental Studies and the idea of a conservation garden explored.

4 As a class decide on '10 ecological commandments' which will involve children in being responsible for the natural world. Make them practical so that you can try to follow them! An example of 10 drawn up by a group of teenagers can be found in B Wood's *Our World, God's World* (Bible Reading Fellowship 1986), pp 80–81.

The pilgrimage to Assisi 1986

This event was organised as a result of the initiative of the Duke of Edinburgh and the World Wide Fund for Nature. The event was brought together by the major religions of the world to rediscover and affirm what their teachers and sacred writings had to say about humankind and nature and to 'repent' for their neglect and abuse of the world. The event is well documented in *Faith and Nature* by M Palmer, A Nash and I Hattingh (Rider Books, Century Hutchinson 1987).

Why Assisi?   Assisi is associated with St Francis. His great 'Canticle of Brother Sun' tells something of his feeling for creation: there is a sense of mystery and wonder, and of relationship.

Pilgrims on the road to Assisi.

The Canticle of Brother Sun

All creatures of our God and King,
Lift up your voice and with us sing
Alleluia, Alleluia!
Thou burning sun with golden beam,
Thou silver moon with softer gleam,
O praise him, O praise him,
Alleluia, Alleluia!

Thou rushing wind that art so strong,
Ye clouds that sail in heaven along,
O praise him, alleluia!
Thou rising morn, in praise rejoice,
Ye lights of heaven find a voice,
O praise him, O praise him,
Alleluia, Alleluia!

Thou flowing water, pure and clear,
Make music for thy Lord to hear,
Alleluia, Alleluia!
Thou fire so masterful and bright,
That givest man both warmth and light,
O praise him, O praise him,
Alleluia, Alleluia!

And all ye men of tender heart,
Forgiving others, take your part,
O sing ye, alleluia.
Ye who long pain and sorrow bear,
Praise God and on him cast your care.
O praise him, O praise him,
Alleluia, Alleluia!

(verse translation from *The Francis Book* compiled and edited by R M Gasnick,
Collier Macmillan 1980, p 108)

Stories are told of St Francis too, which link him with nature. The Wolf of Gubbio and The Preaching to the Birds are both well known. These are both retold by R Brown and P Emmett in *Multi Faith Fables: St Francis, the Birds and the Wolf* (Mary Glasgow Publications 1989).

The Pilgrimage   Here is a brief summary of the great pilgrimage to Assisi:

It didn't seem to matter whether they walked in brilliant sunshine, or were buffeted by the winds and rains which came rolling down from the Umbrian hills. On they came, with banners unfurled, wearing the distinctive sun-and-moon tabards, like some crusader army. The sound of many tongues and the clamour of spontaneous singing rang out as they walked from village to village. At each stop, the message was passed on and shared with villagers, townspeople and the tourists. The message was simple. 'We believe in conservation.' Some believed because they were conservationists, who had studied the impact of humanity on the environment and knew only too well how great is the crisis of our physical world. Others were walking because of the beliefs which their faith gave them. Christians, following the example of St Francis, whose love for all life earned him the name 'the second Christ'. Muslims, exploring the consequences of our being the viceregents of God. Hindus, drawing upon the profound reverence for life which lies at the core of that faith. Buddhists, walking in the path of the Compassionate One. A Maori Elder, bringing testimony of the wisdom contained in the traditional cultures of the world. Zoroastrians, Jains, Sikhs, Baha'is and many others, all walking side by side because of what they believe about nature.

(from *Faith and Nature*, p 52)

When everyone finally gathered in Assisi in the great Basilica of St Francis, symbolic rituals and readings drawn from the faiths brought everyone together. These included Indian dance celebrating creation and the blowing of the *shofar* (usually used on the Jewish Yom Kippur) to call for repentance.

Banners representing world faiths were displayed and each made a solemn declaration and commitment for the future. The Jewish declaration included a story:

Some twenty centuries ago they told the story of two men who were out on the water in a rowboat. Suddenly, one of them started to saw under his feet. He maintained that it was his right to do whatever he wished with the place that belonged to him. The other answered that they were both in the rowboat together; the hole that he was making would sink both of them . . .

. . . We are all passengers together in this same fragile and glorious world. Let us safeguard our rowboat — and let us row together.

(from *Faith and Nature*, p 69)

Activities

1 a Plan walk in your local environment (of Activities on page 136). Make a map so that others can follow it. Pause at different places (1) to enjoy what is there, (2) to reflect on anything that spoils the environment.

   b Design symbols and write a few words to help people think about what they see. Perhaps offer 'Guided tours' to raise funds for a 'Green project'.

2 Paint illustrations for the whole of the St Francis 'Canticle of Brother Sun'; or if it is possible take photographs to illustrate it. Use your paintings/photographs to produce a school calendar for sale.

3 Jewish people returning to Israel in the nineteenth and early twentieth century set out 'to make the desert bloom'; find out about the *Kibbutz* movement and the part it played in making this a reality. (See Resources.)
OR
Find out about Tu B'Shevat—New Year for Trees—in the Jewish calendar, and its annual celebration.

4 Older children may enjoy hearing Jean Giono's *The Man who Planted Trees* (Peter Owen 1989) told simply. This is also available on video, produced by CBC Enterprises and available from Woolworth's and other stores.

Resources

In addition to those mentioned above:

Books
H Exley (Ed), *Cry for our beautiful world*, Exley Publications Ltd 1985
(Poetry, prose, pictures by young people from over 70 nations pleading for the survival of the natural world)
F French, *The Song of the Nightingale*, Blackie 1986
(Children's story inspired by the life of St Francis)
E Haas, *The Creation*, Penguin 1976
(Genesis 1 interpreted by the camera; stunning photographs to enjoy)
T Hughes, *Tales of the Early World*, Faber & Faber 1988
(Collection of creation tales for children)
H Lewin and L Kopper, *Second Chance Books* (four titles), Hamish Hamilton 1989
(Stories celebrating the natural world and highlighting dangers to it. Intended to alert children to ecological issues)
WWF, *Religion and Nature Interfaith Ceremony*, Assisi 1986
(Order of service used on this occasion)
For information on Kibbutzim see the two following:
C Lawton, *Passport to Israel*, Watts 1987
D Bailey, *We live in Israel*, Macmillan 1989
(Picture book about a family living on a kibbutz; for younger children)

AVA
Pictorial Charts Educational Trust:
Creation Stories 1 (Australian Aboriginal, Chinese, Christian, Hindu)
Creation Stories 2 (Humanist, Jewish, Muslim, Yanomamo Sarema)
Philip Green Educational, *Topic Picture Packs*:
P40 *Colours 1*, 'Nature'
P36 *Spring*, P52 *Summer*, P43 *Autumn*, P57 *Winter*
P37 *Shapes 1*, 'Nature'
A Visit to a Kibbutz
(Filmstrip and cassette, available from the Jewish Education Bureau—address on page 25)

SECTION 3: FOR 9–11 YEAR OLDS

19 Water

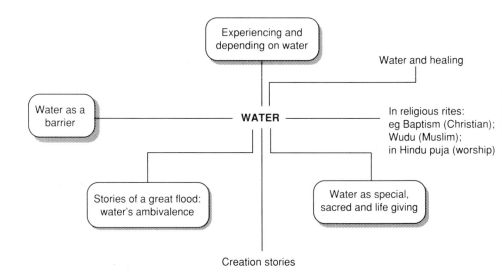

Experiencing and depending on water

Water and healing

Water as a barrier

WATER

In religious rites:
eg Baptism (Christian);
Wudu (Muslim);
in Hindu puja (worship)

Stories of a great flood: water's ambivalence

Water as special, sacred and life giving

Creation stories

Aims | This unit relates to those on light and fire, picking up the theme of elements. It aims to provide children with a variety of experiences of water, so that they can begin to understand its importance as a symbol in the stories and practices of religions.

Experiencing water

Encourage children to reflect on the place of water in human life: what are their own experiences of water? Maybe for swimming, sailing, washing, drinking, fishing, cooking; or perhaps they've been warned of its dangers and have seen its 'power' in floods and storm. *Water 1* (Philip Green Educational, A25) is an excellent set of pictures and poems for beginning this kind of exploration.

The effects of no water can also be explored to highlight human dependency on water. Material from development agencies can be useful here, showing the effects of drought on people, animals and crops. Wendy Davies' *Children Need Water* (Wayland 1987), published in conjunction with Save the Children, provides plenty of ideas for exploring water in this kind of way.

Children might also explore the contrasting 'moods' of water: storm and stillness; lightness, darkness and colour; movement and reflections; ripples and roars.

Activities

1 The importance of water for life may also be explored through story. Two stories from an African context which could be usefully explored and dramatised with children are *Aio the Rainmaker* by Fiona French (OUP 1975) and *Bringing the Rain to Kapiti Plain* by Verna Aardema (Macmillan 1981). The latter, in verse form, would lend itself to dramatic reading by a class.

2 Listen to music associated with the sea which captures its varied character. Children might explore its moods through movement and dance.

3 Display a collection of pictures of water in different moods. Let each child choose the picture she or he likes best and explore in an appropriate way—sound, poetry, prose—what it 'says' to him/her.

4 a Let children carry out tasks which will explore water's sustaining of life; these might be carried out in conjunction with work in science.

b In contrast look at water's destructive power: in storm and flood; in the erosion of coastlines.

Water as special or sacred

Recognition of water as a source of life is often communicated in the stories and practices of religions. Two examples are given here.

The River Ganges

In India, rivers may be the focus of pilgrimage, of ritual bathing and cleansing, and a place where the ashes of the dead are scattered. They are also like 'veins'; after the monsoon they carry water—and so promote life—in an arid land. Among the rivers the Ganga—Ganges—with its many tributaries, is given the name Ganga Mayya, Mother Ganges and is a Hindu goddess: a pointer to the river as a provider and sustainer of life. In Hindu mythology the story of the descent of the Ganges picks up this theme. The story can be found in J Gavin's *Stories from the Hindu World* (Macdonald 1986) and is reproduced on pp 29 and 30 of *RE Topics for the Primary School*.

The practice of well dressing

The tradition of well dressing still continues in Tissington.

In past times, wells, springs and pools of water were often the focus of religious rites and ceremonies; the idea of making an offering at such places probably survives in the apparent urge some people have to throw coins into fountains and pools even today. In places where Christianity superseded 'the old ways', holy wells were often given the names of saints or Mary. Well dressing—the custom of decorating wells with elaborate floral religious pictures—probably reflects both pre-Christian practice and subsequent attempts at its 'Christianisation'. Well dressing ceremonies were common in a number of English counties—among them Staffordshire, Shropshire and Derbyshire. The Derbyshire dressings remain the most well known today. The village of Tissington, which has five wells, dates its festival from 1350, after the Black Death had diminished. The plague had hit Derbyshire badly, but the people of Tissington survived because the well water remained uncontaminated. Wells are decorated with flowers and garlands which often portray biblical scenes. Frames and figures of wood are covered with clay and moss and the surface is covered with flower petals, leaves, buds and berries to form pictures and spell out texts. In Tissington the well dressings are accompanied by a service in church and then a procession to each well, where the water is blessed.

Events of this kind today become tourist attractions, and are perceived as 'quaint customs', but they point perhaps to a basic awareness of dependency on natural elements which is often lost in a country where most people have water at the turn of a tap.

Activities

1 If you are able, obtain from a library some books which show life by the Ganges. A 'coffee table' type book with good pictures to look at is Henry Wilson's *Benares* (Thames & Hudson 1985).

With children, look at some of the pictures and notice all the things that are happening by the river, and note the buildings that are there too. Make a wall picture of the river to illustrate all that happens there. Tell the myth of the descent of the Ganges and discuss the idea of the river as a symbol of life.

SECTION 3: FOR 9–11 YEAR OLDS

2 Make a collection of some biblical passages which suggest that water is a source of life and strength and which would be suitable for quoting in a 'well dressing'. You might for example find the following good starters: Psalms 23; 46:4; 65:9–10.

What pictures do they 'conjure up'? Make pictures done in 'well dressing' style to illustrate the verses; use crumpled tissue paper or mosaic pieces to create scenes if natural materials can't be used. Use them as a focus for an assembly on 'Water: a symbol of life'.

Making a picture from natural materials

---

1 Draw a simple design on paper.

2 Collect leaves, flower petals, buds, seeds, shells and other natural materials.

3 Press 15mm of *damp* pottery clay into a tray. Copy your design onto the tray using a scriber.

4 Use the natural materials to fill in your design and create a colourful picture.

Stories of a great flood

The story of a great flood is found in many cultures. At this stage in the primary school, children might look at a number of stories, compare and contrast the picture they portray and reflect on the symbolism of water in them.

The popular story of Noah usually focuses on the animals when retold in primary school, but this is to look at only part of the story! Many of the stories about a flood point to the ambivalent nature of water: it destroys, but also 'rescues'. It is useful to note too that in some creation stories water covers the earth before plant, animal and human life emerges; so when a flood comes it is almost as if everything reverts to 'the beginning of things', and when it recedes 'new life' can emerge—a fresh beginning.

Here are two 'Flood' stories, one from China and one from the ancient Sumerians; the Hindu story of Manu (retold in *RE Topics for the Primary School*, pp 142–143) is another to look at.

The Flood

The Yellow Emperor was ruler of Heaven, and as he looked down on the earth he was saddened by humankind's wicked ways. He felt he must teach earthlings a lesson, so he planned to send a terrible flood. He sent for Kung-king, the spirit of the waters, to take rain and floods to the earth.

The rains fell and the waters rose. People on earth began to panic — to pack up their belongings and move to higher land. Still the rains fell and the waters rose and many people were drowned.

One of the gods was very sad at all this suffering. He was Kun, grandson of the Yellow Emperor. But his friend, the very old, wise, black tortoise, suggested a plan to save the people.

'Steal some special magic soil from your grandfather and sprinkle it on the flood waters on earth. That will save the people.'

So Kun managed to steal some of the magic soil, and take it to earth, where he sprinkled a few grains on the flood waters. To his amazement, the waters began to dry up until the valleys could be seen again.

The survivors of the flood were delighted. The soil was now dry and firm and they could rebuild their homes and start farming once more.

Saved from the Flood

Many thousands of years ago the gods became troubled about humans on earth. There were too many of them and they were fighting over jobs and food — there was not enough for everyone. So the gods decided to send a flood and drown the people.

But Ea, the water god, warned one of the humans about the floods to come, and he ordered him to build a boat. Utnapishtim did as he was advised and built a wooden boat big enough for his wife, his family, their possessions, their animals and enough food and water for them all.

Then the rains came. The storms lashed the earth for six days until there was no dry land and no beings left alive.

The storm stopped on the seventh day and all that Utnapishtim could see for miles and miles was flat, calm water.

Then the waters began to go down, and the boat hit land. It was Mount Nisir. Still the waters subsided until after seven more days, Utnapishtim sent out a dove. But the dove found nowhere to rest and returned to the boat. The swallow he sent also returned, but the third bird, the raven, found somewhere to rest and something to eat and did not return. Utnapishtim knew it was safe to release his animals and to thank the gods for keeping them all safe from the terrible floods.

(from *Exploring a Theme: Water*, CEM 1987)

SECTION 3: FOR 9–11 YEAR OLDS

Activities

1 **a** Let children compare and contrast a selection of 'Flood stories' and tabulate evidence, eg:

Country	Who/what is destroyed?	For what reasons?	Is anyone saved?	How are things restored to 'normal'?

b Encourage children to put forward their ideas on why people told and continue to tell this kind of story right across the world.

Note: It is worth recognising here that the question of 'Did it really happen?' may occur. For example, within the Christian tradition some Christians will want to answer 'Yes' and some have tried to argue on archaeological grounds that it did happen; others will look just for the meaning of the story.

2 Let children write plays associated with one or more of the stories you explore. If time permits record them on cassette, with appropriate sound effects.

3 Plan a combined RE and Music project and discover and learn (perhaps perform) some of Benjamin Britten's *Noyes Fludde*, which was written with the intention that children could take a large part in its performance.

Water as a barrier

Just as in the flood stories water is often an ambivalent symbol, so with stories where it is seen as a barrier. Sometimes water is seen as something a person must pass through to reach true happiness. In Greek mythology a dead soul had to be ferried across an underworld river, the Styx, to reach Hades. In the Jewish tradition, crossing the Jordan was the last barrier to the people's entry into the land they believed God had promised. In later Christian tradition, Jordan often became a symbol of passing through death to life in a 'new land' or heaven.

Water in this sense is a symbol in other faiths too. The following extract is from the story of *Monkey*. This Chinese story is about Monkey's journey — a quest to bring the Buddhist scriptures to China. It was written by a poet of the T'ang dynasty (sixteenth century CE) who based his epic on the pilgrimage of Hsuan Tang, a Chinese Buddhist scholar, who had himself travelled to India in 629 CE to seek out and bring back the Buddhist scriptures to his own country. The story was given the title *Monkey* by its translator into English. In this passage Monkey and his travelling companions — Tripitaka, Pigsy and Sandy — finally approach their goal, the sacred abode of Buddha — but there is an obstacle to overcome:

Monkey Arrives at the Abode of Buddha

They travelled for many months and became aware that the country through which they were passing was very different from anything seen or imagined. Everywhere were gem-like flowers, magical grasses, ancient cypresses, hoary pines.

In every village were families entertaining priests. On every hill were hermits practising strict rules of self-control. In every wood were pilgrims chanting.

Each night they found a lodging and set out again at dawn. Thus they journeyed for many days until they came at last in sudden sight of a cluster of high eaves and towers.

'Monkey,' said Tripitaka in admiration, pointing with his whip, 'that's a fine place!'

'Considering', said Monkey, 'how often on our journey you have prostrated yourself before the caves and lairs and palaces of false magicians, it is strange you do not even dismount before Buddha's true fortress.'

At this, Tripitaka in great excitement sprang from his saddle.

When they reached the gates a young Taoist came out to greet them.

'Aren't you those who come from the East to fetch Scriptures?' he asked.

The boy was clad in gorgeous brocades and carried a bowl of jade dust in his hand. Monkey knew him at once, and turned to Tripitaka:

'This', he said, 'is the Golden Crested Great Immortal of the Jade Truth Temple at the foot of the Holy Mountain.'

'Well, here you are at last! It is now ten years since the goddess Kuan-yin told me to expect your arrival. Year after year I waited, but never a sign!'

'Great Immortal,' said Tripitaka humbly, 'I cannot thank you enough for your patience.'

Inside the temple, perfumed hot water was brought to wash in and after supper the pilgrims were shown to their sleeping quarters. Early next day Tripitaka changed into his brocaded cassock and jewelled cap and, staff in hand, presented himself to take his leave.

'That's better!' said the Immortal. 'Yesterday you looked a bit shabby, but today your appearance is that of a true child of Buddha! You must let me show you the way. Monkey knows it, but only by air, and you must travel on the ground.'

Taking Tripitaka by the hand, he led him through the temple courtyards to the back and a way that led on to the hill behind.

'That highest peak,' he said, pointing up, 'wreathed in rainbow mists, is the Vulture Peak, the sacred abode of the Buddha. I shall now turn back.'

Tripitaka at once began kotowing, kneeling and hitting his head on the holy ground.

'If that's what you're going to do all the way up,' said Monkey, 'there won't be much of your head left by the time we get there!'

So Tripitaka stopped kotowing and they had climbed some way at an easy pace when they came to a great water, swift and rough.

Tripitaka was just saying 'This can't be the way', when they spied a bridge and a notice which read CLOUD REACH BRIDGE.

When they came to it, it was simply a few slim tree trunks laid end on end, and was hardly wider than the palm of a man's hand.

'Monkey!' cried Tripitaka in alarm. 'It's not humanly possible to balance on it!'

'Yet it's the way all right. Wait while I show you how!'

Dear Monkey! He strode up, leapt lightly on, and was soon waving from the other side.

'I'm over!' he shouted back.

But Pigsy and Sandy just bit their fingers, muttering, 'Can't be done! Can't be done!' While Tripitaka showed no sign at all of following.

Monkey sprang back again and started pulling at Pigsy. 'Fool, follow me across!' But Pigsy lay flat on the ground and would not budge.

'If you don't come, how do you think you'll ever turn into a Buddha?'

'Buddha or no Buddha,' answered Pigsy, 'I won't go on that bridge!'

Just at the height of their quarrel a boatman approached with a boat, crying, 'Ferry! Ferry!' But when it drew near they saw that it had no bottom.

Monkey with his sharp eyes had recognized the ferryman as the Conductor of Souls.

'How *can* you take people across in a battered and bottomless boat?' said Tripitaka.

'You may well think that, indeed,' was the answer. 'Yet since the beginning of time I have carried countless souls across.'

'Get on board, Master,' said Monkey. 'You will find that this bottomless boat is remarkably steady, however rough the waters.'

But, seeing Tripitaka still hesitate, he took him by the scruff of the neck and pushed him on board.

Tripitaka went straight through into the water.

The ferryman caught at him and dragged him up on to the side of the boat, where he sat, miserably wringing out his clothes, emptying his shoes and grumbling at Monkey. But Monkey, taking no notice, bundled Pigsy, Sandy, horse and baggage all on board, perching them up in the same way on the gunwale.

The ferryman had punted some distance from the shore when they saw a body in the water. It was drifting rapidly downstream and Tripitaka looked at it in great fright.

Monkey laughed.

'Don't be frightened, Master,' he said, 'that's you.'

And Pigsy cried. 'It's you, it's you!'

The ferryman, too, joined in the chorus. 'There *you* go!' he cried. 'My best congratulations!'

Safe and sound on the other side, Tripitaka stepped lightly ashore. He had rid himself of his earthly body. He was cleansed and free of all the unwisdom of his earthly years. His was now the highest wisdom that leads to the Further Shore: the wisdom that knows no bounds.

The boat and the ferryman had vanished. And only now did Monkey explain who the ferryman was. When Tripitaka began thanking his disciples for all they had done for him, Monkey interrupted.

'Each one of us is equally indebted to the other,' he said. 'No one of us could possibly have made the journey alone. And the Master would never have got rid of his mortal body.'

With a strange feeling of lightness and joy they set off up the Holy Mountain.

(from *Dear Monkey* by Arthur Waley (abridged by Alison Waley), Collins-Lions 1975, pp 129–130)

Activities

1 The idea of 'passing over' is found in a number of Christian hymns, in songs, and in the Negro spirituals. Children might meet for example the spiritual 'Swing Low Sweet Chariot' and the hymn 'Guide me O thou Great Redeemer' as examples of Christians thinking about 'crossing Jordan'—and as ways of thinking about death. Some children may already know the spiritual 'Michael row the boat ashore', which can be found in *Folk and Vision* by M E Rose and M R Cook (Rupert Hart-Davis 1971).

2 Children might enjoy hearing the story of Christian and Hopeful's approach to the Celestial City in John Bunyan's *Pilgrim's Progress*. They too have to cross a deep river before they reach their goal.

Resources

Books
In addition to those noted above:
C Porteus, *The Well Dressing Guide*, 1978
(Illustrated guide book to the well dressings in Derbyshire, including details of how they are constructed. Available from Derbyshire Countryside Ltd, Lodge Lane, Derby)
J Reeves, *Quest and Conquest*, Blackie 1976
(Retelling for children of John Bunyan's *Pilgrim's Progress*)
B Walpole, *Water*, A & C Black 1988
(General information/topic book in the *Threads* series)

AVA
E724 *Holy Places*, Pictorial Charts Educational Trust
(4 posters looking at places which are special in 4 faiths. Those on Hinduism and Sikhism focus in part on water)

20 Fire

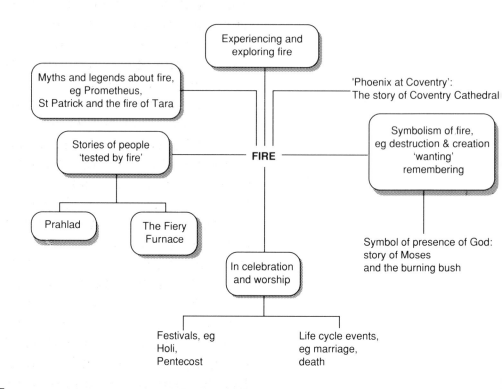

Experiencing and
exploring fire

Myths and legends about fire,
eg Prometheus,
St Patrick and the fire of Tara

'Phoenix at Coventry':
The story of Coventry Cathedral

Stories of people
'tested by fire'

FIRE

Symbolism of fire,
eg destruction & creation
'wanting'
remembering

Prahlad

The Fiery
Furnace

Symbol of presence of God:
story of Moses
and the burning bush

In celebration
and worship

Festivals, eg
Holi,
Pentecost

Life cycle events,
eg marriage,
death

Aims

This is a unit closely related to those on Light and Water; it is intended to provide children with an opportunity for reflection and creative expression in relation to the element of fire and thus to develop understanding of fire as a symbol and as a focus of celebration in religions.

Experiencing fire

Time to reflect on fire, to appreciate its power, its 'life', its destructiveness, as well as its 'creativeness' as humankind puts it to good use; time to identify its uses, to enjoy its colours, changing shapes and sounds, to see it in sun and to feel its warmth—these things and more may be explored to form a basis for understanding the rich symbolism of fire. Apart from warnings about its danger, children's experience of fire is likely to be limited, so reflection on it by way of pictures and poetry is important. To explore something of the importance of fire to humankind the Greek myth of Prometheus might be told. Prometheus has taught humankind all the arts and crafts of life: building, agriculture, domestication of animals; speech, writing, names of living things, and much more. But life is difficult for mortals without fire. He resolves, despite the anger of Zeus which he knows he will incur, to give them fire. He is helped on his way by Athena:

But Athena was always friendly to Prometheus, and interested in his work for Mankind; and so when she knew that he had decided to give them Fire, she led him by the secret paths to the summit of Olympus.

As day drew to an end, Helios drove up in his shining chariot, and Prometheus, hiding by the gateway, needed but to stretch out his fennel-stalk and touch the golden wheel. Then, the precious spark concealed under his cloak, he hastened down the mountain side, and away into a deep valley of Arcadia where he heaped up a pile of wood and kindled it.

The first people upon earth to see the wonderful new gift of fire were the wild Satyrs who dwelt in the lonely valleys. Slowly and shyly they gathered round the edge of the glade in which Prometheus had lighted the first camp-fire; and gradually they drew nearer and nearer.

'Oh the lovely thing!' they cried as they felt the warmth. 'How beautifully it dances; how warm, and gentle, and comforting this new creature is!'

'Oh how I love it!' cried Silenus. 'It shall be mine, mine! See, I will kiss the lovely creature, to prove it!'

With that he knelt down and tried to kiss the tallest and brightest tongue of flame. The look on his face was so comical as the flame scorched him and burnt his beard, that Prometheus sat back and roared with laughter.

But he had more serious work in hand, and when day dawned he began to teach men the uses of Fire. He showed them how to cook meat and bake bread; how to make bronze and smelt iron; how to hammer the hot metals into swords and plough-shares, and all the other cunning crafts of the smith and the metal-worker.

Now that Fire had come upon the Earth, fire could be kindled there whenever it was needed. So Prometheus, with the help of Hermes, invented rubbing-sticks and taught men which woods to use and how to twirl the hard piece in the soft until fire was kindled by the friction.

So Mankind came into his true inheritance: cities began to grow up, and men to practise all the arts and crafts for which Greece was soon to become famous.

(from *Tales of the Greek Heroes* by R L Green, Penguin 1958, pp 33–34)

Activities

1   Explore the many facets of fire, but especially its intrinsic qualities

a Involve children in collecting as many pictures as possible of fire. Try to classify them to illustrate the many facets of fire, eg: warmth and protection; destruction; light; power for . . .

b Listen to music associated with fire. Try to 'capture' its mood in creative writing or in visual expression or movement.

c What kinds of sound does fire itself make? Make music to express the sounds.

d Explore the colours and movement of fire in collage work.

2 Plan a class debate: 'Was Prometheus right or wrong to give humankind fire?' Try to think of the good and bad things about fire.

Exploring the symbolism of fire: stories of 'testing by fire'

This phrase often points to some kind of ordeal a person has undergone; fire is being used as a metaphor. If an object is 'tested by fire', strength, resistance and perhaps also some kind of refinement—such as the removal of impurities—may be in mind. Ideas like these underlie a number of stories from religious traditions. One, the story of Rama's rescue of Sita from the 10-headed demon Ravana—a popular story for Divali among some Hindus—tells how Rama doubted Sita's fidelity whilst she had been the prisoner of Ravana. Sita, dismayed at Rama's lack of trust, ordered a bonfire to be made and bravely walked into it. Miraculously the flames did not consume her, thus witnessing to her purity and integrity. A similar theme is found in the following stories.

The Fiery Furnace (Jewish)

This story is found in the Book of Daniel, chapter 3. It is a story from Jewish tradition, and probably dates from the second century BCE, a period in Jewish history when the Jews were persecuted under Antiochus Epiphanes who wished to stamp out the Jewish way of life. (Details of his rule can be found in the section on Hanukah in *RE Topics for the Primary School.*) The story is set in earlier times—in the reign of Nebuchadnezzar—and is one which is intended to be of great encouragement to those being 'tested' by Antiochus' harsh rule. Some versions of the story include the song of the three men—Shadrach, Meshach, and Abednego—summoning all creatures to praise God. Their song is attractively presented in *The Song of the Three Holy Children* (see page 136).

A Faith to Die For

One day the emperor, Nebuchadnezzar, ordered a huge golden statue to be made—ninety feet high and nine feet wide. He had it set up on the Dura Plain, and issued an edict summoning all the important officers of state—from viceroys to provincial officials—to attend its dedication.

The Dedication opened with a proclamation by the Royal Herald:

PEOPLES AND NATIONS:

WHATEVER LANGUAGE YOU SPEAK, YOU ARE COMMANDED, AT THE SOUND OF THE MUSICIANS AND CHOIR, TO FALL DOWN ON YOUR FACES AND WORSHIP THE GOLDEN STATUE THE EMPEROR HAS SET UP. THE PENALTY FOR DISOBEDIENCE WILL BE DEATH IN THE RAGING FIRE OF A FURNACE.

The music burst on the great assembly, and the vast crowd fell on their faces and worshipped.

Certain Babylonian officials sought an audience with the emperor to lay a charge against their Jewish fellow-officials.

'Long live your Majesty!' they said. 'Your Majesty issued an edict about the Service of Dedication: that at the sound of musicians and choir, the assembly were to fall down on their faces and worship the golden statue; the penalty for disobedience would be death in the raging fire of a furnace. We beg to report that three Jewish officials—royal officials, your Majesty—of the province of Babylonia disobeyed your royal edict. They refused to worship your Majesty's God—or the golden statue your Majesty set up.'

The emperor was furiously angry. He ordered Shadrach, Meshach and Abednego to be arrested and brought into his presence.

'Shadrach, Meshach and Abednego,' he said. 'Tell me the truth. Do you refuse to worship my god and to fall down on your faces before the golden statue? I'll give you another chance. If at the sound of musicians and choir you fall down on your faces before my statue, we will say no more. If you refuse to do so, you will be thrown into the raging fire of a furnace. Who is the god who will rescue you then from my power?'

'Your Majesty,' the three men answered, 'this is no time for words. Our God, the God we worship, can rescue us; and he will rescue us—from the furnace's raging fire and from your Majesty's power. But even if he doesn't, we want to make it plain to your Majesty that we will not worship either your god or your golden statue.'

This made the emperor blaze with anger. His face was distorted with rage at the sight of the three men before him.

He gave orders for the heating of the furnace—it was to be made seven times hotter than usual. His guards were to tie up the three men and throw them into the furnace fire.

The men were tied up just as they were—with their clothes and hats on—and thrown into the furnace. The heat was so great that the execution squad themselves died in the flames belching out of the furnace. The three men fell, bound as they were, into it.

The emperor watched through the side hole of the furnace.

Suddenly he stepped back in alarm.

'It was three men we threw into the fire, wasn't it?' he asked his ministers.

'Your Majesty is correct,' they replied.

'But there are four men there,' he said. 'They are all walking unbound in the heart of the fire, quite unhurt. The fourth man looks like a god!'

The emperor went back to the side hole of the furnace.

'Shadrach, Meshach and Abednego, servants of the Most High God!' he called out. 'Come out and come here to me!'

The three men climbed out.

The emperor and his ministers stared at them: the fire hadn't touched them—their hair wasn't even singed, their clothes weren't scorched, there was no smell of burning.

'Blessed is the God of Shadrach, Meshach and Abednego!' the emperor exclaimed. 'He sent his angel to rescue his servants—men who trusted him, defied my Royal Edict and would rather die than worship any other god than their own God. Let a new edict be issued:

WHOEVER SPEAKS AGAINST THE GOD OF SHADRACH, MESHACH AND ABEDNEGO SHALL BE TORN LIMB FROM LIMB AND HIS HOUSE BURNED DOWN.

'There's no other God who can rescue like this!' he added.

The three men were promoted to high office.

(from *Winding Quest* by A Dale, OUP 1972, pp 371–373)

Holika and Prahlad (Hindu)

This story is one that may be told at the Hindu festival of Holi, a spring harvest festival in India, marked by much fun and hilarity. The lighting of a bonfire is one of its features among Hindus from Gujarat, and has become a popular feature of its celebration in Britain, perhaps because the festival falls around February/March—still a chilly time of year in this part of the world! The bonfire may recall this story:

There was once a demon king called Hiranyakashipu, which means 'dressed in gold'. The King had a son, Prahlad, who refused to worship his father, but instead worshipped the great god Vishnu. Prahlad's devotion to Vishnu sent the King into a rage and he decided to have the boy killed because he would not change his ways. The King ordered an army to cut Prahlad to pieces with their razor sharp swords. As the soldiers advanced, Prahlad called 'Vishnu, Vishnu' and the soldiers lost their strength and were unable to kill the boy. Next, the King had Prahlad thrown into a pit of loathsome, poisonous snakes. Again the boy called the name of Vishnu and the snakes did him no harm. The King tried many other ways to get rid of the boy, once by trying to drown him in the sea and another time by having him trampled to death by a herd of giant elephants who lived in the skies. Every time the boy survived by calling the name of Vishnu. In desperation, the King summoned his sister Holika to help get rid of the boy. Holika was a demoness who once had been given a special favour by Agni, the fire god, so that she would always be protected from the dangers of fire. Holika tricked Prahlad into climbing with her on to an unlit bonfire. When they had climbed up, Holika grabbed the boy and called the King's soldiers to light the fire. The evil demoness cackled with laughter as the flames began to rise. Prahlad called: 'Vishnu, Vishnu'. The power of Vishnu was so great that Prahlad was protected from the flames, while Holika, in spite of her wish, perished in the fire.

(from *Religions through Festivals: Hinduism* by R Jackson, Longman 1989, p 27)

Activities

1 Explore the metaphorical use of the phrase 'tested by fire' and the idea of devotion and loyalty to God: listen to some of the other stories about Prahlad and the dangers to which he was put by Hiranyakashipu. You can find them in *Seasons of Splendour* by M Jaffrey (Puffin 1985) under the title 'The Wicked King and his Good Son'.

2 Discover more about the Hindu festival of Holi. See for example *Holi: Hindu Festival of Spring* by O Bennett (Hamish Hamilton 1987) and *Religions through Festivals: Hinduism* (details above).

3 Build up a picture of life under Antiochus. Then let children be 'underground' reporters at the time of Antiochus; write a series of news bulletins, or prepare a series of cartoon strips based on the story of Nebuchadnezzar and Daniel's three friends Hananiah, Mishael and Azariah (ie Shadrach, Meshach and Abednego)

How might Antiochus' Jewish subjects have responded to the story as they read it? Now let children write letters to the underground press to express their feelings (as subjects) about the story and what it means to them in their situation.

Taking the symbol further

In *RE Topics for the Primary School* the symbolism of fire was explored in relation to Pentecost (pp 116–117) and to the story of Moses and the Burning Bush (pp 186–187) but there are many other facets to explore:

Destruction and creation

Sometimes fire can be utterly devastating; life is extinguished by it. But fire is associated with life too. In Hindu custom, as the body burns on the funeral pyre, the soul or spirit of the person is released to move on to a new life; whilst in Hindu myth the god Shiva symbolises destruction and life.

Look at the picture of the famous *murti* (image) of *Shiva Nataraj*, Shiva Lord of the Dance. Notice how he holds a flame of destruction in his upper left hand; he is also surrounded by a circle of flame representing the universe which he destroys. But notice too the energy of his dance—not dissimilar to the movement and energy of flames—which along with the rhythm of the drum in his upper right hand represents life and creation.

Shiva, Lord of the Dance.

Fire for 'wanting'

If children have seen pictures of a fire out of control—a forest fire for example—they will know how a fire can go on consuming everything in its path, until it is brought under control. The Buddha taught that one of the fundamental problems for individuals was their constant 'craving' (*tanha*) for all kinds of things—material possessions, happiness, long life, wealth, health and so on. Here is part of a famous sermon he preached about this:

Everything is on fire. The eye is on fire; what it sees and how the eye sees is on fire; feelings about how and what the eye sees are on fire. And what are all these things on fire with? They are on fire with 'craving', the fire of passion, of hatred and of greed. They are on fire with birth, death, old age, sickness, hopelessness and despair.

The ear is on fire, as are sounds it hears and the way it hears things. The nose is on fire, and the tongue, and the body and the mind and the ideas . . .

What is this fire with which everything is on fire? With hatred, greed and passion; with birth and death, old age and sickness, hopelessness and despair. These are the fires with which everything is on fire.

When wise disciples *see* this truth they turn away from fire—they turn away from seeing and hearing and tasting; from sights and sounds and tastes; from body and mind. By turning away from all this, the disciple abandons passion and so becomes free, free from being reborn, free from this world.

Fire for remembering

The energy and vitality of fire have made it a suitable symbol for remembrance of life, whilst the light it provides offers a visual reminder of those whose lives have ended. It might be possible to make a collection of places/incidents where a flame is used for remembrance. Here are some examples:

- Yad Vashem   This memorial in Jerusalem is to the victims of the Holocaust. A flame burns constantly as a reminder of those six million Jews, many of them children, who died at the hands of the Nazi regime in the Second World War.
- The Chapel of Saints and Martyrs of our Time   When the Pope visited Britain in 1982, he visited this chapel in Canterbury, and candles were lit to bring to mind the lives of six Christians who have died as martyrs (witnesses) for their faith in this century.
- In a similar way in the present, a lamp burns in the chapel at **Lambeth Palace** especially for Terry Waite, indicative of a community remembering—and hoping.

The Eternal Flame

A country's remembrance may also be symbolised by fire. In the Kremlin in Moscow the Eternal Flame burns at the Tomb of the Unknown Soldier, recalling for a people today those who died—willingly or unwillingly—for their country.

The tomb is often visited by newly married couples, brides leaving their flowers there. Remembrance and the continuity of a community are both given expression.

In many Jewish families the *Jahrzeit* (anniversary) of the death of a loved member of a family will be marked by the lighting of a memorial lamp which will burn for 24 hours: again remembrance and continuity are apparent.

Activities

1   If you are able to borrow a small image of Shiva from a resource centre, set up a small shrine. Let children describe what they see. Tell some of the stories of Shiva: you can find some of these in L Shanson's *Journey with the Gods* (Mantra 1987), especially about his energetic dance. Pratima Mitchell's *The Dance of Shiva* (Hamish Hamilton 1989) introduces children to Bharata Natayam style Indian dance. *Religions through Festivals: Hinduism* has information about the festival of Shiva, Mahashivratri.

2   Discuss the idea of *tanha*: grasping/wanting.

a   Let each person in the class write down the three things they would most like to have. Make a list for the whole class. Discuss the list. Think for example which would make people happy. Might some bring about unhappiness? Which things are just for themselves, which for other people? Are some things of greater value than others?

b   Another possibility might be to get children to do a survey from their television viewing over a week of the things people are encouraged to want, and then to record this research and move into a discussion.

c   Was the Buddha's idea of 'fire' as a symbol of wanting a good one? Why? Is his view that tanha causes unhappiness right or wrong?

3   Explore the idea of remembrance:

a   Light a candle in a quiet place...sit comfortably but still, silent and attentive...focus on it...and let each person think about someone who really matters to them. If appropriate, talk with the children afterwards about whether the flame helped them to focus on the person in their thoughts.

b   Make a list of people your class or school would like to remember. For example: people who are ill from among the school community; or a group of people in the local community; or people a school has been helping here or abroad; or individuals you wish to think about. Plan an assembly when you will remember them. Light a candle/candles as appropriate. Prepare simple words to call to mind who is remembered and why, as each candle is lit, eg: 'This flame is for.....who......'.

c   Yad Vashem and the Holocaust are perhaps difficult areas for primary school children; but many top juniors are likely to have seen films and programmes about the Second World War. If you want to explore this area a little with children, David A Adler's *The Number on My Grandfather's Arm* (UAHL Press 1987), though published in New York, can be obtained in Britain from the Jewish Education Bureau (address on page 25). The book is concerned with a young girl's encounter with her grandfather, who has survived Auschwitz; the child is told something of the horror and difficulties of those days. It has a simple text, and black and white photographs—the grandfather in these is an actual survivor of the Holocaust.

SECTION 3: FOR 9–11 YEAR OLDS

Celebrating in the presence of fire: a Hindu wedding

The power and mystery of fire, as well as human dependence on it, has led to fire itself sometimes being seen as a god or as pointing to God's presence. In the ancient religious writings of India, the *Vedas*, fire is called Agni (from the same word root as ignite or ignition) and many hymns and prayers are addressed to him. The presence of fire is important for many Hindu ceremonies. For example, fire is associated with key events in a person's life: particularly with marriage and death. Marriage takes place in the presence of the sacred fire. In this passage, Sumitra and Susan attend Sumitra's sister's wedding.

Every wedding must be witnessed by Agni, the god of fire, who is the symbol of the sun and power. So a fire, the Sacred Fire, was lit in a metal container. The priest put ghee on the sticks before setting light to it. Throughout the ritual the priest and the couple continued to add ghee, as well as rice and coconut kernel to the fire to keep it going. The priest then took a sheet of white linen and fastened one end of it to the bridegroom's clothes, and the other end to the bride's clothes. After the linen had been removed and they had been garlanded with flowers, he joined their hands together, chanting prayers as he did so, while the bride's elder brother poured rice over their hands. Next he took a cord and placed it around their shoulders. These actions were to show that marriage was a union of two souls which should not be broken. There were many scriptures to be read, much water to be sprinkled and red powder thrown. At last the priest told them to stand and

Throughout a Hindu wedding the Sacred Fire is kept alight; later in the ceremony the bridegroom will lead the bride round the fire and take the *saptapadi* (seven steps).

the bridegroom, linked to the bride by the cord, led her round the fire several times. The guests watched all that happened very carefully, but at no time did they have to sit still and silent; in fact Sumitra and Susan moved more than once to get a better view, and in the middle of one long prayer there was a loud bang when a young man burst a balloon which was hanging from the canopy. Then suddenly a woman began a cheerful song, and the women around her joined in the chorus. Susan wanted to know what it was all about; Sumitra told her that it was a wedding song, telling of the beauty of the bride and the handsome bridegroom. Catching sight of some drinks, she darted along a row of chairs and came back with two beakers of coca-cola.

But now came the most important part of the ceremony. At a nod from the priest, the bride, followed by the groom, took the 'Seven Steps' (*Saptapadi*) around the Sacred Fire, keeping the fire on their right and making promises at each step to honour and respect each other. As he went Govinda said,

> Take one step for food, two for strength, three for increasing wealth, four for good fortune, five for children, six for the seasons and in seven steps be my friend...

The words which Sumitra liked best were spoken by the bridegroom to the bride earlier in the ceremony. They were chanted in Sanskrit, but her father had told her what they meant:

> I take hold of your hand for good fortune, so that with me as your husband you may live to old age. I am the words, you are the melody; I am the melody, you are the words.

(from *Understanding your Hindu Neighbour* by J Ewan, Lutterworth Educational 1977 & 1983, pp 52 and 54)

Activities Look at pictures of a Hindu wedding, or if possible invite a Hindu visitor to school to talk about one. Ask about the importance of the fire in the ceremony.

Resources

Many appropriate resources are listed above, and should be available in the larger RE centres. In addition, the following might be useful:

Books/Booklets
General
Exploring a Theme: Fire, CEM 1986 (address on page 89)
E and T Hadley, *Legends of Earth Air Fire and Water*, CUP 1985

Hinduism
J Jones { *To the temple for arti* / *The Holi Fire* } Blackie 1987
J Solomon, *Wedding Day*, Hamish Hamilton 1981

Judaism
J Neuberger, *The Story of the Jews*, CUP, 1986

Christianity
M Craig, *Candles in the Dark: Six Modern Martyrs*, Hodder & Stoughton 1984
W Purcell, *Martyrs of our Time*, Mowbray 1983
(Both books for teacher reference)

Visuals
A Hindu Wedding (Slidefolio S1526), Slide Centre Ltd, 1986 (address: Ilton, Ilminster, Somerset, TA19 9HS)
Pictorial Charts Educational Trust:
E722 *Marriage Rites* (one poster is on Hinduism)
E748 *Hindu Festivals*

Music
for example:
Handel, 'Music for the Royal Fireworks'
Haydn, *Symphony No 59* — 'The Fire Symphony'
Stravinsky, 'Firebird Suite'

21 Time

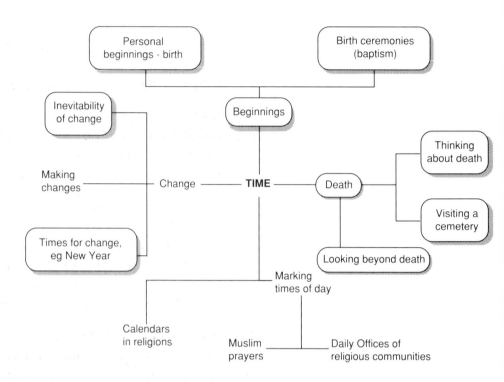

Aims

This unit gives children a chance to reflect on the passage of time through an exploration of the related concepts of beginnings, endings and change which figure so large in human experience.

Exploring beginnings

Beginnings seem always to have had a kind of awe around them for people. New Year, a new home, a new job, starting out on a journey may all be marked in special ways. The journey of a person through time combines many aspects of beginnings. A sense of mystery usually surrounds a baby's arrival, however accustomed people are to birth. Babies are often held to be 'special'—why? What is there about their arrival which evokes this response? Two ways of exploring this mystery of new beginnings are suggested here below.

Prayer before Birth

Louis MacNeice's poem 'Prayer Before Birth' won't be fully understood even by those at the top end of the junior school, but it is accessible enough to prompt serious reflection on the 'specialness' of each new baby. The poem is, as it says, a baby's prayer before it is born, but written with the poet's own perceptions of 'being human'. Key words of each of its verses' opening lines—hear me, console me, provide me, forgive me, rehearse me, hear me, fill me—are followed by 'things that might be'. Older children might follow these 'lead words' by filling out the poem's imagery and hopes and fears from their own experience of the world.

Prayer Before Birth

I am not yet born; O hear me.
Let not the bloodsucking bat or the rat or the stoat or the
    clubfooted ghoul come near me.

I am not yet born; console me.
I fear that the human race may with tall walls wall me,
    with strong drugs dope me, with wise lies lure me,
        on black racks rack me, in blood-baths roll me.

I am not yet born; provide me
With water to dandle me, grass to grow for me, trees to talk
    to me, sky to sing to me, birds and a white light
        in the back of my mind to guide me.

I am not yet born; forgive me
For the sins that in me the world shall commit, my words
        when they speak me, my thoughts when they think me,
            my treason engendered by traitors beyond me,
                my life when they murder by means of my
                    hands, my death when they live me.

I am not yet born; rehearse me
In the parts I must play and the cues I must take when
        old men lecture me, bureaucrats hector me, mountains
            frown at me, lovers laugh at me, the white
                waves call me to folly and the desert calls
                    me to doom and the beggar refuses
                        my gift and my children curse me.

I am not yet born; O hear me,
Let not the man who is beast or who thinks he is God
        come near me.

I am not yet born; O fill me
With strength against those who would freeze my
        humanity, would dragoon me into a lethal automaton,
            would make me a cog in a machine, a thing with
                one face, a thing, and against all those
                    who would dissipate my entirety, would
                        blow me like thistledown hither and
                            thither or hither and thither
                                like water held in the
                                    hands would spill me
Let them not make me a stone and let them not spill me.
Otherwise kill me.

(from *The Penguin Book of Contemporary Verse* edited by Kenneth Allott, 1950)

A baby is baptised

This card, in speaking of a 'christening', recalls the ancient custom of anointing the baptised with holy oil — chrism. The symbol of the fish points to the Greek acrostic

| Jesus   X — Christ   θ — of God
U — Son   Σ — Saviour.

The theme of the Holy Spirit represented by the dove and that of life-giving water are picked up on this card.

Hopes and fears surrounding newly begun life are also picked up in religious practice. The 'specialness' of new human beings finds expression in most of the world's religions: the breathing of the *Adhan* into a new-born Muslim baby's ear and the ritual of *brit milah* in the case of Jewish baby boys have a parallel in those parts of the Christian community which baptise infants. What people do at this time; how the child (and possibly the rest of its friends and relations) is dressed; the celebrations that take place and the gifts that are given are all ways of expressing the 'specialness' of this particular new beginning.

There are many ways of exploring baptism with children: for example, hymns that are sung, baptism cards, ritual acts, prayers. Or you might explore some of the specific symbols associated with baptism: the lighted candle, water, the font, the new garment — all speak both literally and symbolically of what Christians believe about the baby's place in the Christian community and in the wider world.

During a baptism the whole Christian community prays with and for the newly baptised child; children might explore some of the words used, like these from the Anglican tradition. Discuss with children the hopes expressed for the child.

Heavenly Father, in your love
you have called us to know you
led us to trust you
and bound our life with yours.
Surround these children with your love;
protect them from evil;
fill them with your Holy Spirit;
and receive them into the family of your
Church;
that they may walk with us in the way
of Christ and grow in the knowledge of your
love.

(*Alternative Service Book*, 1980, pp 244–245)

Children may know of stories which tell of wishes for a child on its birth. What would the children 'wish' for a new baby as it sets out on a journey through life. Thinking about this might prepare the way for understanding a community's hopes for its new members, expressed in prayers like the one above.

Activities

1 Read 'Prayer Before Birth' to the children. Let children enjoy the words and talk about anything they particularly liked or disliked about it. Explore difficult words and images as far as is appropriate with your class.

2 Produce a collage or mural to make the poem's thought visible. Divide the class into groups; let each group work with one verse, talking out what the hopes and fears of the poem have in common with their own, and how they may best be represented.

3 Invite someone whose baby has recently been baptised to come and

describe what happened, and particularly why they wanted this and what it meant to them for their baby.

OR

With the help of a local priest/minister reconstruct a baby's baptism in a church. Let the children act out the various roles (parents, godparents, Christian community) and learn about the ceremony and its importance.

4   Make a class anthology of poems or stories about birth. Collect prayers or blessings from religious traditions other than Christianity which mark this moment of a baby's setting out on a 'journey through time'. Let children try writing simple blessings themselves to include in the anthology.

5   Discover with children how many beginnings there are in the first five years of life, eg: first solid food; first steps; first words; first haircut; first shoes; first day at school or first religious lesson. You might go on to discover how *some* beginnings are, or have been, marked in religions. For example, first solid food and first haircut among some Hindus; first speaking of the *Shahadah* (the declaration of faith in God and in Muhammad as his prophet) among some Muslims.

Exploring change

If there is something special about beginnings, there is often held to be something unnerving or threatening or saddening about change. Some religions point to what is constant or to be trusted amid change; but all recognise that change is part of living — people die and nature changes too, as does the world around us.

A family photo-chain

Most children are fascinated by their parents' or grandparents' or guardians' stories of 'when I was young'. A display of photographs illustrating, for example, how grandparents, parents (or equivalents), aunts and uncles looked at key moments in their lives, from babyhood to the most recent photos, might be arranged as family trees. This should allow two things to become clear: first, that growing old — and changing — is inevitable; then, in any class, one of the changes will be that some of the people in the family trees have died.

The man who wanted to live for ever

No one lives for ever; nor does anything we know, however firmly established, remain unchanged. A story which can be explored at many levels, and which is a good story in its own right is *The Man Who Wanted to Live Forever*, retold by Selina Hastings (Walker Books 1988). The story is of Bodkin who lived long ago and of his quest for a deathless life; as it should, the story leaves many loose ends and prompts questions about change and decay, life and death; it also opens many doors into the kinds of 'ultimate' question with which religions deal and allows space for them to be explored in many traditions. For example units on the Buddha (and the story of Kisagotami) in the earlier *RE Topics for the Primary School* show how perceiving this truth leads to insight which itself may lead to following the Buddha's Eightfold Path. The units on 'Life Stories' and 'Journeys' (above, pages 106 and 126) also offer related information for this topic.

New Year celebrations

As people experience change, they may also try to take some control of it. The once popular custom of making New Year resolutions is one example of this. In the Christian tradition many Methodists renew their covenant with God each year in January; many Anglicans renew their baptismal vows each Easter. In each case these Christians are reaffirming, at a special moment in time, the kind of person they want to be and how they want to live. In the Jewish tradition *Rosh*

Hashanah, the Jewish New Year, reminds people that God is creator, judge and preserver; that people's actions are 'weighed'; that it is a time for new beginnings. A useful book for exploring this Jewish festival is *A Happy New Year* by José Patterson (Hamish Hamilton 1987). Some features of the festival which children may enjoy are the blowing of the *shofar* (the ram's horn) which summons people to repentance and thus to change; the exchange of cards and greetings; tasting sweet foods—honey cake and apples dipped in honey to focus thought on a good and 'wholesome' year ahead.

This card for Rosh Hashanah shows the shofar (ram's horn) which is blown on the festival and a Torah crown. The inscription in Hebrew reads *Shanah Tovah* — A Good Year!

HAPPY NEW YEAR לשנה טובה

Activities

1 After discussion of the photo-chains, if possible arrange for children to have contact with old people in the community; explore the concept of change with them, eg: What changes have they seen in their lifetime in the local community? In what ways is life easier/more difficult than it was when they were young (this

question allows for both objective and subjective answers)? Or (recognising and accepting change) how could a local community or school help to make life happier or more comfortable for old people?

2   Encourage children to think individually about 'what I should most like to change'. Let them draw up two lists: one for things they would like to change about themselves and one for 'the world'. Use ideas from the lists to paint, draw, write for a class book. It might be done in the style of 'Dear World...' (see Resources, page 89).

3   Design suitable cards or posters for Jewish New Year, incorporating the special greeting and using some of the symbols, eg: the shofar; the scales. Make and enjoy some of the foods associated with the festival—eg: honey cake and apples dipped in honey. Plan an assembly in which they are shared. You may be able to borrow a shofar for the children to see and a recording of it being blown.

4   The story of Jonah is one which is told at this time of year in the Jewish calendar. With its focus on the message to the people of Nineveh, that they must repent and change, *and* on Jonah's need to change his attitude to them—and so change himself—this topic would provide a good context in which to let children enjoy the story. It is retold in *Stories and Legends from the Bible* by K McLeish (Longman 1988).

Exploring ends

Experiencing death

We noted above that a family photo-tree might well show that many children had already experienced the death of someone near to them. It is often hard to know how to handle, in the classroom, the question of death, and many teachers are reluctant to try, though there is a wide range of material available to help them do this. *The Fall of Freddie the Leaf* offers one way into the topic, a topic which is unavoidable if we are concerned with humans journeying through time. This video's way is through the naturalness of death. The video is made in an American arboretum, and follows the brief life of one leaf. The 'story' is open-ended in that it is not religion specific. It follows *one* leaf among others on the tree through the year, ending in 'his' fall in the Fall; the story raises questions about change, death, purpose, meaning, differences and the seasons. People either love the film or hate it, but many teachers *have* used if successfully with a wide range of ages. Make sure you have seen it before deciding to use it, because there is no halfway position about it! On one fact most people are agreed: it is very beautifully photographed and flawlessly produced. This subject offers many possibilities for multidisciplinary topics and opens doors on death and people's responses to it.

As an alternative, *To Hell with Dying* (Hodder & Stoughton 1988) is a book which offers a very different approach; Alice Walker (author of *The Color Purple*) has written an enigmatic and earthy story. Again, you'll need to weigh whether this is the book for *your* class. It is a strong, black American story about dying and death, but also about life and affirming life, and most especially about the power of love to sustain life and survive death. Like the video above, this will not be everyone's choice, but it gets to the heart of many central issues with which religions are concerned.

Looking beyond death

The inevitability of death and what may lie beyond is explored in the following story which children may enjoy and which could be a stimulus for their own creative writing on this theme.

SECTION 3: FOR 9–11 YEAR OLDS

The Island

Petros loved the beautiful and holy island of Crete. He had been born there, and lived all his life there. Now that he was an old man he was ready to leave the earth for heaven, but he did not wish to leave his beloved island, the beautiful and holy island of Crete.

He decided that he would take some of Crete's holy soil to heaven with him. He seized hold of a handful of soil, and kept it firmly gripped in his fist. He sat outside his house, waiting for God to come to collect him, and to take him to heaven.

One day soon God arrived, disguised as a messenger from the king. It is time for you to come with me, said God. Yes, I will come, said Petros. But what do you have in your fist? asked God. It is a handful of soil from my beloved and holy island of Crete, replied Petros, I wish to bring it with me.

No, you can bring nothing with you, said God. Petros refused to open his fist and let the soil drop, and God left him. Petros sat for many more years at the door of his house, waiting for God to collect him, and to take him to heaven.

One day after many years God returned, disguised this time as one of Petros's oldest and closest friends. Petros was delighted to see him. Come, said God, it is time for you to come with me.

Yes, I will come, said Petros, I am ready. But what do you have in your fist, asked God. It is a handful of soil from my beloved and holy island of Crete, replied Petros, I wish to bring it with me.

No, you can bring nothing with you, said God. Petros refused to open his fist and let the soil drop, and God left him. Petros sat for many more years at the door of his house, waiting for God to collect him, and take him to heaven.

One day after many years God returned, disguised this time as Petros's great-grand-daughter. Petros was delighted to see her. Come, she said, it is time for you to come with me. Yes I will come with you, replied Petros. He looked into her eyes, and he saw there also the eyes of all his other great grand-children, and he saw the eyes of his grandchildren, and he saw the eyes of his children, and he saw, as he looked, also the eyes of himself when he too had been a tiny trusting child. I will come with you, he said. But what do you have in you clenched fist, she said. He began to explain, but very gently and sweetly the little child opened his fingers, and he let the soil drop. He went with her to heaven.

And what do you think he saw when he arrived in heaven? What was the very first thing he saw there?

Yes, there, there in heaven, the first thing he saw was his beloved island, the beautiful and holy island of Crete.

A visit to a cemetery or churchyard

Churchyards and cemeteries sometimes become a focus in environmental studies, but their RE potential is not always recognised! Clearly a sensitive approach is needed towards such a visit, not least where a cemetery is still in use for burials. Children might be encouraged to:

- think about the appropriateness of a *special* place for burial and about its importance for relatives and friends of a person who has died;
- look at the inscriptions on head stones and think about the importance for many people of remembering (see page 76);
- notice symbols used and the beliefs about death and life to which they point.

Follow this up in a Christian context with readings, hymns or prayers used at a funeral service and thinking about why a family might find them comforting. The custom in a Western Christian tradition of remembering on All Souls Day (2 November) members of the community who have died might also be explored. Some churches have a memorial book on display which is open each day or week at the page which recalls those who have died in earlier years on that date. (See also 'Remembering', page 74). This kind of exploration could usefully be undertaken at Hallowe'en (literally All Hallows Eve).

Activities

The approaches above lend themselves to discussion as *appropriate to the children* at the time when 'death' is handled. In addition children might:

1 Make a collage about change, death and life (in human and animal life), thinking of as many expressions of this as they can: seasons; natural world—plants, stones, trees, mountains etc.

2 Find out about religious rites surrounding death in different faiths; see for example Jon Mayled's *Death Customs* (Wayland 1986) but be careful to check out its limited text against more substantial information like *Death* edited by J Prickett (Lutterworth Educational 1980), which offers information at the teacher's level.

3 A topic on 'the passage of time' might be brought to a finale by drawing on the well-known words from Ecclesiastes chapter 3, perhaps in the popular version of Pete Seeger. This can be found in *The Complete Come and Praise* (BBC 1990). The song could perhaps provide a focus for a week's Collective Worship in school, drawing on children's work done in the course of this topic.

Resources

Books
In addition to those listed above:
J Mayled, *Birth Customs*, Wayland 1986
(Pupil book, interesting pictures but text rather too brief)
J Prickett (Ed), *Initiation*, Lutterworth Educational 1978
(Survey of initiation ceremonies in different world faiths)
B Ward & Associates, *Good Grief 2* (1989)
(An impressive handbook for 'Exploring Feelings, Loss and Death with under 11's'; available from Good Grief, 19 Bawtree Road, Uxbridge, Middlesex UB8 1PT)

AVA
E720 *Birth Rites* (Christian, Hindu, Muslim) ⎫ Pictorial Charts Educational Trust
E723 *Death Rites* (Christian, Sikh, Buddhist) ⎭
(2 sets of each of 3 charts, with notes; pictures, line drawings, short text on each chart)

RE ACROSS THE CURRICULUM 5–7 SECTION

TOPIC	Religions drawn upon	Life questions	Celebrations	Values	Community	Symbol & Communication	Key figures	Sacred writings	Creative expression
1 MYSELF	Sikhism	✓		✓	✓		✓		
2 FAMILY	Judaism Christianity	✓	✓	✓	✓	✓			✓
3 BEGINNINGS	Hinduism Islam Sikhism Christianity Judaism		✓		✓	✓			
4 ANIMALS	Judaism Christianity Islam Hinduism Sikhism	✓		✓		✓	✓		
5 COLOURS	Christianity Hinduism		✓	✓		✓			✓
6 PATTERNS AND SEASONS	Islam Buddhism Christianity	✓				✓			✓
7 PLACES	Islam Christianity		✓		✓	✓			

RE ACROSS THE CURRICULUM 7–9 SECTION

TOPIC	Religions drawn upon	Life questions	Celebrations	Values	Community	Symbol & Communication	Key figures	Sacred writings	Creative expression
8 HOMES	Christianity Hinduism Islam						✓		✓
9 REMEMBERING	Christianity Hinduism Islam Judaism	✓	✓		✓	✓		✓	
10 SENSES	Buddhism Christianity Hinduism Islam	✓	✓			✓			
11 IMAGINATION	Christianity Islam Sikhism			✓		✓			
12 COMMUNICATION	Buddhism Christianity Hinduism Islam					✓		✓	
13 DIFFERENCE	Islam Sikh Buddhism Christianity Judaism Hinduism	✓		✓	✓				✓
14 LIGHT	Christianity Hinduism Judaism		✓			✓			✓

RE ACROSS THE CURRICULUM 9–11 SECTION

TOPIC	Religions drawn upon	Main areas of religion touched upon							
		Life questions	Celebrations	Values	Community	Symbol & Communication	Key figures	Sacred writings	Creative expression
15 LIFE STORIES	Buddhism Christianity Judaism Sikhism	✓				✓	✓	✓	
16 COMMUNITY	Buddhism Christianity Islam			✓	✓	✓			
17 JOURNEYS	Buddhism Christianity Islam Judaism Sikhism	✓		✓		✓	✓	✓	✓
18 THE NATURAL WORLD	Christianity Islam Judaism (North American Indian tradition)		✓	✓		✓		✓	
19 WATER	Buddhism Christianity Hinduism	✓				✓		✓	
20 FIRE	Buddhism Hinduism Judaism (Greek mythology)	✓	✓	✓		✓			
21 TIME	Christianity Judaism	✓	✓		✓	✓			

CHARTS

These tables should help to identify other topics or curriculum areas to which the topics in this book might contribute. Only the most apparent of these have been included.

RELATED CROSS-CURRICULAR TOPICS IN 5–7 SECTION

	TOPIC	Related cross-curricular topics	Specific religious topics
1	MYSELF	Family. Local environment. Senses. Homes	Birth ceremonies. Naming ceremonies
2	FAMILY	Remembering. Where we live. Local history. Homes. Birth. Children	Worship. Special days. Times. Places. Festivals. Birth. Weddings. Funerals
3	BEGINNINGS	Birth. New life. Moving. Change. Growth	Stories of creation. Rites of passage. Celebration. Key figures
4	ANIMALS	Courage. Friendship. Conservation. Homes	Stories from religions. Hindu gods. St Francis
5	COLOURS	Tessellation. Rainbow. Myself. Environment. Signs and symbols	Calendar. Dress. Art and Sculpture. Buildings. Symbols
6	PATTERNS AND SEASONS	Cycle of seasons. Environment. Colours. Rhythm. Trees. Birthdays. Anniversaries	Calendar. Buildings. Art and Design. Dress. Worship
7	PLACES	Environment. The past. Homes. Particular countries	Pilgrimage. Jerusalem. Makkah. Buildings. Worship

RELATED CROSS-CURRICULAR TOPICS IN 7–9 SECTION

	TOPIC	Related cross-curricular topics	Specific religious topics
8	HOMES	Myself. Imagination. Family. Meals	Home rituals. Special days. Childhood stories of Jesus. Muhammad. Krishna. Heaven
9	REMEMBERING	Myself. Family. Making judgements	Festivals. Memorials. Death rituals. Sacred books
10	SENSES	Human Body. Measuring. Myself. Music. Textures. Food	Worship. Ritual. Places of worship. Meditation
11	IMAGINATION	Consequences. Making calculations. Making hypotheses. Artistic expression. Stories. Time	Religious images. Islamic patterns. Ideas about God, heaven, paradise
12	COMMUNICATION	Books. Relationships. Community. Signs and symbols	Sacred books. Myths. Religious imagery and language
13	DIFFERENCE	Community. Myself. Handicaps. Race relations. Individual beliefs	Religious buildings. Religious diversity
14	LIGHT	Sun. Fire. Symbolism. Darkness. Day and night	Festivals of light. Parsees. Easter

172

RELATED CROSS-CURRICULAR TOPICS IN 9–11 SECTION

TOPIC	Related cross curricular topics	Specific religious topics
15 LIFE STORIES	Famous people. Leaders. Writing biographies. Remembering. Discovering stories: saga, myth, legend etc.	Key figures: Buddha, Jesus, Guru Nanak etc. Teachings of key figures. Writings about such figures.
16 COMMUNITY	Belonging. Sharing. Living together. Family. The local community. Life-style. Commitments. Rules.	Religious orders. Ideals for living — values. Church (Christian community); Umma (Muslim); Sangha (Buddhist)
17 JOURNEYS	Life journeys. Exploration. Mythical journeys. Journeys of discovery.	Symbolism. Rites of passage. Pilgrimage. "Ways of Life', eg Buddhist Eightfold Path.
18 THE NATURAL WORLD	Creation/Evolution. Caring for the environment. Responsibility. Animals and plants. Caring for pets. Interdependence.	Creation myths. Religious symbols drawn from natural world: trees; rivers; sun etc. Harvest celebrations. St Francis of Assisi.
19 WATER	Elements. Water for life. Drought and famine. The Sea. Rivers and floods. Barriers. Life and death.	Symbolism. Rites of passage, eg Baptism; Death rituals. Sacred places/Rivers.
20 FIRE	Elements. Energy. Mystery. Remembering. Persecution. Light. Candles.	Symbolism & ritual, eg Sacred Fire in Hinduism. Easter and Pentecost (Christian). Holi (Hindu).
21 TIME	Change. Birth and death. Continuity. Pattern. Seasons. Beginnings. Endings. Calendars. Sun/Moon.	New Year celebrations. Rites of passage. Weekly celebrations, eg Sunday; Shabbat. Religious calendars.

Index

Acknowledgements

We are grateful to the following for permission to reproduce copyright material:

Advaita Ashrama for an adapted version of the story of Krishna's birth from *Cradle Tales of Hinduism* (second illustrated impression, 1972); Amaravati Publications for extracts from their literature, © Amaravati Publications; Andersen Press Ltd for *Badger's Parting Gifts* by Susan Varley; A & C Black (Publishers) Ltd for a shortened version of *Don't Forget Tom* by H Larsen; The Central Board of Finance of the Church of England for a prayer from *The Alternative Service Book* (1980), copyright © The Central Board of Finance of the Church of England; Chester Music Ltd, a division of Music Sales Ltd, for 'Canticle of the Sun' translated by William H Draper, English translation copyright J Curwen & Sons Ltd; Christian Education Movement for the short stories 'The Flood' & 'Saved from the Flood' from *Exploring a Theme: Water* (2nd edition, 1990); CollinsDove Publishers, a division of HarperCollins Publishers, for an extract from *Petook: An Easter Story* by C Houselander; Evans Brothers Ltd for an adapted extract from *Nadeem Makes Samosas* by S Stone (English/Urdu edition, 1987); Faber & Faber Ltd for *Maria* by Catherine Brighton (1984) & the poem 'Prayer Before Birth' from *Collected Poems of Louis MacNeice* by Louis MacNeice; Grafton Books, a division of HarperCollins Publishers, for the negro spiritual 'Michael Row the Boat Ashore' from *Folk & Vision* by M E Rose & M R Cook (Rupert Hart-Davis, 1971); The Islamic Foundation for an adapted version of the story 'The Little Ants' from *Love All Creatures* (1981); The Lutterworth Press for extracts from *Understanding Your Hindu Neighbour* by J Ewan (Lutterworth Educational, 1977 & 1983); the author, Patricia Middleton for the song 'The Rainbow Warrior' from *Sing for Your Life* chosen by S Kerr (A & C Black (Publishers) Ltd, 1987); The National Council of the Churches of Christ in the USA for extracts from *Revised Standard Version Common Bible*, copyright 1973 by the Division of Education of the National Council of the Churches of Christ in the USA; Orchard Books, part of The Watts Group, for the adapted poem 'From Me To You' from *From Me To You* by Paul Rogers (1987); Oxford University Press for the extract 'A Faith to die for' from *Winding Quest: The Heart of the Old Testament in Plain English* by Alan T Dale (1972), © Oxford University Press, 1972; G P Putnam's Sons, the Putnam Publishing Group, for the poem 'Everybody Says' from *Here, There & Everywhere* by Dorothy Aldis, copyright 1927, 1928, copyright renewed © 1955, 1956 by Dorothy Aldis; Random Century Group for the poem 'First Day at School' from *In the Glassroom* by Roger McGough (Jonathan Cape Ltd); Simon & Schuster Young Books for the poem 'Puddle Splashing' by Frank Flynn from *Four Seasons Poetry Book: Summer* compiled by J Wilson (1987) & an adapted version of the story 'The Donkey & the Tiger Skin' from *Stories of the Sikh World* by R J Singh (1987); Spindlewood, on behalf of Era Publications, Australia, for *Arthur* by Amanda Graham & Donna Gynell (1984), copyright © 1984 Era Publications; Stanley Thornes (Publishers) Ltd for the story 'Mr Rashid Packs His Bags' from *Westhill Project, Muslims 1* edited by Garth Read & John Rudge (1988); Unwin Hyman, a division of HarperCollins Publishers, for an extract from *Dear Monkey* by A Waley (1975); Wayland (Publishers) Ltd for an adapted version of the story 'How Ganesh Got His Elephant Head' from *Hindu Stories* by V P (Hemant) Kanitkar (1986).

We have been unable to trace the copyright holders in the following & would appreciate any information that would enable us to do so:

'The Rainbow' by Dineshi Kodituwakku; 'Holi, Festival of Colour' by Punitha Perinparaja; 'Colour Song'; 'Some things don't make sense at all' by Judith Viorst and 'The Island'.

We are grateful to the following for permission to reproduce photographs and other copyright material:

Andes Press Agency, pages **35, 59, 102**; Mohamed Ansar, page **88**; Barnaby's Picture Library, pages **71** (photo: Mavis Ransom), **78** (photo: Gunter Reitz), **91** *above right* (photo: Sarah Thorley), **94**; Duncan Beal, page **112**; from: *Worship*, Unwin Hyman, a division of Harper Collins Publishers, page **132**; from *Sing for Your Life*, A & C Black, London, page **137**; Allan Cash, page **33**; Cephas Picture Library, page **145** (photo: D Burrows); illustration by Dominic Robinson of the Chartres Cathedral Maze from *Question Marks Series: Doing & Being*, Christian Education Movement, page **55**; illustration by Pauline Baynes from *The Silver Chair* by C S Lewis, Collins, 1989, page **84**; Cam Culbert, page **16**; Peter Fisher, page **139** *below*, Richard Gardner, pages **23, 24, 101** *below*, **123, 139** *above*; Sally & Richard Greenhill, pages **19, 80**; © Michael Holford, pages **103, 104, 157**; Geoff Howard, pages **30, 46**; The Hutchinson Library, page **38** (photo: Chandana Juliet Highet); Greta Jensen, page **54**; National Maritime Museum, Greenwich, page **96**; Bury Peerless Slide Resources & Picture Library, page **110**; illustration by Pauline Baynes from: *Prince Caspian* by C S Lewis, Penguin Books, page **83**; illustrations from *Iconography of Religions* by G H Moore, SCM, page **108**; illustrations from *Prince Siddhartha* by J Landaw & J Brooke (Wisdom Publications) 1984, page **109**; David Rose, pages **13, 14, 89** *left*; Peter Sanders, pages **29, 62, 87, 89** *right*, **92** *below*, **122** *above*; Tim Smith, pages **48, 75, 121** *above* (photo: Guzelian), **122** *below* (photo: Guzelian), **160**; Tantra Designs, pages **53** (photo: Peter Douglas), **69**; illustrations from *Religions of Man*, by J R S Whiting, Stanley Thornes (Publishers), 1983, page **40**; John Twinning, page **91** *left*; The Uphill Ski Club of Great Britain (photo: Glynis Edwards) page **99**; WWF/ICCE 1987, page **140**; Regional RE Centre, Westhill College, Birmingham, pages **100, 101** *above*; Jerry Wooldrige, page **91** *below left*; John Robert Young, page **76**.

Cover photo: by Camilla Jessel.
Illustration on page 13 by Darin Mount.

For teachers:

For pupils:

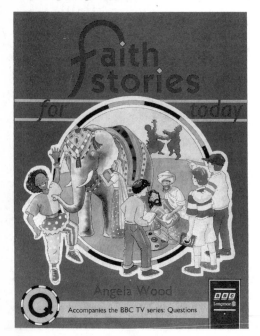

Here are four more books for help with Religious Education across the curriculum and for assemblies:

Religious Education Topics for the Primary School
582 00334 2

Assembly Kit
582 06783 9

Faith Stories
582 06783 9

Festivals in World Religions
582 36196 6

176